Contents

Preface

I was well into the third year of my PhD research (British Attitudes to Nuclear Proliferation 1952-1982) at the Politics Department, University of Edinburgh when, in November 1984, I spotted an advert for the post of Senior Research Officer in the Arms Control and Disarmament Research Unit at the Foreign and Commonwealth Office. I thought I might apply, but had absolutely no expectation that I might be successful. Four months later I started work in the FCO on 19 March. The post was originally for a term of three years, with the prospect of an extension for a further two years after which the contract would end. It occurred to me that this timeline worked well for my then intention of teaching and researching in a university after my PhD. Experience of 'working on the inside' would be a great value in any future job application, or so I thought. Plans can change and opportunities open; my post had been made a permanent one by the FCO in 1989 and the variety and interest of the work seemed to offer much more than a career in academia, so I stayed and enjoyed several personal promotions into the bargain. Thirty-five years later I retired from the FCO after a great career working on nuclear, chemical, biological weapons arms control and disarmament. A significant part of my job focussed on the verification challenges of weapons of mass destruction disarmament treaties and this story forms the basis for this book. It was one of the main reasons that the FCO had for converting my post into a permanent one – the need to develop and sustain long-term expertise inside the Office when most diplomats only stayed in post for an average of three years before moving on. This enabled me to play a part in over thirty years' worth of on-site inspection exercises across nuclear, chemical and biological weapons disarmament.

BRITAIN AND WEAPONS

OF MASS DESTRUCTION
VERIFICATION

For Holly, Grace, Mia, Freya and Rosie.

We tried to make the world a safer place.

BRITAIN AND WEAPONS
OF MASS DESTRUCTION
VERIFICATION

JOHN R WALKER

Pen & Sword

MILITARY

AN IMPRINT OF PEN & SWORD BOOKS LTD.
YORKSHIRE - PHILADELPHIA

First published in Great Britain in 2025 by
PEN AND SWORD MILITARY
An imprint of
Pen & Sword Books Limited
Yorkshire – Philadelphia

Copyright © John R Walker, 2025

ISBN 978 1 03612 591 2

Typeset in Times New Roman 11/14 by
SJmagic DESIGN SERVICES, India.
Printed and bound in the UK by CPI Group (UK) Ltd.

The Publisher's authorised representative in the EU for product safety is
Authorised Rep Compliance Ltd., Ground Floor, 71 Lower Baggot Street, Dublin
D02 P593, Ireland.
www.arccompliance.com

For a complete list of Pen & Sword titles please contact
PEN & SWORD BOOKS LIMITED
George House, Units 12 & 13, Beevor Street, Off Pontefract Road,
Barnsley, South Yorkshire, S71 1HN, England
E-mail: enquiries@pen-and-sword.co.uk
Website: www.pen-and-sword.co.uk

or

PEN AND SWORD BOOKS
1950 Lawrence Rd, Havertown, PA 19083, USA
E-mail: uspen-and-sword@casematepublishers.com
Website: www.penandswordbooks.com

Acknowledgements

It was my great privilege to have worked with so many fine and able colleagues over the years, and not just from the UK but from all over the world. It would be invidious to single out any one or two. They represented a broad range of disciplines and expertise – academic, diplomatic, scientific, engineering, industrial, military, police and legal. I learned a lot from them over the years. A few are mentioned in the following chapters, and to them and everyone else a big thank you. Sadly, some of them are now no longer with us.

I am most grateful to Graham Hand, Senior Sensitivity Reviewer at the Foreign, Commonwealth & Development Office for expediting the clearance of my manuscript around Whitehall for publication.

After I retired from the FCO I was invited to serve as a Trustee for the Verification Research, Training and Information Centre (VERTIC) and I would like to thank Larry MacFaul, its Executive Director, for permission to draw on material that I had published previously in VERTIC's journal 'Trust and Verify.'

The folks at Pen and Sword – Lisa Hoosan, Jon Wright, Charlotte Mitchell, Harriet Fielding – deserve a shout out too for their efforts in bringing this manuscript into book form. I am also very grateful to copy editor Margaret Moran for improving the text and removing all the spelling and grammatical errors that I had missed. I have always been a hopeless proof reader.

In writing this book I also drew upon state papers in The National Archives at Kew and contemporary UK working papers and reports that were submitted to various meetings of the Conference on Disarmament, Non-Proliferation Treaty, Comprehensive Test Ban Treaty Organisation Preparatory Commission and the Biological and Toxin Weapons Convention. A lot more detail and background can be found in these sources, many of which are cited in the bibliography. Sadly, at the time of writing – spring 2024 – the FCO's Arms Control and Disarmament Department files from 1988 to 2004 on the UK's chemical and biological on-site inspection exercises are still not available at The National Archives at Kew. Of course all errors of fact and interpretation remain the sole responsibility of the author. Apologies too if I have spelled anyone's name incorrectly. This work is not in any way an official history, neither are the views expressed here necessarily those of my former employer – the Foreign and Commonwealth Office as was.

Chapter 1

Introduction

It was unseasonably cold; the wind was up and you could feel the tent sides moving with the force of it. At least the sleeping bag was warm, there was no heating in the tent as it had not been thought necessary to bring any heaters. Late summer/early autumn should have been warm enough. At this point I realized that I should not have had that extra beer as nature was calling and that meant venturing out of the six person tent – we each had our own little cubicles – and into the cold and a short trek to the Scandinavian electric toilets, or alternatively just a respectable distance away from the tent making sure to check the wind direction first. That meant unzipping yourself from your sleeping bag, unzipping the cubicle door and then the inner and outer doors to the tent. It was at this point that I realized – once again – that there is no substitute for practical experience. Similarly, negotiating arms control and disarmament treaties in Geneva in the Palais des Nations, a task invariably and largely done by diplomats, is one thing, but the only way to learn how to do it, to see what works and what is required to design and then implement an effective on-site inspection regime is by conducting realistic exercises. In August/September 2008 the Comprehensive Nuclear Test Ban Treaty Organisation conducted its first large-scale field on-site inspection exercise at the former Soviet nuclear test site at Semipalatinsk, colloquially known as the Polygon.[1] I was present playing the role of the Inspected State Party Representative as well as one of the control staff to help run and steer the exercise to ensure that it met its objectives. All the exercise players lived and worked in a temporary camp site located a short distance outside the Polygon and some three hours journey from the nearest town at Kurchatov. We were there for over a month. This exercise, known as IFE08 – Integrated Field Exercise 2008 – was designed to help the CTBTO's On-Site Inspection Division develop methodologies and procedures and equipment for conducting a real on-site inspection once the Treaty had entered into force. A good deal was learned during this exercise, including quite a bit on how not to do things. For me this was only the latest in a long series of practice inspection exercises that had begun in March 1989. The United Kingdom had, since the 1950s, always regarded effective verification as a crucial requirement for any arms control and disarmament treaty. Indeed, even in the mid-1950s the UK conducted practical verification exercises to see how one might go about verifying a treaty for the cut-off in the production of fissile material for weapons purposes. This was known as Operation CIRCUS and involved exercises at the United Kingdom Atomic Energy Authority's Windscale plutonium production reactors.[2] In the late 1950s and early 1960s UKAEA scientists at Aldermaston (and then Blacknest) also undertook pioneering work on teleseismic research in order to work out how to verify effectively a comprehensive nuclear test ban treaty.[3] So it was very much within this tradition that the UK embarked on a series of practice challenge inspections during the Chemical Weapons Convention (CWC) negotiations. The basic aim of these exercises was to see whether the UK itself could live with the sort of intrusive verification measures essential if a CWC were to be effective and to help design the specific measures for challenge inspection that were then under negotiation in Geneva. The first of these took place in October 1988, with the second one in March 1989 and this was my first involvement in what was to become a career in the Foreign and Commonwealth Office in which biological, chemical, nuclear weapons arms control verification was to loom large. Over the years until I retired from the FCO at the end of May 2020 I participated in over seventy on-site inspection national and multinational exercises, the results of which not only shaped UK policy, but also helped inform the negotiations for the CWC and the ultimate content of the Convention's Verification Annex. Although negotiations on a Biological and Toxin Weapons Convention verification Protocol ultimately failed in July 2001, British work on inspection and investigation procedures had an influence on the Protocol's provisions on on-site visits and investigations. Nuclear disarmament verification research became a significant British contribution to work on strengthening the 1968 Nuclear Non-Proliferation Treaty (NPT); and this effort, which was undertaken jointly with Norway, led to a pioneering verification exercise focussing on aspects of a nuclear warhead dismantlement process. Following conclusion at long last of a CTBT in 1996, a new organization was created to build up the treaty's complex verification system consisting of some 321 seismic, hydroacoustic, infrasound and radionuclide stations and sixteen radionuclide laboratories across the globe. The CTBTO was also tasked with building up a capability to mount an on-site inspection after entry into force of the treaty, and although the poor relation compared to the International Monitoring System, the On-site Inspection Division went on to do much sterling work where field exercises were instrumental in building up on-site capabilities. As a nuclear weapon state and strong supporter of the Treaty, the UK made important and sustained contributions to this effort. I ended up becoming a Joint Task Leader on the OSI Operational Manual along with Malcolm Coxhead from Australia. When the Ottawa Convention on Anti-Personnel Landmines was agreed in 1997,[4] the UK went on to be the only state party that conducted practice fact finding missions (FFM) – the term of art for this Convention's main verification procedures. These will not be separately discussed in their own chapter since many of the lessons were either identical or similar to those learned during the CWC PCIs. As with earlier work on the CWC and BTWC, these were designed in part to ensure that the UK would be able to handle a real FFM. Given my previous experience with the CWC exercises, I was closely involved in the practice FFMs as well, usually as control staff or host state party representative.

Over the years then, the UK spent a good deal of resources, time and effort on developing on-site procedures learning how to plan, conduct and report them whilst ensuring that legitimate national security interests unrelated to the object and purpose of the relevant treaty could be protected. Much of this empirical work produced results and lessons that often did not sit well with the attitudes of many delegations in Geneva, The Hague and Vienna, not just during the relevant negotiations in the 1980s and 1990s, but also subsequently in the implementation phase when procedures and provisions were further elaborated during the Preparatory Commissions for both the CWC and CTBT.

This book has two main objectives: first of all, it is to chart the UK's role in developing and shaping thinking and measures on on-site inspection for biological, chemical and nuclear arms control and disarmament over an approximate 30 year period between 1988 and 2020. The second objective is to recount my own modest role in this process as I was lucky enough to be directly involved over the same time span, taking a wide range of roles in the exercises. I was probably the only person who ended up playing all the possible positions from inspector to control staff. Moreover, this second objective offers a more personal account that highlights the nature of the insights gained by the UK over the years as well as the anecdotal and humorous side of the story that amplifies the more academic or practical lessons identified and learned during the various exercises.

The subsequent chapters will provide a largely chronological and thematic account of UK work on on-site inspections starting in Chapter 2 with the UK's initial CWC practice challenge inspection programme that ran from October 1988 through to April 1990. This entailed six inspections exercises at a wide range of defence and intelligence related facilities; it will also address the managed access follow up work at nuclear sites as well as a smaller number of practice inspection exercises at civil chemical industry, and two exchange exercises with the Federal Republic of Germany at defence sites.

Chapter 3 will address the UK's practice compliance inspections programme mounted in support of work underway in Geneva on verification measures for the Biological and Toxin Weapons Convention (BTWC). This programme was much more modest in comparison with the CWC PCIs as only four exercises took place at a range of pharmaceutical and biotechnological sites. Nevertheless, it was a pioneering effort that influenced the UK's approach to the eventual negotiations in the Ad Hoc Group (AHG) on a BTWC verification Protocol between 1995 and 2001, especially the development of its Annexes containing the detailed provisions for on-site investigations. UK research work was not confined to challenge on-site inspections, but also explored other types of on-site activity that would be needed in an overall comprehensive approach. This also entailed exercises in the UK and Brazil. These examples encouraged other states parties to run their own on-site activities. The chapter also discusses the relevance of the Russian visit to Evans Medical in 1994 to the UK's work on BW verification.

Once the CWC had been concluded in September 1992 and opened for signature in January 1993, the Ministry of Defence decided to embark on a new series of exercises designed to ensure that defence sites across the UK would be able to cope with a real challenge inspection after entry into force. These will be the subject of Chapter 4. The key aims here were to be able to demonstrate UK compliance with the Convention whilst protecting national security sensitivities at the same time. Once the CWC entered into force, attention turned to ensuring that the Organisation for the Prohibition of Chemical Weapons (OPCW) Technical Secretariat would be able to mount an effective challenge inspection if ever requested to do so. Chapter 4 will thus also look at the work the UK did in this context as well as various exercises conducted in Germany, the Netherlands, Switzerland and Sweden. There was also an important exercise conducted at AWE Aldermaston in August 1992 that addressed the problem of clandestine sampling.

Chapter 5 focusses on development of CTBT on-site inspection operational capabilities by the Preparatory Commission's Provisional Technical Secretariat in 2008. The UK contributed expertise and provided some hardware in the shape of a mobile radionuclide laboratory. In terms of expertise that was essentially experts from AWE Aldermaston and me, though the CTBTO also recruited British experts from academia and industry to help the process. The chapter's main focus will be on IFFE08 and its aftermath.

Chapter 6 switches to nuclear disarmament verification and the UK work with Norway, known as the UK-Norway Initiative (UKNI). This entailed a serious examination of the challenges of how one might go about verifying the dismantlement of a nuclear weapon whilst protecting warhead design information, but providing enough access and information to assure inspectors that the warhead had in fact been dismantled and its fissile material accounted for. What made this exercise more challenging was that Norway played the role of a fictitious nuclear weapon state whilst the UK was the non-nuclear weapon state. The main exercise took place in 2009. Almost ten years later, another larger exercise took place, this time involving the US and Sweden with inspected state party and inspection team members drawn from all four participating countries. What added to the interest and verisimilitude of this exercise, known as Letterpress, was that it took place at a former RAF real nuclear weapons storage site – RAF Honington – and used a UK WE177A tactical nuclear bomb inert training round to simulate a live weapon.

Chapter 7 reverts to the CTBTO and its substantial work on on-site inspections between 2012 and 2014, culminating in the very much larger and more ambitious IFE14 in Jordan. This chapter will include the three key Build-Up Exercises (BUEs) that were an important precursor and preparation for IFE14. It will also have a word or two about an exercise conducted on the launch phase of a CTBT OSI that took place at the end of 2019. I ended up heading the external evaluation team for the BUEs and IFE14, one of the five key roles in the exercise: the others being the heads of the inspection team and inspected state party, the exercise director and the head of the Scenario Task Force.

Chapter 8 will offer some general observations and lessons identified during the UK's work on on-site inspections. There will be a clear personal view here as I was the only expert in the UK, and as far as I know elsewhere, who was closely involved in work on the verification practicalities of chemical, biological and nuclear (both disarmament verification and test ban treaty on-site inspections) arms control and disarmament. UK experts and those elsewhere in Australia, China, France, Germany, Russia, Sweden Switzerland and the US, for example, all tended to be either chemical or biological (occasionally both) or nuclear – but not all three. My involvement was unique at the level of detail described in these chapters, and hopefully as such that adds some value to the overall concluding observations and insights on on-site inspections that I make in this chapter. In essence, I became an expert in how to plan, conduct, conclude and report arms control and disarmament inspections, something that I could not have envisaged when I joined the FCO on an initial three year contract. There was also a link between the field research represented by the exercises, arms control policy making in the FCO, representing the UK at the treaty negotiations and further elaboration of procedures at Preparatory Commissions – OPCW and CTBTO – since I was closely involved in these activities too.

All the on-site inspection exercises discussed in this book were performed in strict role play; namely, individuals would assume the role of inspectors, inspected state party escorts, and requesting state observers. Site personnel played their own roles. However, exercises also require other players – directing and control staff, evaluators and observers. Over the years I played all the roles possible: inspector, deputy chief inspector, chief inspector, inspected state party (ISP) escort, deputy ISP representative, the ISP representative, requesting state observer, directing/control staff, evaluator and head of the evaluation team. This meant that I saw the issues and problems from different perspectives, and that provided unique insights into the overall process that were probably not available to others. It was very much a continuing learning process as there was always something new as each exercise threw up new problems as well as solutions. These exercises were a validation process too as the importance of specific and often the same or similar measures, strategies, tactics and techniques were frequently demonstrated across the different areas – chemical, biological and nuclear. That will hopefully become apparent as the book unfolds. The general applicability of lessons and approaches that could be used by both inspectors and inspected state was one of the key observations that struck me over the years. There were of course specific solutions and approaches particular to each subject matter area, and some that were even site specific given the nature of the facilities and activities underway at such places.

A word about sources used for this book: a good deal of the book is based on memory. Memory is of course fallible and not always reliable and some of the events described are over thirty years old. Having said that, my job in the Arms Control and Disarmament Research Unit at the FCO often required a revisiting of previous exercise experiences and reports for training courses for both inspectors and escorts and for the design of exercise scenarios. So a lot of the past was ever present in more contemporary settings and in some cases we revisited some sites several times. However, the UK generally went to great lengths to report its findings publicly, so there are many primary sources too to support the narrative and analysis here. There was no point in keeping the results secret as one of the key UK objectives over the years was to influence and persuade other states that intrusive inspections were both possible and could be managed in such a way to protect legitimate national security and commercially confidential information unrelated to CB weapons, or the purpose of the inspection. Inspection programme results were usually reported in national Working Papers submitted to the Conference on Disarmament (CD), the BTWC Verification Experts Group (VEREX), the Ad Hoc Group, the NPT Review Conference and its related Preparatory Committee meetings and other fora such as both the CWC and CTBT Preparatory Commissions' Working Group B. Results were also published in academic outlets (see bibliography). The MOD CWC challenge inspection preparatory exercise reports post 1993 were not normally published, but rather the subject of reports was used to shape policies and to make any amendments to internal procedures set forth in national guidance documents. British contributions to the development of CTBT OSI operational capabilities were not reported publicly, but appeared directly in UK contributions to the Preparatory Commission's Working Group B (WGB). As head of the external IFE14 evaluation team I had to draft the high level report to WGB based on the detailed contributions from other members of the team. This document was submitted as a Provisional Technical Secretariat Information Paper, which was provided to CTBTO member states. All the Build-Up Exercise reports were provided to the PTS' On-Site Inspection Division only and not circulated beyond that.

One final point here: these exercises in addition to being stimulating intellectually and pioneering activities in the field of arms control and disarmament, were always great fun to do. Over the years I must have worked with hundreds of people – not just UK diplomats, civil servants, military, industry and academic individuals, but many other European, North and South American, Asian, Australasian and African experts from the same communities. That diversity and divergence in perceptions, approaches and cultural perspectives certainly shaped my views over the years, and was certainly a large and important part of the never ending learning process. A good thing was that we could often have a laugh whilst doing so, even though we were dealing with serious issues in trying in our own modest ways to make the world a safer and more secure place for everyone.

Chapter 2

Chemical Weapons 1988–1992

The Chemical Weapons Convention negotiations and the UK Practice Challenge Inspection Programme

Introduction

When the UK Foreign Secretary, Douglas Hurd, signed the Chemical Weapons Convention in Paris in January 1993, the occasion marked the successful conclusion of some twenty years of effort and negotiations in the Conference on Disarmament in Geneva. An effective Convention had been a major objective of UK arms control and disarmament policy since the conclusion of the Biological and Toxin Weapons Convention (BTWC) negotiations in September 1971.[1] Indeed one could even argue that aspirations for a global ban on chemical warfare stretched back to 1899 when The Hague treaty sought to prohibit asphyxiating gases in war, a prohibition that did not survive the First World War, which witnessed extensive use of a wide range of toxic chemicals. Indeed, by the end of that war almost one in three of artillery projectiles fired contained a chemical agent fill.[2] In the years following the First World War further international efforts were made to prohibit chemical warfare, but these only ended up with a more limited set of constraints contained in the 1925 Geneva Protocol, which was little more than a prohibition on the first use of chemical weapons; many of the signatories reserved the right to retaliate in kind if ever attacked by states using them.[3] Although chemical weapons were rarely used in the Second World War, even though extensive stockpiles existed in all the major belligerents, post war efforts on disarmament sought to go beyond the Geneva Protocol. Cold War rivalries and suspicions invariably put paid to the grandiose three stage plans for general and complete disarmament in the 1950s and early 1960s where chemical disarmament usually sat in step two out of three. One of the biggest obstacles was verification: for Western powers effective verification was essential in any disarmament treaty and that meant extensive rights for on-site inspections on the territory of the parties. In contrast, the Soviet Union insisted that national technical means of verification were all that was needed and generally regarded onsite inspections as espionage, and something that would actually highlight their weaknesses. Such a position was always going to present a problem for the cause of chemical weapons disarmament, and certainly for the British since disarmament under effective control had long been an absolute requirement if there was ever to be agreement of far-reaching measures. Soviet opposition to on-site inspections had scuppered efforts to secure a Comprehensive Nuclear Test Ban Treaty between 1958 and 1963.[4] Given the nature of chemical weapons, primarily their comparable ease of production and storage – certainly compared to nuclear weapons – and that the key ingredients were readily produced and available within the civil chemical industry, the only way to deter and detect cheating would be through extensive on-site inspections. Arguments over verification – its scope, procedure, and provisions – would dominate discussions in Geneva in the 1970s and well into the 1980s. When the CD finally agreed a formal negotiating mandate for a Chemical Weapons Convention for 1984, a meeting of minds on verification was nowhere in sight and when the United States tabled a draft CWC on 18 April 1984 the divergences on verification could not have been made clearer.[5] This treaty contained what its drafters assumed would be a killer provision (i.e. the Russians would reject it): a no right of refusal short notice challenge inspection procedure aimed at state owned facilities. Any refusal to admit inspectors would be an automatic breach of the CWC. It was this aspect that gave the UK most concern.[6] MOD and FCO officials had to consider the implications for the UK of such a measure.[7] Now whilst such a provision would undoubtedly be a critical verification tool in any treaty – the UK had proposed challenge inspections in its own draft treaty in 1976 and again in a CD working paper in February 1984 – the US focus on state owned facilities was aimed at the Soviet Union. Inevitably the Russians rejected such a provision and, coupled to wider arguments in the CD over what sort of verification arrangements might need to apply to the chemical industry, it was clear that rapid progress in the negotiations was not going to happen.

Thus, prospects for a CWC were grim. However, that was about to change following the emergence of new developments in the Soviet Union where General Secretary Mikhail Gorbachev and his Foreign Secretary Eduard Shevardnadze saw the need to find ways to end the East-West arms race and make substantial progress on arms control, especially nuclear arms control. This was going to be a key feature in their foreign policies, but it would require a volte face in traditional Soviet attitudes to verification if they were to convince the West that they were serious. In the CWC context this meant that the Soviet Union was now willing to support short-notice challenge inspection, and Shevardnadze announced this change to the CD in 1989: a position that put the US on the spot. The Russians were not supposed to accept; and the US was not even sure that it could live with such intrusive inspections at its own defence and other facilities. Consequently, the US had second thoughts about the wisdom of its original proposal. The UK itself had tried to find alternative ways of ensuring that the CWC might contain effective challenge provisions and had tabled some ideas to this effect in the CD in its working paper CD/715 in 1987. Prime Minister Margaret Thatcher wanted to see an effective CWC that addressed the problem of Soviet CW capabilities, which were believed to be extensive. She also worried too whether the UK itself could cope with instructive inspection at places such as AWE Aldermaston (the UK's nuclear weapons research and production facility) and GCHQ (the government's signals intelligence centre) if the US Article X provisions were ever to be implemented.[8] For this reason the UK felt that there ought to be some initial right to refuse such an inspection in exceptional circumstances, but there would still need to be an obligation to demonstrate compliance.[9] Until there was an agreement on both the principle of short-notice challenge inspection and on how such inspections were to be conducted, there could be no breakthrough in the CWC negotiations. London's dilemma was to find an effective alternative to the US Article X proposal that would stand a chance of being negotiable with the Soviet Union. There were other issues of course such as the scope of industry verification and the powers and functions of the policy making organs such as the Executive Council, but challenge inspection was seen, certainly by the UK, at the time as the key to breaking the log jam in the negotiations. This is where the UK's practice challenge inspection programme exercises would come into the process of finding a practical solution to the problem, the first of which took place in autumn 1988. This chapter will discuss and describe the programme, the key lessons identified and how these fed into the Geneva negotiations and final shape of the future CWC's provisions on challenge inspection. It will also recall some of the anecdotes from these exercises as many of them actually illustrate key points on how to go about conducting a challenge inspection; and indeed, as well as how not to go about conducting such an inspection.

The CWC Practice Inspection Programme 1988–1990

In the aftermath of the UK's Working Paper on challenge inspection tabled in 1986,[10] which set out how there should be an obligation to demonstrate compliance on a state party receiving such an inspection, attention in Whitehall started to shift onto the practicalities of how a challenge inspection might work in practice. There was one key question that needed to be addressed: could sufficient access be given to a site such as the Atomic Weapons Establishment Aldermaston to enable international inspectors to determine that no illicit CW activity was taking, or had taken, place whilst protecting nuclear and other national security sensitive information? As far as we knew, no one else had looked in detail at the practicalities of how one would go about conducting a short notice challenge inspection, certainly in the UK. This would prove an important step in linking empirical work with diplomatic negotiations. It would provide an evidence base for countering those negotiators in Geneva who argued that something would not work or be effective. The Ministry of Defence's Defence Arms Control Unit (DACU) therefore began planning a series of exercises that would look at three key questions: first, to assess the security implications of challenge inspections under a CWC; second, to examine ways of demonstrating compliance with a CWC while protecting legitimate security interests unrelated to chemical weapons; and third, to draw any lessons for how challenge inspections under CWC might be conducted.[11] What became known as the Practice Challenge Inspection (PCI) Programme therefore began in autumn 1988. This necessarily became a cross Whitehall effort involving various military and civilian branches of the MOD, such as the Commitments Staff, Land Command, Strike Command, Defence Intelligence Staff, the Foreign and Commonwealth Office (the Arms Control and Disarmament Department – ACDD and me from the Arms Control and Disarmament Research Unit –

ACDRU), the UK Delegation to the Conference on Disarmament – UKDis Geneva), and importantly the Chemical Defence Establishment Porton Down.[12] In fact, the joint exercise control staff consisted of Dr John Bartlett Superintendent of the Assessment Trials and Range Division (S/ATRD at Porton) and Ian Manson, who was head of the CWC section in DACU. They were responsible inter alia for creating the overall scenario. One of the major objectives of the programme was to look at a range of different types of defence facilities with the ultimate aim of running an exercise at Aldermaston; an unstated assumption amongst many of us was that if we could manage to conduct an effective exercise there, then there would be no site in the UK that could not cope with a real inspection. DACU therefore wanted the programme to cover ammunition storage sites, an operating air base, AWE, a proofing and experimental establishment and a facility with an unavowed intelligence function. All this would take time, not least of which was the need to convince the relevant commands and directorates in the MOD to make one of their facilities available to host a PCI. This would not always be easy as we shall see. However, the imperative that an effective CWC was an important foreign policy objective for the Conservative government, and that the Prime Minister herself took the matter very seriously helped to shift the obdurate.

PC1 Kineton – a land services ammunition depot

The overall organizational plan for this, and future exercises, was to assemble a small inspection team (the IT) with the necessary skills and expertise drawn from appropriate departments or services within the defence and foreign policy community. The IT would be matched by a home team (HT) who would provide the escorts and link between the IT and the facility personnel. Senior site personnel would participate either full time or as required in the HT as did a couple of CDE experts to advise on chemical warfare aspects and ways to demonstrate compliance. One person was selected to play the Requesting State Observer (RSO), of which role more anon. Finally, there were two control staff to ensure that the exercise ran to time and met its objectives; they would only intervene if things started to go off the rails and there were impasses between the IT and HT. And this point highlights a key feature of the PCI programme: all the exercises were run in strict role play in order to maximise the realism of the process as far as possible. This included housing the IT and HT in separate hotels so there were no out-of-exercise debates or re-runs of disputes earlier in the day in the bar over a refreshment or two. We wanted the IT to think and act like inspectors for the duration and the HT to think and act like national escorts and site managers/commanding officers. Each exercise would run for two full working days, with a short 'hot-wash up' with all the players at the end of the second day. The head of each team would then provide a summary of the key points and lessons identified during the exercise. Afterwards Ian Manson (DACU) would prepare a draft report, then circulate it to all participants for comment and any corrections. The aim in good British civil service tradition was to produce a consensus report at the end that would serve as the formal record and would be used to help draft an overall programme report, which could be submitted to the Conference on Disarmament in Geneva. A consensus report most definitely did not mean the lowest common denominator, there was genuine broad agreement on many of the issues and it proved remarkably easy to reconcile different perspectives in the majority of cases.

I was not included in the teams for the first exercise at Kineton. This was one of two large land services conventional ammunition depots that stored munitions for the British Army – the other one was at Longtown, of which more later as it also hosted a PCI after conclusion of the original PCI programme. The Chief Inspector for PCI 1 was Dr Graham Cooper – a chemist from CDE Porton Down on secondment to the FCO to provide technical advice to the UK CD delegation in Geneva. Graham was resident in Geneva full time – he was assisted by three other inspectors, including Lieutenant Colonel Alan Morley, a Senior Ammunition Technical Officer. Graham would continue as Chief Inspector for the rest of the programme and Alan carried on to provide the munitions expertise. Continuity was going to be important as although additional experts were drawn in as needed, the core IT could then see how things developed across the programme and at different types of site. PCI 1 was largely a scoping exercise in the sense that it provided a first look at the nature of a CWC challenge inspection and how to go about it. Issues such as physical access to buildings and munitions, documentation and interviews, working out what sort of information needed to be protected and how that protection would be applied were all to the fore in PCI 1. All were to become recurring themes in the further five inspections.

PCI 2 Royal Naval Ordnance Depot (RNAD) Crombie

The planning meeting for PCI 2 in early 1989 was my opportunity to take a role in the exercise programme. This was the sort of thing that ACDRU should be doing – practical field research into how one would go about verifying a disarmament treaty. It would never be enough to just sit in an office and review documents and think in terms of principle and concepts. MOD's PCI programme could be the start of something for the long term as verification would continue to be a key requirement for UK arms control and disarmament policy. At first it seemed as if the planning process was only going to stick with four inspectors as at Kineton. I had already indicated to my colleague from ACDD and then the head of the CWC section David Powell that I would quite like to take part. So just when it seemed as if I had missed the boat, David suggested that I should also be included in the IT for PCI 2. Fortunately, that was quickly agreed as I think it was recognised that an extra pair of eyes and boots on the ground would be extremely useful. And as Crombie was on the River Forth that would mean a trip back home to Scotland.

RNAD Crombie had originally been built on the north shore of the River Forth during World War I to store ammunition for the Grand Fleet based at Rosyth a few miles up the coast. In the Cold War it served the same purpose, though it also stored ammunition taken off navy ships heading to Rosyth dockyard for repair and refurbishment. It had a long jetty out into the Forth for such purposes, though when we were there for PCI 2 a new more modern and longer jetty was being constructed to replace the WWI vintage one. The depot itself was long and thin across the foreshore with munitions storage bunkers built deep into the hill side; it also had various ammunition processing buildings, an integrated weapon complex for guided weapons, numerous storage and administrative buildings, a small burning ground at the top end of the site; it was also connected to the British Rail network, though by this stage not used much. RNAD Crombie initially had a narrow-gauge railway to move the munitions to and from the bunkers and processing buildings, but sadly by the time of our PCI it had long since been decommissioned otherwise one of the first tasks would have been to request a ride on it.

The inspection began with a briefing by the site superintendent; this covered a general overview of what went on the facility, what its purpose was, its organizational structure coupled with a health and safety briefing.

This was followed by a site windshield tour as the IT was driven around the site to provide an orientation and which also enabled us to identify areas of possible interest for further, more detailed, inspection. One of the key features to look for in a munitions store was the fire division hazard symbols posted outside the bunkers driven into the hillside as this would give a clear indication of the nature of the ammunition and explosives stored inside. [13] The distinct symbols are there to help firefighting personnel easily recognize the type of hazard and apply proper techniques to control it. Other symbols of interest would include a blue breathing apparatus, which would indicate some sort of respiratory hazard in the event of fire. Now of course if a state were cheating and a site under inspection was in fact producing or storing CW, it would not necessarily be marking things correctly or indeed at all. However, one of the early lessons we saw here was that a challenge inspection is an opportunity for a state to demonstrate its compliance with the Convention, and one of the best ways of doing this is ensuring that everything the inspectors see is consistent with the stated purpose of the object or location. So, in this case at Crombie, when we selected some of the bunkers indicating Fire Division symbol 1.1, we expected to see storage boxes and containers consistent with these markings and that the individual boxes selected for opening were all correctly marked for high explosive content – for example, a yellow role band marking on the munition in line with NATO Standard Regulations.[14] In this regulation chemical weapons should be painted grey with a green role band to indicate a nerve agent fill. We also noted one marking of some interest, which momentarily led to some excitement. 'GD' was stencilled onto many of the standard brown storage boxes – GD is the short code name for the WWII German nerve agent soman.[15] However, on being questioned our hosts said that GD stood for Glascoed, which was a Royal Ordnance Factory in Monmouthshire, Wales.[16] Now whilst anything could have been stencilled on a projectile or missile to make it look like a conventional piece of ordnance, how would an inspector know for sure that its content was not a chemical warfare agent? Whilst storage boxes could be opened in a bunker, the munition inside could not be broken down any further, largely for explosive safety reasons. If they were to be x-rayed or further examined, they would need to be moved to an Ammunition Processing Building (APB). We selected a few at random for just such examinations. This would be a key part of the deterrent aspect of a challenge inspection. In this exercise the IT only consisted of five inspectors, so we could have only sent an escort to accompany the munitions at the expense of further inspection activity elsewhere on the site. Alternatively, we could have attached tamper indicating seals and tags that could be verified on arrival at the APB, thereby leaving inspectors free to inspect other parts of the site. As we had none available in this exercise, it was decided that notional seals would be placed on the munition boxes. The IAEA had been using tamper indicating seals and tags reliably for years in safeguards at nuclear facilities, so we did not think this was unrealistic. That said, there was the separate question as to where you would place the seals and tags, but that was something for further consideration.

There were three things in this particular exercise that struck me at the time as important outcomes and which would go on to shape the design of future exercises and the content of the future CWC Verification Annex. The first of these concerned out of bound areas. One of the site features that attracted the IT's interest was the existing pier, but also the new construction of a modern replacement; however, the exercise control had agreed with the site that the construction area would not be part of the role play exercise. A major concern was that too much interference with the construction could be presented as an excuse for late project completion. This frankly was a bit over the top because this could have been factored into the exercise play and physical access controlled and set under agreed parameters that would not cause undue disruption and still probably provide inspectors with what they needed. The lesson for future was that these real-world issues should be factored into the exercise, and in the event of a real challenge inspection they would need to be handled not ignored; big exclusion zones were not at all ideal in any kind of challenge inspection regardless of Treaty.

The second event arose in the site's small burning/demolition ground; many such sites had an area where disposal of waste or small quantities of explosive or propellants were permitted. Why would this be of interest to CW inspectors? If there were a need to dispose of incriminating evidence quickly, then this would be one place that could be used *in extremis*. So, on this occasion two of us went off to have a look and rummage through the remains of a recent incineration of some waste materials. We asked the site representatives to explain what activities were routinely conducted at this location. Once there we found the remnants of a CW respirator canister (in this case it looked like the standard British Armed forces version – an S-10), so what was this doing there? And if there were no chemical weapons on the site, why had there been a need for CW protective equipment? At this passage of time I do not recall exactly what the explanation for this unexpected discovery was. It might have been for force protection in case of a terrorist attack using CS. Respiratory protection for fire fighters was required since some of the ordnance, such as propellants, stored on the site would give off hazardous gases if they had gone on fire; canisters have a shelf life and it may have been that the one whose remains we had found was time expired. A key lesson out of this episode was that inspectors could well find even small indicators of CW activity and that a site could not be sure it could conceal all traces of clandestine activity. One respirator canister does not make for an offensive CW capability of course, but what it does do, as in this case, is to open up new avenues of inquiry for the inspectors. Much will depend on the level of detail, its plausibility and technical credibility that the team manages to elicit from the site personnel and escorts. Responses may be satisfactory or simply not forthcoming or inadequate, in which case suspicion will grow, thereby making further probing necessary. Content will be everything. In this case everything else on the site appeared to be clearly consistent with the stated purpose of the site – naval ordnance storage and maintenance – and the site cooperated with the inspectors. Thus, one minor issue with a plausible explanation did not assume any significance when set against the wider picture.

The third issue that arose during PCI 2, and the most significant, concerned the first test of a managed access approach. The core problem is how to protect sensitive information unrelated to offensive chemical weapons whilst still providing sufficient access to enable inspectors to be confident that nothing illegal was being concealed. Managed access' origins in the UK context went back to 1984 when officials were first tasked by the Prime Minister to come up with an alternative approach to the US 'anywhere any time, no right of refusal' challenge inspection process as proposed in CD/500. Paul Schulte in the Defence Arms Control Unit developed the concept of iterative managed access, a sort of peeling off of the onion skin layers. The idea here was to show only a portion of an inspected area or object in the hope that this would be enough to persuade the inspectors that nothing untoward was being concealed. This could be done in increasing levels of access until a bottom line was reached beyond which no further access and/or information would be provided. Paul told me that he got the idea initially from reading about childbirth in the eighteenth century, 'when men-midwives worked blind, practising under bed sheets, tied bib-like around their necks, to obscure women's genitalia and to preserve their modesty.'[17] The concept was taken no further at the time, with the concept of 'alternative arrangements' in the UK's CD Working Paper CD/715 the preferred option. By the time we got to

RNAD Crombie the control staff and the home team decided to exercise for the first time a practical managed access scenario.

As inspectors we had selected a particular storage shed that looked to be of potential interest. On arrival at the entrance, we were told that managed access would be necessary and that only the Chief Inspector would be allowed into the building. From an inspector's perspective this was far from satisfactory as the range of expertise within the team might well be needed to assess the building's contents. If we wanted access, then we had to agree to what was on offer. As Dr Cooper approached the doors, it was at this point that the senior home team escort – Lieutenant Colonel Terry Taylor from DACU – whispered to Graham – in jest we assumed: "Well Dr Cooper, this is where we offer you the half-million pounds and a ticket to Rio." PCIs always had their humorous moments and this was PCI 2's. Returning now back into role play, the Chief Inspector was faced with a large floor space in the middle of which was a very large, shrouded object – it was covered completely with a large tarpaulin, sufficient in size to be possibly concealing a significant number of ammunition storage boxes. On asking what was under the shroud, Graham was told that no further information could be provided as the shrouding was necessary to protect national security information. Clearly this was not enough to convince us. After much negotiation both sides eventually agreed that other inspectors could also access the building and that it would be possible to touch the shrouded object, lift the corner of one end of the tarpaulin and use a chemical agent monitor (CAM) briefly to see if any chemical warfare agents, either G series or sulfur mustard, were present.[18] From what we could see and assess the tarpaulin was covering standard British munition storage boxes, which were painted brown. It looked in the main to be small arms ammunition. No information or explanation was offered. In fact, we learned in the wash up discussions that the boxes were all empty, they had been placed there in order to simulate a possible managed access scenario. A key lesson here was that in future this sort of approach does not really work as the home side has no real credible story to tell or secrets to keep. An important aspect of managed access was knowing exactly what needed to be protected and that would then allow some details of a lower classification to be divulged if that was needed to convince the inspectors. This proved easier in the case of the handful of boxes that we had asked to be opened in the APB. Once there we could view the projectiles and missiles, but there was no further facility for breaking them down. An x-ray could reveal whether there was a liquid fill present, which would be indicative of a chemical warfare agent fill.

In the exercise the home team offered to transport the selected items under IT escort for explosive demolition at Otterburn in Northumberland – about 100 miles away, which was the nearest licensed facility permitted to do this for this class of munition and the UK's largest live firing range. This would clearly show the absence of a chemical fill. In an ammunition storage depot, this sort of random but informed selection of buildings, storage bunkers and munitions for closer inspection was going to be a key part of the overall hoped-for deterrent element in a challenge inspection. An inspected state party and facility could never be sure exactly what inspectors might pick, and if items and activities prohibited by a CWC were being hidden, they would run a risk of discovery, or having to deny sufficient access to inspectors as well as obstructing or failing to cooperate with the process. This in itself could be significant, and as we were to see later in Iraq and Russia in the 1990s, refusal to provide access without any credible explanation and effort to demonstrate compliance did betoken non-compliance.

The draft CWC proposed that the Requesting State Party could send its own observer (RSO – Requesting State Observer) to monitor the inspection conducted by the Technical Secretariat.[19] A crucial consideration here would be the RSO's role in ensuring that inspectors looked in all the right places and asked the right questions. This was driven by the expectation that a request would be informed by national intelligence information, and the hope that the presence of an RSO would add to the overall deterrent effect of a challenge inspection and give the requesting state greater confidence in the outcome from the process. All this was to become more and more contentious during the CWC negotiations in Geneva, but for this exercise (and all subsequent ones in the initial programme) an MOD Lieutenant Colonel from the Central Staff – Robin Waters – played the role. Robin by default basically ended up serving as an additional surrogate inspector and shared the same working areas as the IT; he was privy to all our tactical and strategic planning discussions, and made a lot of frankly helpful suggestions. Although the observer was escorted separately and was not given the same access to buildings as the IT, we were to learn later that an RSO was not necessarily a useful thing in the overall inspection process. More on that lesson later, but that of course was part of the programme: learn how to conduct inspections from both an inspector and home team perspective.

So that was PCI 2, the next exercise in October 1989 was to prove one of the most important to date as it was the first time that we ran an exercise in a nuclear weapon related facility.

PCI3: RAF Honington – operating air base for Tornado GR1 Tactical Weapons Conversion Unit and a nuclear weapons Supplementary Storage Area (SSA)

The inspection and home teams for PCI 3 were largely the same, though Dr Richard Soilleux – a CW expert from Porton Down – joined the IT in place of his Porton colleague Tim Rubidge. Richard acquired an aerial photograph of the airfield from Suffolk County Council before the exercise began, something which was going to create a bit of a stir later in the exercise. I also did some research into the history of RAF Honington and prepared a background brief for the IT, which was to help us to work out in advance what we might expect to see on the site and to inform our initial planning. This was years before the arrival of the Internet and Google Earth made such a task so much easier and quicker.

As before the inspection began with a site briefing which described the overall purpose of the base, although it was conspicuously silent about the existence of the SSA and its content. The MOD's longstanding policy had always been to neither confirm nor deny the presence of nuclear weapons at any particular location and time. The exercise control staff had designed this exercise so that we would inspect the Hardened Aircraft Shelters (HAS) and other parts of the site on day one with the focus on the nuclear part of the site on day two; in fact, one HAS was set up in advance with a standard munition load for a Tornado GR1 aircraft laid out for us to see, though I think these were training and inert rounds. We would magically select the appropriate HAS randomly after making our initial inspection plan following the obligatory windshield tour. The control staff told us which one to pick. The airfield was divided into zones: for example, aircraft engineering and maintenance hangers; a western and eastern HAS compound; a conventional munitions bomb dump, the SSA – both on the northern side of the airfield and administration, training, command and control and living quarters on the southern side. There were also two bulk fuel installations (BFIs). The key events of this inspection took place in the Eastern HAS area and in the SSA, which was the main reason for coming to this site in the first place. In fact, the part of the RAF responsible for Honington, AMSO – Air Member for Supply and Organization – took a bit of persuading to let us play on their turf.[20] The general feeling amongst the FCO and MOD CWC officials was that if it was possible to provide access to a nuclear weapons storage site, provide sufficient information to the inspectors and protect weapon design and stockpile numbers, then we could almost certainly cope with a challenge inspection anywhere else in the UK – defence or commercial.

After the general windshield tour and formation of the initial inspection plan, the IT headed towards the Eastern HAS area to inspect the 'randomly' selected shelter. As we drove round the outer perimeter road, the station's senior escort officer said that we could inspect all of the HAS, but it was only time constraints that prevented such a prospect. This statement was to come back to haunt him. We duly entered the selected HAS and noted the standard array of conventional ordnance laid out next to a Tornado aircraft. The item of most interest was the JP233 anti-runway and area denial bomb, which contained a large number of sub-munitions that had to be delivered by a very low-level approach over an enemy runway. Sub-munitions would also be an ideal way of delivering chemical warfare agent, so how could we be sure what the content really was? This was the problem of the sealed container that we had first encountered at Kineton and Crombie. A discussion ensued between inspectors and escorts on how we might deal with this problem as there was no facility for breaking down the JP233 on site – another trip to Otterburn might be in order. Clearly some form of non-destructive evaluation would be required in future that could provide an elemental composition of the weapon content under examination. It was this experience that eventually led to UK interest in, and a research project on, neutron activation analysis (NAA) as an analytical technique for future use by OPCW inspectors. NAA could provide an inspector with an indication that if the contents were high in nitrogen, this would indicate high explosive; however, a higher reading of say phosphorus and fluorine would be suggestive of a nerve agent. All that was for the future, but a key lesson from these early UK PCIs was a need to deal with the problem of accessing sealed containers, especially munitions such as the JP233.

As we were leaving the HAS, we decided that it might be worth running the CAM over a few fifty-five gallon oil drums outside the adjacent HAS – this was in part to use up some spare time in the exercise as we had completed our work in the HAS quicker than the time planned for, but also to see whether the escort team would agree. The CAM was our one piece of inspection equipment. So off I went with the hand-held detector to see what reading it gave and to my great surprise it read three bars on G following my running it over the tops and sides of the drums, which would suggest the presence of a nerve agent. Now this was evidently a false-positive and as the device was designed for battlefield use rather than as a precise measurement instrument for on-site inspections, better safe than sorry. However, we decided to push our luck with the escorts and requested immediate access to the HAS – clearly with potential indicators of non-compliance activity we could do nothing else. The control staff let us push the exercise envelope a little even though the rest of the HAS compound was supposedly out of bounds. This rattled the home team and a negotiation between the two sides ensued; no further access was to be allowed was the response. We reminded the senior site escort that he had previously said that we could inspect all the HAS, it was only a shortage of time that we could not do so. Now the moment some potential non-compliant activity had been discovered, he was denying access. We suggested that this did not look good and would certainly appear so to an international audience that read our inspection report. At this point the control staff finally intervened. We were taken aside to hear the decision. Apparently overnight an aircraft carrying sensitive equipment had arrived and was parked inside the HAS, and the RAF did not want us to see it. Two major lessons were identified out of this experience: first, choose your words very carefully when speaking to inspectors – do not give any hostages to fortune.[21] Second, careful thought would have been needed to go into developing suitable managed access strategies for such eventualities had this been a real inspection. One option would have been following the positive CAM reading, to permit a more thorough analysis of environmental samples collected from the HAS exterior and ground surrounding it. A simple refusal of access to such a large potential storage space would be something to avoid for any home team wanting to demonstrate compliance with the CWC. Exclusion zones needed to be kept as small as possible.

Day Two finally saw us negotiating access to the SSA. Now things started to turn really serious – the SSA was storing live nuclear weapons, which meant that security was strict. We were not allowed to take any equipment into the HAS and had to surrender our notebooks and pens, and were handed paper and pencils instead. We were brought in through the gate that led to the airfield rather than the main entrance. The main rationale here was that we would not see the normal security arrangements and equipment in use; armed RAF Police were out in force too, complete with a few angry looking Alsatian dogs. I had mentioned earlier that Richard Soilleux had acquired a colour aerial photograph of the SSA, something which caused the site security officer palpitations. (His palpitation rate increased further when we noticed that contractors working on an adjacent part of the airfield had created a temporary gate of their own nor far from the SSA through which a large lorry was entering.) From Richard's map we could very clearly see the layout of the SSA and that there were two main types of revetted storage igloos plus what looked to be a handful of administrative looking buildings. No doubt, Soviet satellite photo reconnaissance also had a good picture or two of the site. At that stage my knowledge of the UK nuclear weapons programme suggested that the larger igloos had been used for the first and second-generation nuclear weapons, whilst the more modern looking ones set around the SSA in a herring bone pattern were for the WE177 tactical nuclear weapon that first entered service in September 1966. Clearly such a highly secure explosive storage compound could equally be used to hide chemical weapons. In order to protect nuclear stockpile numbers and the exact figure held at Honington the home team had devised a new strategy that rejoiced under the unfortunate acronym RANSAC – Random Selective Access. Ransacking a site was perhaps not the best message to give to site representatives, but it was a neat acronym. Clearly, being allowed to inspect all igloos would reveal total numbers held on site, instead we were invited to choose any two ourselves. The psychology behind this is important. If inspectors are offered a choice, then this is better than being told what you can inspect. The issue then becomes one of what percentage of a number offers the highest level of assurance and deterrence; this is not a precise science, but clearly more than two out of some twenty-five igloos would provide higher levels of comfort. Equally the home team would ideally set a bottom line, but would certainly not offer that first – it might then appear generous when it acquiesced to inspectors' request for further access. We did not resolve this matter during PCI 3, but the principle was established and the concept appeared to work well in practice on the ground.

Once inside the few igloos we noted that one was empty, so we requested another one to examine instead. Once inside one of the more modern looking igloos we saw three trolleys that had what appeared to be two weapons on each one under a tarpaulin. We asked if the tarpaulin could be lifted in part, and this was agreed to after some discussion by the escorts, but before being allowed to look we had to leave the igloo whilst some preparations were made. This was all part of the managed access approach. We were allowed to stand outside so nothing could be taken out unobserved. There were some shrouds placed on the ballistic casing of the weapon to cover up some classified details that the hosts did not want us to see. We were of course confronted with the problem of how to be sure that this object was in fact nuclear and did not contain a chemical warfare agent fill? Handling procedures for nuclear weapons were extremely strict for sound safety and security reasons, and no unauthorized equipment could be used anywhere near such a weapon, certainly nothing electrical or which contained a radioactive source in it. So how could the home team demonstrate compliance? In this case the tentative proposal put to the inspection team would be that a gamma spectrometer owned and operated by the hosts might be used to provide an indicative reading to show that the readings were consistent with the publicly known characteristics of a nuclear weapon system. Furthermore, the gamma spectrometer could be calibrated against plutonium stored under IAEA seals at BNFL Sellafield in order to show that the spectrometer was functioning reliably and that there was no attempt to provide a false signal. All this would take time to arrange, even in the event of a real inspection, and would require seals and tags to keep objects under inspector chain of custody. In terms of the PCI this solution was the adopted one, coupled with perhaps some environmental sampling from the igloo (such as the plant room filters) and surrounding areas in the SSA.

Once the role play part of the PCI was over and the hot wash up completed, we were interviewed by an RAF security officer to find out exactly what we had discovered and deduced from our time inside the SSA. A continuing Cold War concern was what could be revealed to an inspector working for a hostile intelligence agency and who then passed his information to experts who might make more of the information than he/she could. There were, moreover, concerns about compromising physical security arrangements, and there was still at the time a terrorist threat from PIRA, which also had to be considered. We were asked what we thought the total stockpile was in view of the access we had received and what had we deduced about the weapon design and other features. All we could say was an estimate based on the fact that each of the modern igloos could likely hold eight such weapons as a maximum and as there were nineteen such igloos that might make for a theoretical total of 152 weapons. We could not say for sure what number might be stored in the larger older igloos as no weapons were seen inside the one we inspected; it only had some trolleys and a tractor unit. As we had seen one empty igloo, we could not be sure that all the others were full or what number they might hold – it could be anything from one to eight. So overall the stockpile could be anywhere between 8 and 152, and we certainly did not know how many other such SSAs the UK had for nuclear weapon storage, no doubt the Soviet Union knew as these facilities were built to a standard design and would be observable to photoreconnaissance satellites. As for warhead design we were none the wiser, all we could say was to give an approximate estimate of the size of the warhead within the ballistic casing. We were not allowed to photograph or measure the weapon casing. No doubt the RAF security chap went away quite assured and this exercise went a long way to showing that the UK could live with highly intrusive inspections at even very sensitive sites.

Now there is an interesting footnote to all of this. A lot of trouble had gone into designing an effective managed access strategy for RAF Honington and to protect classified details about the WE177 weapon system. Nine years later the last four RAF WE177As were withdrawn from RAF Marham on 22 April 1998 and returned to AWE Burghfield for dismantlement. The final weapon was broken down in September that year. Since then, more and more details about the WE177 programme have emerged in papers held at The National Archives, and I was eventually able to publish a detailed history of the programme.[22] We now know that there were in fact three variants of the WE177 – the A, B and C. Each had a different yield, including a depth bomb version of the WE177A. The B and C variants used the same ballistic casing, and were physically longer than the WE177A. Keeping this secret from the inspectors had been the RAF's main aim in 1989, and they had succeeded. And as for the total stockpile, the UK appears to have built 252 weapons.[23] Of this we had not a sniff back in October 1989, which just goes to show that managed access can work. This also shows that pressing security concerns can be and are transient, especially in the context of weapons systems withdrawn from operational service. The JP233 also ended its service life in 1998.

There is one more legacy from PCI 3; the SSA finally closed as an operational nuclear weapons storage site in 1998 once the last Polaris Chevaline warhead, being held there temporarily, was moved to Burghfield for dismantlement. However, we were to return four more times for CWC exercises (including once when it was still operational) and for a multinational nuclear disarmament verification exercise in 2017 – almost thirty years since my first visit, but that is for subsequent chapters.

PCI4 AWE Aldermaston – nuclear weapons research and components manufacture

From the outset the aim had been to conduct an exercise at Aldermaston, essentially on the assumption that this was likely to be the hardest nut to crack, but if we did the way would be clear to conclude confidently that no other defence site in the UK would present a problem. The task of convincing AWE management and its MOD counterparts in London fell to the Defence Arms Control Unit as planners and sponsors of the PCI programme. As might have been predicted this was far from easy as the initial reaction was that "you cannot come in here," and the notion that ultimately foreign inspectors under a future CWC might be allowed in was an absolute anathema. There was then a very strong culture in the nuclear weapons community that non-cleared personnel, even if holding a positive vetting security clearance, were to be kept well away from nuclear weapons secrets. A strict need to know policy applied; there were also concerns that an exercise might interfere with the Trident warhead production programme. Another acute anxiety extended to concerns about compromising the 1958 UK-US Mutual Defence Agreement.[24] This agreement was critical in underpinning the UK nuclear weapons programme as a good deal of warhead related information, components and materials were provided by the US. AWE and the nuclear branches of MOD, notably ACSA (N) worried that access for future international inspectors could lead to the inadvertent release of US owned classified information, which the UK was legally obliged to protect. Furthermore, there was a perception that any such leak would also breach the 1968 Nuclear Non-Proliferation Treaty under which the UK was prohibited under Article I from in any way assisting, encouraging, or inducing any non-nuclear-weapon state in the manufacture or acquisition of a nuclear weapon. As at RAF Honington, site physical security and the terrorist threat added to the anxiety levels as intrusive access might reveal protective measures and potential vulnerabilities. All these and other concerns were of course legitimate. One concern apparently was that inspectors might see how many toilets there were, which could give an insight into the number of personnel working in key buildings, thereby enabling some deductions to be made about potential outputs. This was not a legitimate concern and would require some tremendous powers of deduction to rival Sherlock Holmes. However, the whole point of conducting a PCI in the first place was to see whether these concerns – no matter how daft – could be addressed whilst still leaving sufficient access that would likely convince international inspectors that nothing was being concealed. DACU took about two years to talk our way into Aldermaston with a few days in February 1990 finally being agreed as suitable to hold the exercise; however, there was to be a compromise as a condition which would see a hybrid exercise combining physical access to parts of the site and a table-top component that would simulate access to one of the key manufacturing buildings – A45, which was used to produce HEU weapon components. There would be a site brief, windshield tour and, like Honington, access would be provided to a pre-selected building that would hopefully give a clear insight for the inspectors of the sorts of features that would be encountered in a radioactive components manufacturing facility such as glove boxes used to handling and working with plutonium. In this case the building was A1.1, which had been used to produce the plutonium components for the UK's first nuclear device that was tested at Montebello in October 1952 as well as Chevaline.[25] A1.1 was in the process of being decommissioned, so there would be minimal disruption to real on-going production work. The table-top element proved to be an interesting combination of floor plans, still and video photography. We were shown a building plan that had certain areas hashed out to conceal sensitive details and invited to select several laboratories for inspection. We would then be shown a video of a walk down a corridor and then through the laboratory doors and then around the lab itself – the video would stop at certain points and we had to ask for its continuation or for additional views. We could also ask our hosts about what we were seeing as well as explanations for the various features observed, such as the criticality cages, used to keep fissile material a safe distance apart to prevent the inadvertent assembly of a critical mass. All the photos and video footage had been taken over one weekend when A45 was not in use. We only found out about this sometime afterwards, and complained that had we known we could have conducted the exercise for real over a weekend instead of collecting photographic materials for the table-top. From what we could see, it seemed clear that this building was designed and used for metal bashing, there was nothing to suggest any capability for either the manufacture or storage of chemical weapons.

Looking at the facility floor plan that clearly showed the layout of corridors and laboratories we could see that one large space had been divided into multiple sub-divisions as part of the site's managed access strategy. We were not going to be allowed access to every laboratory, only a percentage at our choosing. But it was not clear how we could access the very large space with the multiple managed access zones that had been created. It seemed that this space might be one of two things: either the place where final warhead component assembly took place, or the storage vaults for completed warhead components. As it transpired it was the latter and the irony of the situation was that the managed access strategy developed to protect this location had drawn attention to it. This would be one of the major lessons from the PCI programme, sometimes it would be better to hide things in plain sight and that managed access strategies would need to be carefully applied in practice to wherever possible avoid drawing undue attention to particular places or objects. For AWE, the major concern was that access had revealed the location of the component storage area and it was where this was in the building in relation to other external features of the site that was the problem. This was going to have a major impact on the overall PCI programme report that the UK would ultimately present in Geneva in the summer of 1990.

As at RAF Honington, the inspection team was debriefed after the role play part of the exercise had concluded. We saw nothing that gave us any indication of warhead design, component shapes and geometries or any idea of through-put – of course our views were constrained by sight of photographs and videos only, but that said we were shown what we would have likely seen had we been physically present; for example, all the glove boxes viewed had no warhead components on display, moulds and other fixtures or furniture such as cradles that could have given some insights were not on display. Apparently there had been some anxiety that if we had seen one particular piece of equipment – an isostatic press – and worked out where in the production process this sat, then this could have revealed some insights. We did not know whether there was single or multiple production lines in the laboratories, so we could make no sensible deductions about throughput; neither would we have had sufficient details that would have enlightened a more knowledgeable person. Nor was anything done that posed a threat to the 1958 MDA or likely place the UK in breach of its NPT Article I obligations. We did correctly work out that A45 was used to produce radioactive components – using HEU in this case – for weapons, but that was hardly likely to be unknown to the Soviet Union since photoreconnaissance satellites would have revealed quite a bit about the layout of the site. A45 was clearly a contained building designed to handle radioactive components.

PCI 4 was a major milestone in the overall PCI programme, and arguably in the UK's overall approach and work on arms control and disarmament verification to date. It had established a vitally important precedent, namely that physical access was indeed possible in even the most sensitive sites. Whilst comprehensive access to every nook and cranny was never on the cards, PCI 4 had shown the way forward and proved the point that there was no site in the UK to which some form of access was not possible. The use of the word site is quite deliberate, and that will become clearer when we reach the overall conclusions from the PCI programme, and what that entailed for the UK's next steps on CWC challenge inspection verification.

PCI 5 Proofing and Experimental Establishment (PEE) – Shoeburyness

When considering the UK defence facilities that we would need to examine, a testing range for ordnance came into the reckoning. Shoeburyness on the Essex coast near Southend thus became the venue for PCI 5. A proofing and experimental range was also the sort of site that might feature prominently in the types of places that an offensive CW programme would need for some of its work. The Shoeburyness site provided a closed and controlled environment for testing weapons systems at various stages of development, for safe disposal of expired ammunition and for live ammunition training in Explosive Ordnance Disposal techniques. It also had, at the time of our exercise, environmental test chambers in which pieces of ordnance could be exposed to specific climatic conditions for a given period of time, the object of which was to test how the weapon stood up the strains and stresses of extreme heat, humidity or cold in order to replicate the kinds of conditions the weapon would encounter in its service life. As a bonus, the overall range included AWE Foulness, which meant that we could include a third nuclear weapons related facility in the PCI programme. Foulness itself covered over 2,000 acres, was adjacent to the PEE test range at Potton Island and was needed to undertake hydrodynamic experiments with larger quantities of conventional explosives than were permitted at Aldermaston or on the range at Porton Down. Tests conducted at Foulness were concerned primarily with improvements in safety and the approval of new weapons designs. The site also contained a blast tunnel that was used to simulate the effects of a nuclear explosion.[26] Foulness had also been used in the late 1950s and early 1960s for experiments connected to seismic research for the detection of underground nuclear weapon tests.[27] So here some thirty years later the site was contributing once again to the development of a verification regime for another arms control and disarmament treaty. I had not realized that at the time. PCI 5 was set for March 1990.

One of the key techniques in a CWC challenge inspection would be sampling and analysis; we had not really addressed this topic in the previous PCIs, though we did on occasion request permission to take one or two environmental samples. Indeed, in PCI 4 I had suggested that we should ask to retain the white protective over shoes that we were required to wear by our hosts whilst inspecting building A1 at AWE. This request was promptly denied, probably out of concern about what else might be detected if the dirt on the overshoes were analysed. For PCI 5 we were tasked to think more about where an inspection team might wish to collect samples – all of this would be done notionally as we had no capacity to collect real samples. There were essentially two main reasons for requesting a sample: to confirm information provided by the hosts, or because we had reason to be suspicious about an object or location given other contextual information collected by the inspectors. In the end we requested some sixty-six samples over the two days.[28] One of the reasons for doing so was to see to what extent such requests might impinge on classified information unrelated to chemical weapons. After the exercise Dr Paul Norman from Porton Down's Chemistry and Decontamination Division told us that this number of samples would keep an analytical laboratory, such as Porton, busy for three months. So clearly much more thought and focus would be required for real sample collection in a challenge inspection. There were two sample requests that were to prove noteworthy. The first of these concerned a 155 mm projectile that we found in a ditch on one of the firing ranges. Our request was that a small explosive cutting charge should be used to punch a hole in the casing so we could see whether the projectile had a liquid fill. We left a notional inspector to keep an eye on the item and headed off elsewhere to continue our physical inspection. A short while later we heard a huge explosion, the EOD team assigned to the task had decided to destroy the object rather than cut it open. This appeared to be an attempt to destroy incriminating evidence – echoes of the 1969 film 'The Italian Job' and Michael Caine's immortal line, 'You were only supposed to blow the bloody doors off,' but had such a situation occurred for real we

31

could probably have recovered the fragments and had these analysed for the presence of a chemical warfare agent or its degradation products.

The second sampling scenario concerned our selection at random of two 155mm projectiles from one of the explosive storage houses for closer examination; our hosts agreed that these could be subject to explosive demolition to demonstrate that they did not contain chemical warfare agents. As was the way of it there were two lot-expired projectiles that were already scheduled for explosive demolition and these were substituted for our selected items as part of the control staff's exercise play. The two 155 mm projectiles were placed on cradles in a shallow pit, which was then filled with diesel fuel. The pit itself was surrounded by a breeze block lined berm to contain any fragments. Things did not quite go to plan; one of the shells, which had been wired with a small demolition charge, failed to fire fully – 'low ordered' to use the technical term whilst the other one detonated in full – 'high ordered' – and shot off the cradle, bounced off the inner wall and back into the fuel fire ignited by the charges. Once it was safe to enter the demolition pit we were able to collect some fragments that could have been analysed. The size of the explosions provided pretty conclusive evidence that the 155mm projectiles contained HE. Our Senior Ammunition Technical Officer in the inspection team (Alan Morely) had witnessed the placing of the charges, hence our confidence. That said, this was quite an extreme way to demonstrate compliance and once again highlighted the need for an effective non-destructive interrogative technique to confirm the contents of sealed containers such as artillery projectiles.

PCI 5 threw up three other vignettes that help illustrate the sort of problems that could arise in a challenge inspection They also reveal how the deterrent function of such an inspection and the chances of discovery of illicit activity are in reality quite high in so far that a state cannot be sure that everything will go to plan and its concealment plans remain water tight throughout an intrusive inspection. Example one: we encountered an extremely large – almost a sports hall equivalent in dimensions – revetted storage building in a remote part of the site, and which could certainly be used to store ammunition, especially if one were not too fussy about safety. On entry we found this space piled high with sandbags in a large square. The sandbags were on pallets. We wondered whether these were being used to conceal objects at the centre of the stack, so the request was made to have one side of the square removed. This required a fork lift truck, but unfortunately the driver was not fully trained – he was the only one available at the time – and on his second attempt, a stack of sandbags fell off the pallet and split open. However, this was sufficient for us to see that the box was hollow, the piles of sandbags were only one pallet deep. One does see some strange things on military sites. The willingness to move the sandbags scored highly on the cooperation scale and showed a commitment to demonstrate compliance.

Example two concerned the environmental test chamber encountered at the north end of the site. On the day a long-term exposure trial was underway and no access would be possible otherwise months of expensively acquired experimental data would be wasted. Now one could argue, as indeed was done subsequently, if such an occasion were ever to arise for real and access by inspectors was the only thing that would demonstrate compliance, then the experiment would be written off. Ministers would undoubtedly prefer the UK to receive a clean bill of health. During the exercise we looked at alternative methods to deal with the problem, and these included a review of experiment documentation and a briefing on the nature of the experiment itself, which was a test for the new UK man portable anti-tank weapon LAW 80 that had entered service in 1987. There were also viewing ports that allowed us to look inside and see what was being held in the environmental test chamber. All in all, these sorts of alternative methods would probably be sufficient, and were convincing enough for us.

The final example concerned our inspection of AWE Foulness, which although within the wider Shoeburyness Proofing and Experimental Establishment perimeter, was situated on an island linked by a causeway. As its name indicated it was part of the Atomic Weapons Establishment, it was also the first example of what later became known as the 'lodger unit' problem, though strictly speaking on this occasion this was not true. Nevertheless, the point here is that challenge inspection was being designed to apply to a specified geographic area – it was not going to be defined by institutional affiliation, so we could have a situation where multiple entities reporting to different command authorities might occupy a facility or physical space. There might also be commercial or private properties. Although there might be a predominant or principal player on the site, they would not necessarily know exactly what was going on within a lodger unit, or even have the authority to enable access without prior agreement. On this occasion our senior escorts facilitated access to AWE Foulness, which was much less sensitive than its parent site at Aldermaston. Testing of implosions systems would contain classified shapes and the results of the experiments were the main sensitivities, but none of this was underway during our inspection. Our main interest was in the explosive storage houses, the engineering workshops and the range given the exercise scenario. It became clear that there were no chemical warfare signatures present, and our senior AWE Foulness escort told us that there were no chemical labs or facilities on site, and as he said this we turned a corner in the main engineering workshop and there in front us was a chemical fume hood. Our response was instant: in which case why do you have a chemical fume hood? His response was genuine – 'I had no idea that we had that.' On closer examination it was clear that the hood was no longer in a serviceable condition and evidently had not been used for years. There was no power and it contained a handful of very old crusty brown jars with faded labels. No one had got round to removing it and there it stood gathering dust. From an inspector's perspective looking for the incongruous, the anomalous and the unusual is a key task. Assessing any explanations provided for such features for their scientific and technical plausibility and credibility is essential, and on this occasion the wider context of our discovery suggested that it was nothing worth investigating further. PCI 5 had provided a good deal of new insights as well as reinforcing earlier lessons. Perhaps the main outcome was that much more thought was going to be needed on the sampling and analysis issue both in terms of its practical and resource implications for inspectors and home teams.

PCI 6 – a government communication facility

At the time of the original programme and in the UK's two reports in our Working Papers for the CD we did not reveal the identity of the facilities involved, though the description of PCI 4 would have left the reader in little doubt as to the location. The elapse of some thirty years means that the names can be revealed; however, this does not apply to PCI 6. One of the Prime Minister's initial worries about the US challenge inspection provisions in CD/500 back in 1984 was the potential adverse impact on AWE and GCHQ. So, at some stage we needed to look at how a CWC CI might impact on an intelligence facility, hence the need for what became PCI 6. First the location was only chosen after much debate and argument with representatives of the UK intelligence community, whose initial reaction was similar to the one that we heard from AWE: 'You can't come in here.' They were persuaded eventually, largely because an effective CWC was a key foreign policy objective endorsed by Ministers, and the Prime Minister herself. We did not go to Cheltenham for PCI 6. PCI 6 would now take place in April 1990.[29] There was a strong pressure to complete the programme and provide the results to the summer session of the CD in Geneva and hopefully shape the direction and outcome of the negotiations on the CWC's challenge inspection provisions. These were going to be key to whether the CD could produce an effective Convention.

As it transpired the facility at PCI 6 posed few access problems for the inspection team – the same core group of experts were present once again. The main reason for this was that there was nothing at all on the site that had a chemical signature or would unduly raise the curiosity of a CWC inspector; the most that we could tell was the work done there was evidently related to communications technology. Two elements of this exercise stood out. The first of these concerned the opening site briefing. We had already seen in the earlier PCIs just how important the briefing was in setting the scene and addressing questions raised by the inspectors. One of the key elements in demonstrating compliance was showing that everything seen and encountered on the site was fully consistent with its stated purpose, and good and detailed briefings played an important part in this. We therefore eagerly anticipated the site briefing at PCI 6. We had already noticed that the site representatives were wearing name badges with only first names shown – no surnames or roles or titles. These were the days before PowerPoint when old fashioned overhead projectors were in use with large, printed transparencies. Much to our surprise it quickly became clear that this was going to be a silent brief; all we were going to be told was what was written briefly in about ten or so slides, each one remaining on screen for a few moments only. The principal reason for this was to make sure that a carefully limited presentation was made conveying the essentials; we all know that when speaking to slides people can add in more detail than is needed or desirable or just drone on and at a sensitive intelligence related site there could be a risk that gratuitous information could be provided. On reflection this seemed a sensible approach and one that could be recommended in future use for comparable challenging sites. It would have helped though if the inspectors had been prewarned that it would be a silent briefing.

The second event proved to be a very imaginative use of managed access; in this case a large object was carefully shrouded in a laboratory – it was certainly large enough to be hiding fume hoods and or chemical laboratory glass vessels, so we felt that we ought to probe more deeply. Part of the scenario alleged that clandestine development of CW was taking place. After an initial request to raise part of the shroud was rejected, our hosts suggested that they might be able to offer something, but would require some time to make a few adjustments. If we were to return after lunch, then an alternative access option might be ready. So, after leaving a notional inspector or two to monitor the lab door to ensue nothing came out, we headed to our working space to consider our next steps over a sandwich lunch. An hour later we returned to find that the large, shrouded object now had an entrance on one side that we could walk through to reveal an empty space, the other side of the shrouded object carefully screened with the same cream coloured hessian cloth as the rest of the structure. It was essentially a box. We could collect some environmental samples if we wished and use the CAM. This appeared satisfactory as once again the willingness to offer a workable solution placed alongside the contextual nature of this managed access case provided assurance that whatever this object was, it had nothing to do with chemical warfare. PCI 6 thus concluded on a high, so it was time to draft and agree the overall programme report for the CD, which the Foreign Office Minister of State would present during his visit to Geneva in July.

The final report to the CD

There was a good deal to report, much of it positive. The final report had been much heralded in Geneva; indeed, a short video of PCI 2 had been made by Porton Down and this had done the rounds of CD diplomatic missions in Geneva and an earlier working paper summarising the findings from the first two exercises had already been tabled in June 1989.[30] The film, which was shown to the CD on 19 April 1990,[31] highlighted key features of a challenge inspection such as perimeter monitoring, dealing with munitions and managed access. When Dr Cooper took it to the Bulgarian mission the third secretary at the mission had failed to load the right video and when the film started it seemed to Graham that what came up looked like John Ford's great 1939 Western 'Stagecoach' with native Americans chasing a stagecoach through Monument Valley; cowboys and Indians seemed one way of summing up a challenge inspection he commented. On more serious matters, the FCO Minister of State William Waldegrave addressed the CD on 11 July in order to present the analysis of the results from the PCI programme.[32] The UK Working Paper went into a good deal of detail, starting with a summary of some of main security concerns encountered in the programme.[33] The first of these was physical security, which was a common concern across all the sites; certain intelligence advantages accrue from gaining physical access to a site beyond those available from other sources. Presence and location of sensitive stores was the second main concern since the UK's policy was neither to confirm nor deny the presence of nuclear weapons at any single location. Stockholdings, throughput and capacities were acute anxieties at PCIs 3 and 4. Worries about compromising nuclear warhead design information also figured prominently, particularly given the risk of compromising Article I of the NPT. On the other hand, CWC inspectors would need sufficient information and access to satisfy themselves that any weapons they encountered were not chemical weapons.

The PCI programme identified a range managed access techniques for dealing with the security concerns about sensitive buildings, rooms, equipment, processes while still enabling a good deal of information to be made available to help inspectors determine whether the area was concerned with undeclared activities relevant to the CWC. The UK divided these into two categories: routine managed access measures for use at most sites, and exceptional measures for sites where especially sensitive national security concerns were at stake.[34] Routine measures included shrouding of sensitive items, but there was an important caveat here. It would be essential to ensure that the 'keep out zone' is kept to the smallest size possible. Wherever possible inspectors should be allowed to touch through the shroud and use instruments to sample the air in and around the shrouded object. The impact of shrouding on the inspectors would vary from case to case. A small, shrouded object in an otherwise open electronics laboratory or drawing office is less likely to arouse inspectors' suspicions than a large, shrouded area in an ammunition storage facility. Other techniques include the use of instrumentation such as x-ray equipment to demonstrate whether ammunition has a solid or liquid fill – a liquid fill would be indicative of a chemical agent. The Working Paper went on to report that the UK had commissioned a project looking at neutron activation analysis as a non-intrusive alternative to x-ray analysis. This was a project that I had convinced our FCO Assistant-Under Secretary John Goulden to fund at Porton Down. Another possible technique was gamma ray spectroscopy to address whether sealed containers held nuclear materials. Gravity meters and other geophysical techniques could be useful in detecting concealed underground storage facilities.[35] The UK had in fact already presented a working paper setting out the value of instrumentation in CWC routine and challenge inspections.[36]

In the UK vision exceptional measures would be required in specific circumstances. In order to prevent the compromise of highly classified information about stockholdings, throughputs and capacities – a particular concern at nuclear weapon facilities – something which could be deduced by an inspection team if allowed access to all the relevant buildings on a particular site, a system of Random Selective Access was developed. Under this approach only a given percentage of buildings within a site or rooms within a building and/or items within a room were available for inspection at the inspectors' own choice. During the four exercises where this approach was deployed that percentage was normally twenty per cent, though it need not be set at that level. It could be deployed in two different ways, with pros and cons for each. One option would be to let the inspectors negotiate access to buildings or parts thereof on a step-by-step process until they are satisfied or until they have reached the percentage limit. Another approach would be to state from the outset that within the challenged site or parts thereof only x per cent would be allowed at the inspectors' choice. There was no clear-cut advantage to either option. The disadvantage of the former is that inspectors would have to negotiate every level of access, which if protracted could create suspicion. Indeed as Dr Graham Cooper had commented in 'The Chemical Weapons Convention Bulletin', 'The UK learned lessons about unhappy inspectors during six national practice challenge inspections (PCIs). During early PCIs, inspectors became increasingly frustrated at having to fight repeatedly for access inch by inch, particularly so if hard-won access, say to a building, revealed it to be entirely empty. This frustration usually led to renewed and heightened suspicion and to increasingly vigorous demands for greater access.'[37] The main disadvantage of the latter would be that more access might be given to inspectors than in normal circumstances might be necessary. Making sure that inspectors had the choice was the key to an effective deterrent; preselected choices foisted onto the team would not serve at all. Overall, the UK concluded that random selective access as part of a managed access scheme represented a major contribution to meeting security concerns while at the same time giving inspectors sufficient access at their choice to enable them to conclude with a high degree of confidence that the location or item subject to managed access was not related to chemical weapons. Moreover, the UK had often found that areas of greatest concern to the challenged state from a security perspective were of little interest to a CW inspection team. Despite this, the working paper went on to record that within certain sites (i.e. AWE Aldermaston) clarification was needed as to whether managed access might have to include denial of access to a very limited number of highly sensitive buildings. This was clearly highly unsatisfactory from the point of view of the design of an effective CWC challenge inspection regime as it would grant the unscrupulous ample scope to cheat, and certainly further investigation of this problem was going to be needed. We will return to this problem in the next section. That said, the UK concluded that there was no site so sensitive from a national security perspective that it could not allow some form of access within the site, appropriately managed, to an international inspection team under a future CWC. In most cases, normal work would have to cease to facilitate such levels of access, though this was an assessment that would change in future. Of course, we did not imagine that the application of managed access would prevent the loss of some sensitive information that a state party might have preferred to shield. However, the extent and importance of this would vary from site to site. These factors would need to be weighed against the value of having a more effective CWC and the overall gains for national security from permitting such access.

A few other key points were discussed in CD/1012. One of these noted the demonstrable value of all facilities likely to be the subject of a challenge inspection preparing and exercising beforehand a reception plan including the preparation of shrouding and managed access strategies and fallback positions for instances where the inspectors are not convinced by the initial levels of access. Such decisions should not be left to the day of a real inspection as this can cause major problems and delays which would only arouse inspectors' suspicions. This insight was to form the basis for a new round of practice challenge inspection exercises at defence sites after the conclusion of the CWC, and these will be discussed in greater detail in Chapter 4. A site briefing on the work and layout of the facility was picked out as being of value to inspectors, especially when conducted over a map or model. A briefing would help orientate inspectors and tell them what activities and facilities they should expect to see. A site tour immediately after the briefing was essential too. Sampling modalities would also require further thought and would also entail significant resource implications for both inspectors and sites.

Managed access follow-up

However, there was one contentious issue left over from PCI 4 at AWE Aldermaston as alluded to in CD/1012. Whilst it was evident from all the sites used in the PCI programme that there was no site where we could not offer some form of access, the problem was that the security concerns at Aldermaston surrounding one building meant that the then official position had to be that on some very few and exceptional cases, access to a building might need to be denied to inspectors. Despite this the CD report contained a good deal that was to help shape the negotiations and demystify challenge inspection.

The business over the need to exclude buildings from inspection, even only under very exceptional circumstances, remained unsatisfactory. This was not the ideal outcome as it could potentially provide a state party in future with an easy excuse to keep inspectors out of areas where cheating was in fact taking place. Indeed, given the size of the building in question at AWE and its other features, such as its containment and air handling, this was the sort of place that had some attributes that could suggest that it might be related to chemical warfare. Clearly that was unwelcome from a national UK standpoint; there was also the small matter of making sure that the future CWC's challenge inspection provisions were effective. The ideal position would be that no building was so sensitive that some form of access could not be provided to international inspectors. For this reason, the MOD with full FCO support embarked on a managed access follow-up programme to look at how this problem, particularly the one at AWE, could be resolved. This new approach was endorsed by the Whitehall interdepartmental Chemical Weapons Convention Steering Group (CWCSG), chaired by FCO Assistant Under Secretary of State John Goulden. The CWCSG was the policy making body that oversaw and directed the UK's negotiating strategy. This would entail a series of visits to civil and military nuclear sites in the autumn of 1990: British Nuclear Fuels Limited (BNFL) Sellafield, which had been the subject of a separate invitation from the BNFL's Head of Security and Safeguards – Dr Roger Marsh, BNFL Springfields, the Naval Reactor Test Establishment (NRTE) HMS Vulcan at Dounreay, AWE Aldermaston and AWE Burghfield. These were not role play practice inspections, but rather what became known as 'walk-through, talk-through' visits in which CWC experts walked through difficult parts of the facility and discussed and identified potential ways and means of providing sufficient access for international inspectors under the future CWC. Our key objective was to see whether we could devise bespoke managed access strategies for these nuclear sites that would enable inspectors to be given access to every building, though in some cases the level of access might need to be quite constrained. The BNFL sites presented their own challenges, but we saw nothing that would prevent access to all buildings and structures; for example, by constraining the viewing angle on the spent naval reactor fuel store ponds at Sellafield and HMS Vulcan we could protect the classified design of the fuel elements; the radioactively contaminated areas where direct physical access was not possible could be readily demonstrated as such with their configuration and space totally unsuited to CW production or storage. We worked out too how we would manage access to the store at Springfields of UK nuclear material held outside IAEA safeguards for the defence programme. At AWE Burghfield an application of random selective access, rigorous shrouding and ensuring that all classified warhead shapes and components and warhead component cradles were not on display when inspectors were allowed access would work; environmental sampling would be possible too subject to case by case negotiations and if push came to shove, we could offer gamma spectroscopy to show that the contents of a loaded warhead transport container possessed features consistent with known characteristics of a nuclear weapons system without divulging specific design details or precise isotopic ratios of the fissile material present in the weapon.

The main obstacle remained that one building at Aldermaston, and it was quite clear that we were going to need to develop a specific set of measures to enable access. In PCI4 we had played this building in the exercise through a combination of floor plans, videos and still photography; this time we were able to enter and walk-through the facility, and could quickly see ways and means of creating a managed access plan, which in part built on the initial random selective access strategy used back in February. Access could be offered at the inspectors' choice of a small percentage of the separate laboratories in A45 with no attempt to sub-divide the storage area. Environmental sampling of the building perimeter and possibly inside too, again subject to case-by-case negotiations, could also be offered. Overall, the context of the access and the nature of the building itself ought to be sufficient to demonstrate that it was a radioactive materials and metals facility, and thus not being used or capable of being used for CW purposes.

This seemed to be a workable solution and enabled us to conclude that there would be no building in the UK so sensitive that some form of access could not be offered; this was going to be an important message to give to the CD negotiations. However, plans to report the results of the managed access follow-up work were ultimately abandoned in 1991 as the MOD became overly nervous at publicly stating a position that could embarrass the US and potentially jeopardise UK-US nuclear cooperation. The Americans were still reviewing their challenge inspection policy having rowed well back from their initial anywhere anytime 1984 proposal. This is not the place to chart the tortuous nature of the US policy review process and the end game of the negotiations on the CWC's challenge inspection procedures; however, many of the detailed provisions in the Convention's Verification Annex Part X on challenge inspection, especially on managed access, do owe their origins to the work done during the initial UK PCI programme and managed access follow-up work.

Exercises in the chemical industry

It was of course not just a case of military or defence related sites that would be subject to challenge inspection – any site on the territory of a state party in theory could be inspected. The chemical industry was going to be under an extensive regime of routine inspections, and many states in the CD had started to conduct practice routine inspections to see how these might work and to assess the potential impact on commercial confidentiality and the normal and safe functioning of chemical plants.[38] The UK had already conducted one national trial inspection in Avonmouth, which was a simulated routine Schedule 2 facility inspection.[39] However, we needed to see how an industrial site could stand up to the strains and stresses of a challenge inspection. Fortunately, the UK chemical industry was strongly supportive of efforts to negotiate a CWC and there had long been regular government-industry consultations on the elaboration of the CWC's declarations and inspections provisions affecting industry. After the Canberra Government-Industry Conference in 1989 a more formalised structure was set in place with the creation of a UK Government-Industry Group consultative meeting process – the Government Industry Working Group (GIWG). Industry was represented by the UK Chemical Industries Association (the CIA – not to be confused with the Langley, Virginia version) with participation from ICI and Astra Zeneca. When the request was made for a volunteer to host a CWC challenge inspection exercise, the CIA did not need too much convincing and undertook to find some volunteers. ICI Grangemouth and Rhone Poulenc at Avonmouth stepped forward; we did not need nor were likely to have six separate sites in an industry PCI programme volunteered up by the CIA. We agreed with the CIA that Grangemouth would host a full role play exercise whilst Rhone Poulenc would provide its site for a 'walk-through, talk through.' ICI Grangemouth was a multipurpose batch production site whilst the focus at Rhone Poulenc was their single continuous dedicated production line, which produced potassium fluoride (KF). The Grangemouth PCI and Rhone Poulenc exercises were set for January and April 1991 respectively with the aim of reporting the results to the CD during its summer session. This time round the lead government department was the Department of Trade and Industry rather than the MOD. We planned to stick with largely the same personnel in the inspection and home teams, but also needed to supplement them with some additional expertise. For the Grangemouth exercise we recruited an expert from the Health and Safety Executive's Industry inspectorate branch (Paul Robinson) to play the role of the requesting state observer, and for the inspection team we added one of the very last surviving chemical engineers who had worked on the UK's offensive CW programme in the 1950s and was still working at Porton Down. In this case Dai Morgan who had worked on the sarin pilot plant at Nancekuke, Cornwall. That had ceased nerve agent production in 1956 when the UK's offensive programme had been terminated following a Cabinet Defence Committee decision that year.[40] The site was used for other chemical defence related work until finally dismantled in the 1970s. Members of the CD were invited to visit to see that the facility had indeed been decommissioned and dismantled.[41] As a former CW Production Facility it would eventually be declared and inspected under the future CWC even though it had long ceased to be a chemical plant.

The Grangemouth exercise began in the same way as the previous six exercises at government sites with a team of government advisers assisting the senior site personnel in their preparations. Inspectors were provided with a site briefing setting out in general terms the history and activities of the site, and we were then given a quick tour of the facility in what by then was the customary minibus. We asked some questions and identified areas of possible interest for closer inspection when we made our initial inspection plan; we asked for lists of the chemicals held on site and their quantities, a list of accidents and their nature and the capabilities of the medical facilities on site. At which point we struggled to work out exactly how we should go about inspecting the various plant sites and other laboratories. Things had seemed much clearer on the defence sites, especially those storing munitions; Dai Morgan suggested that the best option would be to select one of the production processes and follow the pipe work and reactor vessels through from start to finish; the aim would be to check whether the chemical engineering and associated safety processes were suitable for either mustard or nerve agent production (the non-compliance scenario alleged CW agent production) as presently configured, or would be readily adaptable for such purposes. We could also look to see whether there was any pipework that might allow the diversion of chemicals for unknown purposes. Checking the list of chemicals held and produced on site would also indicate whether the raw ingredients needed for nerve agent production were available. This seemed to be sensible and as it turned out pragmatic way to proceed; we were also interested in accounting for batch runs and maintenance records to explain plant down time. We also noted a storage area for redundant or damaged reactor vessels, pipework and flanges, a good place for environmental samples as indeed were the waste and effluent disposal plants, to which we also paid close attention. Our colleague from the HSE, who was playing the role of the challenging state observer, was also a great help in suggesting the sort of things that we should look for. In fact, this was exactly one of the key roles envisaged for the observer as he/she could gently steer the inspectors onto the areas of greatest non-compliance concern to the requesting state. There were, however, negative aspects too, as we were going to discover later in this exercise. We quickly released that the UK regulatory framework that governed health and safety and environmental protection required the keeping of numerous records and standards. These could be requested by inspectors for review and could help build up a picture of the nature of legitimate activities at the site. Records could of course be falsified, but to sustain a complete parallel set covering all aspects of site production batches, inventories, raw materials, finished production, maintenance, quality control and even accident records covering months would be an impossible challenge; a site could never know exactly what records inspectors might request to see. Any inconsistencies or gaps would likely quickly unravel under scrutiny, which would leave the site with some explaining to do to convince the inspection team that all was well. On the subject of records, we had asked for and had received two copies of a list of chemicals held on site covering both raw materials as well as finished products: one copy for each IT sub-team. At one point when we were heading off to inspect part of the site, I noticed that one copy was missing. I assumed that it was buried in the masses of paper that we had acquired, but as time was pressing we had no chance to look for it. In the exercise hot-wash up we found out what had happened to it; the RSO, who shared our working area space, had secretly purloined one copy, and then proudly unveiled it during the wash up. The observer was following his brief to acquire as much information about the facility as possible – it was this incident that convinced me that an observer was a bad idea and posed a greater risk to confidentiality than the inspectors. We would be better off without an RSO. In future exercises after the signing of the CWC we made sure that the Requesting State Observer was always escorted, and housed and transported separately from the inspectors. Access would be limited as required with only periodic meetings with the Chief Inspector allowed in order to meet the minimum requirements set forth in the CWC's Verification Annex. This experience also highlighted the need to keep control of, and account for, all documents provided and self-generated during an inspection; this lesson applied to both escorts and inspectors and would become more and more important in future exercises, not just chemical ones as will hopefully become clear in subsequent chapters. It was clearly essential to keep track of all documents requested and handed over as well as oral and written questions that were put to the escorts, especially those that remained unanswered.

The final leg of the UK's work on challenge inspection at civil chemical plants was an extended 'walk-through, talk through' at Rhone Poulenc's Avonmouth plant that specialised in fluorine chemistry. Our focus was on the dedicated production plant for potassium fluoride (KF), a chemical that could be used in the production of GB (sarin). Avonmouth was of course not making chemical weapons or precursors for their production elsewhere – KF has multiple peaceful uses as a fluorinating agent and for etching and frosting glass, making silver solder flux and insecticides. The focus became the production and raw material records to see whether it would be possible to detect any diversions of KF and account for all production runs. Although material balances were one of the key methods used in nuclear safeguards, such fine accounting would not really work in the chemical industry given the very large volumes of materials involved in the production processes. The chemical industry was of course interested in making sure that processes were as efficient and economical as possible, but chemical weapons inspectors could not rely on highly accurate measurements that would account for chemicals down to the last gram in industrial scale production. It would come down to an overall assessment that things looked about right and that there were no troubling anomalies, which is what we concluded after a review of the KF plant at Avonmouth.

Although the UK pioneered practice challenge inspections, other CD member states looked to conduct their own. By the end of the negotiations in September 1992 the US, Netherlands, Canada, Poland, Switzerland, West Germany, East Germany, the USSR, and France all had conducted similar exercises with similar objectives.[42] The West Germans were particularly keen and suggested that the UK and Germany might conduct a joint exercise, which we quickly agreed. The plan would be for a UK inspection team to conduct the first PCI at a West German military facility in May 1990, in this case a Luftwaffe airbase at Pfedersfeld in Bavaria, whilst the return leg would be hosted by the UK at the Central Ammunition Depot at Longtown, near Carlisle in June. Both teams flew to the locations in military aircraft, in the British team's case we were met at Bonn-Cologne airport and ferried down to Pfedersfeld in a Transall C 160 whilst the German team flew to Carlisle airport direct in a Luftwaffe C 160. The Germans brought some verification equipment, which was used to check the contents of sealed containers such as a device for hydrogen concentration measurement. At Pfedersfeld the UK team, led this time by Richard Hoskins from the MOD's Central Staffs, rehearsed sample taking from various locations on the airfield, including from some railway oil tanker wagons. We also identified the fire engines at the airfield fire station as sample targets – our rationale was that if there had been any chemical warfare agent spill, particularly sulfur mustard, and the fire engines had been deployed to help decontaminate the mess, there might be a good chance that the rubber tyres might have absorbed some of the agent. Rubber was a good sample matrix. Our escorts agreed that we could do so. When we were about to slice a few slivers off one of the tyres with a scalpel, our host suddenly had an abrupt change of mind. It turned out this fire engine belonged to the US Air Force, which had an enclave on the airfield. US facilities were out of bounds in this exercise. We were invited to choose another target on the grounds that the first one did not exist for exercise purposes. We could see the funny side, but there was a serious point here in that lodger units could cause real issues in the effective handling of an in-bound inspection. We would encounter this problem again in future exercises, and would become a real challenge when it came to dealing with US bases and assets in the UK.

To say that we were not properly dressed for such activities would be an understatement. Once the CWC entered into force OPCW inspectors would be fully kitted out in NBC protective suits when collecting suspect environmental samples, we were just looking to see what was permissible and to work out future modalities. One of the main outcomes of the UK inspection at Pfedersfeld was my suggestion that we should write a full inspection report as if it had been a *'real inspection'* in order to give the CD some idea on what might be expected if ever a report was presented to the Executive Council for its consideration. I wrote the report which was agreed by the British side and then was cleared by our German colleagues and then included as an annex to the Working Paper that we presented to the CD.[43] At that stage of the CWC negotiations, it was largely agreed that the inspectors themselves would not make any compliance judgments, they would simply report the facts. Any decision on whether the state was non-compliant would be for the Executive Council's members to determine on the basis of the IT's factual report. That is how things ended up in Article IX, but I had felt that a detailed report describing the comprehensive and meticulous nature of the inspection would speak for itself, especially if the inspectors could comment on the nature and extent of the inspected state party's cooperation. Thus, if a state persistently refused access to buildings and locations, failed to answer questions and those that they did were not credible, rejected requests for samples, generally delayed and obstructed the inspection process and failed to demonstrate compliance, then the conclusion that one would draw from such a performance would be clear. As Robert Burns said in his 1786 poem 'A Dream': 'Facts are chiels that winna ding.' Facts do not lie.

There was also one further joint exercise hosted by the Germans, this time a multinational event designed to convince many of the doubters in Geneva that challenge inspection could be handled without undue disruption and compromising classified or commercially sensitive information. The Germans arranged for several Ambassadors from the CD to witness the exercise, which took place at the Luftwaffe base at Bad Kreuznach.[44] The British contingent was me on the inspection team and an RAF air traffic controller from the Joint Arms Control Implementation Group (JACIG) as the RSO, the tri-service body established by the MOD to conduct and host inspections under conventional arms control agreements in Europe. The RSO made such a nuisance of himself – well within the exercise rules of course – that our German hosts presented him with a medieval ball and chain in the wash-up discussions, which would be needed to provide greater control in future. All this did was to reinforce further my own scepticism of the value of an RSO. We were also provided with an aerial overflight of the airbase as part of the inspection, and it is the only airfield that I have been on where we taxied up hill to the main runway, which also had a slight dip in it, which was a bit disconcerting on landing. Ideally an overflight should be conducted in a helicopter – we had used one at PCI5 and during the German inspection at Longtown – as this affords the best view of the ground, assuming the flight was flown with that objective in mind. British experts on the exchange visit to the Soviet CW facility at Shikhany in 1988 were treated to an overflight that managed to avoid flying over anything of interest. Things were much harder in a fixed wing aircraft where the passenger seats were parallel to the fuselage and you had to turn your head to look out of the small windows. The Germans only had a Dornier 28 Skyservant plane available, and as that was better than nothing so up we went – inspectors first. This is a short take-off and landing aircraft, so we took off with a very sharp angle of attack, which was rather abrupt to say the least and not at all like the gentler ascent one has in a civil airliner. And to add to the discomfort, the pilot was making very sharp turns so that we could obtain a good view of the airfield and its facilities. This proved a bit much for my RAF colleague who asked if the pilot could take it easier on the turns; as noted he was not aircrew so being airsick was not surprising. All these aerobatics were noted with some apprehension by the waiting CD Ambassadors on the ground as they were also going to go aloft after we had landed. Word was duly passed to the young pilot to take it easier on the take-off and aerial manoeuvres over the airfield. The key point here however is just how important an overflight would be at a large inspection area (and some areas here were wooded) as it would enable inspectors to orient themselves and identify targets for inspection that might not be readily visible from the ground. We should recall here that this was in 1991, long before Google Earth, which today would allow inspectors to come prepared with some detailed high-resolution imagery of the location that they were to inspect. That said, ground truth could well have changed since the time the satellite or aircraft was last over the location, so the easier availability of high resolution imagery today does not obviate the value of a helicopter overflight during an inspection of large complex sites.

Conclusion

The PCI programme represented a major effort to plan, organise, conduct and report nine full inspections exercises, plus a detailed 'walk through, talk through' visit not to mention the multinational trial at Bad Kreuznach. The managed access follow up work at military and civil nuclear facilities was no less important as were all the other visits to defence and civil sites as part of the selection process for finding suitable facilities for the main PCIs.[45] All this practical work to inform national understanding of the problem and to shape the outcome of the CWC negotiations was very much in the tradition of British policy on disarmament verification going back to the 1950s and 1960s. It was fascinating at a personal level to be directly involved in all of this work and to have contributed to the development of concepts and techniques that would shape the final content of the CWC's Verification Annex. Despite all the practical effort, the final negotiated text on Challenge Inspection in the Convention's Article IX was not what many of us would have preferred to see. As in any multinational negotiation it represented a compromise between the ideal and the achievable. It was to some extent ironic that the weakening of the original concept of challenge inspection as proposed by the US in CD/500 was down to the Americans themselves. The Department of Defense (DOD), Joint Chiefs of Staff and Department of Energy found that they could not live with their own proposal, and wanted extra safeguards introduced to give them more time to prepare sites for inspection; hence the convoluted perimeter negotiation process and the extend timelines, originally set at 184 hours before inspectors would be permitted access to a site. The 184 hours was whittled down to 108 in the final stages of the negotiations, however the interpretation of the finally agreed text would lead to future disagreement. In the British view once the inspection team accepted the inspected state party's proposed alternative perimeter, then that would become the final perimeter and the inspection could begin, a period of time that could well be considerably less than 108 hours. There were two major conclusions for me from all of this. First, no matter how sound the technical arguments and even one supported by extensive pragmatic field work, such as our PCI programme and managed access follow up, that might not be enough to shift friend or foe alike in arms control and disarmament negotiations when they had convinced themselves that a much less ambitious and effective outcome was more in their national security interests. The second major conclusion was that the UK would likely have to expend a good deal of diplomatic, scientific and technological as well temporal effort in trying to convince the US that the British approach was better in any future arms control negotiations. And this was about to come to pass as international attention now turned to trying to strengthen the Biological and Toxin Weapons Convention by adding a verification Protocol in order to close its compliance machinery deficit that had haunted the Convention since the conclusion of the original negotiations in September 1971.[46]

Chapter 3

Biological and Toxin Weapons Convention 1992–1998
The UK's work on practice compliance inspections and other on-site activities

Introduction

BW verification was and remains problematical both politically and technically. This was undoubtedly true during the immediate origins of the Biological and Toxin Weapons Convention in August 1968 when the United Kingdom proposed that the Eighteen Nation Disarmament Committee (ENDC) should address the problem of CBW arms control by dealing with biological weapons first, leaving the much more difficult matter of chemical weapons disarmament for later. UK ministers and officials recognised at the outset the problems posed by dual-use technology, materials, equipment and expertise in the biological sciences for effective verification, though they rarely used the term dual-use at the time – they certainly understood the concept well enough. However, contextual considerations also framed the debate in the UK's Foreign Office, Ministry of Defence and Cabinet Office and ultimately in Geneva as these constrained not only what was possible to negotiate and agree in the 1960s and early 1970s, but prevented progress on the one measure that the UK believed to be essential in a meaningful BW disarmament treaty – namely investigations of alleged biological weapons use. As it turned out neither the Soviet Union or the US were ready to accept such a provision in a BW treaty, so the final text that was agreed in Geneva in September 1971 contained no provisions for the investigation of alleged biological weapons (BW) use.[1]

We would have to wait another twenty years before verification returned to the active agenda of the BTWC at its Third Review Conference in 1991. Substantial progress being made in the CWC negotiations, the ending of the Cold War, the threat from Iraq's offensive BW programme that was being uncovered by the UN Special Commission (UNSCOM) and the revelations about the Soviet offensive BW programme combined to enable the Review Conference to establish an Ad Hoc Group of Government experts (VEREX) open to all States Parties to identify and examine potential verification measures from a scientific and technical standpoint.[2]

VEREX was tasked inter alia to examine potential verification measures in terms of several main criteria, namely their:

- strengths and weaknesses based on, but not limited to, the amount and quality of information they provide, and fail to provide;
- ability to differentiate between prohibited and permitted activities;
- ability to resolve ambiguities about compliance;
- technology, material, manpower and equipment requirements;
- financial, legal, safety and other organizational implications; and,
- impact on scientific research, scientific cooperation, industrial development and other permitted activities, and their implication for the confidentiality of commercial proprietary information.

The UK had been fully behind this outcome and had pressed hard for the establishment of such a group. VEREX was mandated to hold one meeting in 1992 and others as it determined, but with a view to completing its work by the end of 1993. If a majority of states parties so decided, then a Special Conference could be convened to review the VEREX report and decide on any further action. It was certainly the British hope that all of this would ultimately lead to a negotiation on a verification Protocol. Experience from UNSCOM's early BW inspections in 1991 certainly highlighted the value of on-site measures as indeed had the joint UK and US visits to Soviet BW facilities between 1989 and 1991 following the defection of a key Soviet BW scientist to the UK.[3] The UK presented a working paper at the first VEREX meeting that summarised the findings of the second UNSCOM BW set of inspections in Iraq. Although I drafted the paper and cleared it with UNSCOM it was presented by Dr David Kelly of Porton Down who had led the first UNSCOM BW inspection at Salman Pak and was a key member in the second mission that visited ten different sites, one of which – Al Hakam – even at that stage stood out as a probable BW production plant.[4] The VEREX process eventually concluded in 1993 that some form of verification would be useful.[5] It took another year following a majority of states parties calling for a Special Conference for such an august body to be convened in September 1994 to review the report and decide on next steps, setting the context for the UK decision to conduct a series of practice compliance inspections (PCI) in the biotechnology and pharmaceutical industries.[6] The idea originated with Dr Tony Phillips at Porton Down who had assumed the role of its main expert on BW arms control measures. Dr Graham Pearson as Director-General also saw the importance of these measures, and was supportive. He had also established a separate set of experts at Porton to provide Whitehall with the necessary scientific and technical advice to underpin UK work on the CWC and BTWC.[7] They were to become integral to all that the UK did on CBW in The Hague and in Geneva. I supported the idea of a PCI programme since I had seen the benefit the experience and results had had for the CWC, and Tony started to sound out some companies in industry to see if there would be any willing volunteers. As with the CWC where close cooperation and consultation with industry had been essential, we saw the vital importance of engaging the biotech industry too if there were likely going to be negotiations on a BTWC verification Protocol. In this case our main contact was the Association of the British Pharmaceutical Industry (ABPI), who at that time were conveniently headquartered at the top of Whitehall by Trafalgar Square. Fortunately, it proved comparatively easy to find volunteers to host the practice inspections, no arm twisting or Ministerial requests were required. Our aim was to cover a range of pharmaceutical and biotechnology sites in order to gain a deeper insight into the potential challenges and to see whether the managed access concepts originally developed for protecting nuclear weapons related secrets might also work in such a different environment. Our starting hypothesis was that they probably would, but we would need some empirical evidence from the planned exercises. As in the case of the CWC, the hope was that positive lessons from practice inspections would be key in securing agreement on a BTWC verification protocol where anxieties over commercial confidentiality were even more acute than they had been in the chemical industry. The programme envisaged four exercises: one each at a pharmaceutical research and development site, a large-scale production site; a large-scale R&D and manufacturing site, and finally a vaccine production plant. These were held in October 1993, December 1993 and two in March 1994. As in the CWC PCI programme we were divided into three teams: an inspection team led by me, which included technical experts from Porton – Dr Lorna Miller and Amelia Jones; a home team (mostly MOD's Proliferation and Arms Control Secretariat – PACS the new name for the old DACU.[8]) to advise the site personnel and a control staff to ensure that the exercise ran smoothly and its objectives were met. The exercise was run in role-play with a scenario prepared to set the scene and context and lasted two days with a hot-wash up on the key lessons learned at the end. We also prepared a detailed verification Protocol that laid out procedures for the conduct of a challenge type inspection; this was split into several parts and drew in large measure from the CWC's Verification Annex Part II General Provisions and Part X on challenge inspection. It also reflected some of the lessons from UNSCOM and visits to Russian BW facilities. We thought that many of the details would likely work just as well in a pharmaceutical plant – indeed the CWC had been drafted with such plants in mind and had been shaped by lessons from the UK as well as other states' inspection exercises. We also updated this document in light of the experience gained during the programme.[9] A key part of this exercise Protocol was the section on managed access as we were keen to see how this might work in a pharmaceutical or biotechnological facility. As we have seen, managed access had been absolutely crucial in ensuring that we could let inspectors into the most sensitive of defence sites. A detailed draft exercise report was prepared and then checked and cleared with the company before finalising with a copy also going to our main ABPI contact Dr Jeff Kipling.

The programme, like the CWC one, had three objectives:

(1) to test the effectiveness of verification inspections at pharmaceutical and biotechnological facilities, especially those that are large, multipurpose, flexible compatible with pathogen work and where there are substantial concerns about commercial confidentiality;

(2) to examine the issues that arise for industry, for the UK and for the administration of such a verification measure under the BTWC; and,

(3) to test whether sufficient access within the plant and to documentation could be given to demonstrate compliance with the BTWC, without unacceptable compromise to commercial confidentiality.[10]

Practice Compliance Inspection 1: Smithkline Beecham, Epsom

The first exercise in the sequence took place at Smithkline Beecham's R&D site at Epsom. This was very much a first attempt looking at basic ideas and to learn how to go about conducting a BW related inspection where there was a non-compliance concern expressed about a particular site. Prior to the exercise we had heard a good deal from ABPI and industry representatives we had consulted that there were acute concerns about sampling and analysis (S&A). Industry's fear was that this posed the greatest threat to commercially sensitive proprietary information as S&A could reveal the identity of strains of microorganisms being worked on in the company's research programmes seeking biologically active molecules that could be turned into drugs to treat a range of diseases. Bob Imrie, the lead Smithkline Beecham expert in the home team, was particularly concerned about this risk. Bob was initially disposed to reject any request for samples that might be made by the inspectors. This seemed to be an absolutist position, not too dissimilar to initial reactions at Aldermaston in refusing access, however, the result was different here. Inspectors asked for a sample to be taken from a 300 litre fermenter in one of the laboratories, as it happened there was no production run underway and there had been nothing especially sensitive in recent batches either. So much to Bob Imrie's surprise we were able to have our sample – collected notionally as was the sample anti-body test performed in the facility's own laboratory under close supervision by the inspectors. So rather than having to insist on absolute blanket refusal to sampling, we could now see that in some circumstances it might be possible. We would however have to think more about how to address genuinely sensitive samples, perhaps the same sort of approaches applied in the CWC's managed access provisions in the Verification Annex Part X, where sampling would be limited to Scheduled chemicals only. In a BTWC context we might have to work from an agreed list of agents, something that was going to consume an inordinate amount of time in the future Protocol negotiations. Ideally, samples should not leave the site in order to protect commercially sensitive information and should be, where possible, analysed on site with the inspection team's own equipment. This was to be the preferred option in the future CTBT's inspection Protocol. Furthermore, we also concluded much the same as we had done during the CWC PCIs that samples should not be requested at each and every location. Instead they should only be sought where there were significant ambiguities or concerns or to confirm statements made by an inspected state party. [11]

As we saw in the CWC PCI at ICI Grangemouth, the UK's regulatory framework governing health and safety at work, environmental protection and product licensing require the production and retention of extensive documentation, some of which is even in the public domain. The pharmaceutical industry was of course subject to the same level of control, and possibly even more so given the tight regulatory control to ensure that new drugs were not only efficacious but also safe. In practice this meant that any company before it could bring its new drug to market had to be able to demonstrate safety and effectiveness through three stages of clinical trials to the UK regulator, the Medicines Inspectorate[12]as it then was, not to mention the prior work before a drug was even ready for a clinical trial phase 1.[13] Massive amounts of records had to be kept to sustain all of this, and some of these could be requested by inspectors as they would lend credence to the claims that all that was being done, and had been done, was for purely peaceful purposes. During this inspection for example inspectors asked to see records on the culture collections held at the site as well as the site's own Genetic Manipulation Safety Committee, which recorded discussions and decisions on experiments. Inspectors were offered a random selection of four pages from the culture collection lists to see whether there were any agents of BW interest held. The same approach was applied to laboratory logbooks. We could observe too that the fermentation halls and laboratories were not equipped for the safe handling of Hazard Groups 3 (such as bacillus anthracis) and 4 (such as Ebola Virus) pathogens as designated by the UK's own Health and Safety Executive's Advisory Committee on Dangerous Pathogens. In discussion following the exercise, the company experts thought the Health and Safety Executive inspection process was more rigorous than that anticipated of a future BTWC inspectorate. Indeed, they posed a greater threat than the theoretical risk to commercially sensitive information from a crooked inspector. The HSE could impose a prohibition order on further work on the site if they had evidence of serious unsafe practices, or there had been a major accident that led to fatalities or life changing injuries. Such a prohibition order would cost serious money, delays to the research and production programme, and significant reputational damage. A prohibition order would not be lifted until remedial action had been taken to the HSE's satisfaction. While this sounds draconian, which it is, the HSE generally preferred to work with companies through guidelines and advice in order to prevent serious safety problems arising in the first place.

PCI 2 Dista, Speke

Our second exercise was held at the large-scale pharmaceutical production facility run by Dista, part of the US pharmaceutical giant Eli Lilly. We had decided to invite experts from Canada, France, Germany, Netherlands, New Zealand, the US, Sweden and Switzerland to participate as members of the inspection teams in the remaining three exercises. At Dista we had Tom Dashiell from the US, Gordon Vachon from Canada and Jan Gebrandy from the Netherlands. I remained as chief inspector whilst Lorna and Amelia transferred to the home team advising the site management. Dista's John Cornfield had been most anxious about the potential adverse implications for commercial confidentiality prior to this exercise. The focus for the inspection team was to establish whether the facility was doing what it claimed to be doing, so we made the most of the opening briefing and site tour along with what we could establish about the site prior to the inspection. As usual a specific non-compliance concern had been generated that gave something for the inspectors to focus on, but was not drawn too narrowly (production of bacillus anthracis and then filling into spray tanks for example), which would make it easier for the home team to refute. This exercise worked to the advantage of the inspection team: we felt that we had gained access to all the information we needed to build up an accurate picture of the nature of the biological activities on the site and thereby came away with a high level of confidence that the site was in fact doing what it claimed as we could find no major ambiguities or uncertainties that might be suggestive of non-compliant activity. However, the company felt that it had somehow lost control over the flow of information and was worried that aggregation of individual bits of information would enable the inspectors to obtain too great an insight into the site's capabilities, capacities and commercial objectives.[14] This problem of aggregation had been evident too during the CWC PCIs and would be a recurring anxiety in years to come. Prior preparation, including devising managed access strategies, would be one of the best ways of countering this risk. I used to think that this problem was overdrawn, however as it was an important perception by some so we had to find ways of dealing with it. In short, John Corfield feared that he had given away the store, though he and other Dista personnel could not point to anything specific that might have contributed to such an outcome. We had therefore succeeded with only one side of the inspection equation: inspectors were happy, but we had failed to provide reassurance for industry colleagues. This was not a good outcome since we would clearly need pharmaceutical industry support if we were going to succeed in negotiating a verification Protocol. In the CWC context, support and endorsement from the civil chemical industry were critical; indeed, UK industry became extraordinarily strong supporters of challenge inspection as we saw in chapter 2. We would need to do better next time in PCI3, which we had scheduled for the large Pfizer production and R&D site at Sandwich in Kent. In fact the home team were already onto the problem and had started to think about how they were going to manage and control the flow of information and access next time round.

One other key lesson that we re-learned the hard way concerned the handling and accounting for documents and papers acquired during the inspection. We were seeing quickly just how much paperwork could be generated and acquired – site diagrams, lists of chemicals and other raw materials, accidents, summary of research programmes, batch records, interview notes and national regulatory requirements covering health and safety, environmental protection, Good Manufacturing Practice, Good Laboratory Practice, Quality Control and Quality Assurance records, and photographs. Keeping track of all of this and making sure that we carefully reviewed and used this information to inform inspection planning was a major task, and a small inspection team struggled to keep up. In future there would need to be a documentation officer to keep tabs on it all. I was using a site map that laid out the building numbers and their functions and it was proving a bit of handful as we conducted our activities around the site as well as trying to take careful notes of our observations and comments made by the escorts. After exiting one complex building I realized that I must have put my copy of the site map down somewhere and forgotten to pick it up – how embarrassing. I do not think John Corfield was impressed, and rightly so. But he who never made a mistake never made a discovery as the nineteenth century Scottish author and reformer Samuel Smiles once noted.[15] In future exercises control of documentation would therefore be a priority and over time we developed a well-oiled process that worked well in future CWC, Ottawa Convention, nuclear disarmament verification and CTBT on-site inspections as we will see in subsequent chapters.

PCI3 Pfizer, Sandwich

Our third site was down in Kent at Pfizer's large R&D and pharmaceutical production plant; this was a modern site with large scale production capabilities as well as some interesting work on developing anti-flea and tick products for domestic pets – more on that later. The home team (Dr John Noble from PACS, MOD and Dr Lorna Miller from Porton) this time decided to be much more restrictive in terms of information that would be provided to the inspectors, driven by the experience at Dista. They planned to use managed access measures more rigorously in order to reassure industry. Each and every inspector request for information would be asked for a justification before a response in writing would be provided – that only became apparent to the inspection team as the exercise unfolded. I was joined on the inspection team by Richard Manchee from Porton's Biology Division. Richard had amongst other things been closely involved in the 1980s decontamination of Gruinard Island off the west coast of Scotland, which had been the location of the UK's WWII BW experiments with anthrax.

Work with experimental animals, especially non-human primates, is a key activity in both biodefence and offensive BW programmes. The nature and extent of the trials and experiments would be of key interest to BW inspectors. In a biodefence programme trials would be used to test the development and validation of medical countermeasures such as vaccines, anti-microbial and anti-virals as well as detection systems. They might also be needed for threat evaluation to see whether a biological agent could be effective if used in warfare; for example, would it be stable in the environment and how effective would it be as an anti-personnel agent. An offensive programme would be more interested in the lethality of an agent and the explosive dissemination of the agent. Thus any work with animals would be a key target for early attention in a BTWC on-site inspection, so after the site briefing, tour and presentation of initial inspection plan we headed for the animal house. Work with experimental animals was controversial in the UK, and animal rights activists were known to have targeted sites doing such work and even attacking the scientists involved. For these reasons the physical security around animal houses was usually strong to prevent break-ins. Furthermore, the Home Office heavily regulated such work under the provisions of the Animal (Scientific Procedures) Act 1986. This Act controls the use of protected animals in any experimental or other scientific procedure which may cause pain, suffering, distress or lasting harm to the animal. It is an underlying principle of this Act that animals bred, supplied and used for scientific procedures are cared for in accordance with the best standards of modern animal husbandry. The regulated procedures covered by the Act are controlled using a triple licensing system enforced by the Home Office. All this meant that a tranche of site documents was kept for national regulatory purposes that we could request and which would provide critical insights into the nature of the experimental work being performed by the scientists; for example, the project licence which was a requirement under the Act. The licence holder must send to the Home Office, before 31 January each year, a report giving details of the number of procedures and animals used, and the nature and purpose of the procedures performed under the authority of the project licence during the calendar year.

Our first port of call was the flea and tick breeding laboratory – these were produced to infest experimental cats and dogs to test the efficacy of new treatments. The explanations were all clear and informative and consistent with the site briefing; we saw no evidence of any work with pathogens making use of fleas and ticks as vectors. Several breeding trays were shown to the inspection team and we were reassured that the fleas could not jump off and light upon the gazing inspectors. As we were leaving the laboratory, I took the opportunity to ask the lab manager a last innocuous question: 'have you ever worked here with non-human primates?' Back came the response: 'We used to do that some years ago.' My interest was piqued and the look on the face of the senior site escort standing behind the lab manager was a picture; in fact I think he even put his head in his hands. This opened a new line of questioning and on a sensitive matter too. It highlights what can be uncovered when site personnel are questioned, useful pointers or facts can slip out, which of course is what makes states nervous about interviews. Asking killer questions on the point of departure after seemingly putting the suspect at ease was a technique used by the US TV detective Columbo – he of the shabby raincoat. 'Oh and just one more thing' was his standard line. This experience at Pfizer was a key moment as it helped to underline the vital importance of national regulatory frameworks and the great utility of interviews and discussions with site personnel. Dr David Kelly had already told me that in his experience in Russia and Iraq, interviews were the most valuable tool for BW inspectors. In fact, the two together were vital tools for inspectors. The UK went on to present a working paper on auditing during the eighth session in 1997 of the future Ad Hoc Group, which drew in part on the experiences of document reviews in the PCIs. Auditing had in fact been one of the verification measures examined during VEREX. We had concluded considering the lessons from the BTWC PCI programme (and reinforced by the earlier experience in the CWC PCI programme) that information obtained by auditing reinforces and builds confidence in the consistency and plausibility of information acquired by other measures such as interviewing, visual inspection and identification of key equipment.[16]

The home team made things hard for the inspectors during PCI3; every question or request was queried – Why do you need to know that? What do you mean by dryers? Can you be more precise? This was all designed to control the flow of information so that the company could be reassured that sensitive commercial proprietary information was not compromised. There was also a plus side as it did force the inspectors to make sure that they were clear in the articulation of both their oral and written requests. The grudging release of information did lead to one amusing incident when one of the inspectors – Dr David Langley a biologist from the MOD – had a potentially embarrassing sartorial incident when the seat of his trousers split. In my next visit to the home team office to check on the state of our outstanding questions, I also asked if we could borrow a needle and thread, and before they asked I told them a needle was a small, long sharp silver pointy object and that a thread was an elongated piece of very thin cotton used to stitch or sew garments. During the exercise wash-up when each of the teams offered its initial comments and lessons, Richard Manchee asked the home team if it had been their intent to annoy the inspectors, because they had certainly done so. As Graham Cooper had commented on the early CWC PCIs, inspectors became increasingly frustrated at having to fight repeatedly for access inch by inch, particularly so if hard-won access, say to a building, revealed it to be entirely empty. This frustration usually led to renewed and heightened suspicion and to increasingly vigorous demands for greater access.[17] So here again the same sort of lesson had emerged. In fact such was the constraint on the flow of information during PCI3 that the inspection team, in sharp contrast to PCI2, were unable to say with any confidence whether the site was compliant. We simply had been unable to collect sufficient facts to prepare a detailed report. The pendulum had now swung too far in the opposite direction. We would need to strike a balance between access and control and keep both sides happy at the end of an inspection. We had one final PCI to do this as next up was Evans Medical at Speke.

PCI4 Evans Medical

Thus far we had not looked at a vaccine production plant. A vaccine production plant was of keen interest since it had the capabilities to produce pathogens in large quantities in fermenters or in eggs in safely contained facilities. Thus vaccine plants had an inherent potential for misuse. The BTWC Confidence Building Measures (CBMs) had been extended at the Third Review Conference in 1991 to include the declaration of licensed human vaccine plants for this very reason. Evans Medical's main production process focused on influenza vaccine, which it manufactured using chicken eggs; it also made yellow fever and tetanus vaccines, and formulated anthrax vaccines that had been made at CAMR Porton Down. The UK therefore declared Evans under the annual CBM Form G returns. For this exercise we needed to strike the right balance between ready access sufficient to demonstrate compliance and control to protect commercial proprietary information. This task fell primarily to the home team of Dr Lorna Miller and Dr John Noble as the main technical advisers to the company senior managers, who entered the spirit of the process very proactively and were transparent and cooperative throughout the exercise. Access to the production facilities and records proved to be straightforward with review of randomly selected batch runs across the various stages of vaccine production and maintenance records proving extremely useful for the inspectors. The deterrent effect in this is the heart of the matter; a site would not know in advance which weeks or days the inspectors would check. Moreover, to obtain a manufacturing license for human vaccines meticulous records must be kept as part of GMP and QA and national regulatory requirements. As we had seen elsewhere, such records proved to be of an inestimable value. This approach did not compromise any company sensitivities as we did not threaten any commercially sensitive information. Even looking at the work done with the experimental animals, essential to test vaccine efficacy and safety, raised no problems. Interviews with company personnel, especially the senior site manager Tony Colegate, once again highlighted the critical value of interview material in helping to confirm and validate information extracted from documents and inspector observations of equipment and activities. In short, everything seen was commercially and technically consistent with the plant's stated purpose; there were no anomalies or uncertainties that would have created suspicion or left large areas of activity unaccounted for. More to the point from Evans' perspective is that the inspectors, in the words of one senior manager, 'didn't come close to compromising commercially sensitive information.' This exercise had finally shown therefore that we could square the circle of being able to demonstrate compliance whilst protecting industry's legitimate interests. We were sure that this had not been a one off, but a result of experience from the previous three exercises and careful site preparation and planning. Our exercise at Evans had an important footnote that helped reinforce the specific lessons that we had learned and went on to shape our overall assessment of how one went about demonstrating compliance with the BTWC at a commercial biological facility. More on that later, but what were the overall conclusions from the programme?

Programme conclusions

There were four main interrelated issues in the PCIs: access to facilities, personnel and documentation; compliance assessment; commercial confidentiality; and logistics. The key programme lessons fell under these headings.[18] Managed assess techniques aided negotiation on a range of facilities and documentation, the level of access depending on the individual case. Bespoke managed access solutions might be needed for more challenging issues.

We did not expect that in any future verification regime that inspectors themselves would make formal or final judgments on compliance, they would be there to gather facts for a future Executive Council to determine whether there had been non-compliance as was the case in the CWC's Article VIII. However, we had to see whether inspectors would be able to gather sufficient information that could lay the basis for such a determination at the political level.

Crucially from an industry perspective, it was clear that commercial confidentiality could be protected through use of managed access and prior preparation, although as noted above some case specific circumstances would require their own bespoke solution. Much would also depend on the overall level of access and information provided elsewhere during the inspection, so that a few managed access cases would not prevent inspectors from doing their job effectively. Broader cooperation and transparency and readiness to find alternative ways of meeting inspectors' access and information requirements would be the keys to the successful management of an intrusive inspection.

Overall the UK programme concluded that in-depth BW inspections were a practicable proposition where auditing, interviewing and visual inspection of key equipment were all essential tools of the trade, but a single element was not likely to be useful as their integration was the key to an effective BTWC inspection. (Integration would also be a vital concept in future CTBTO on-site inspections, but that is for chapters 5 and 7.) Provided sites used managed access and preparation in advance (e.g. developing managed access plans for known difficult areas at the facility, identifying key documents ahead of time and assembling briefing packs), the risks to commercially sensitive information could be significantly reduced. We also came to similar conclusions having participated in a joint Canadian-Dutch practice inspection at veterinary vaccine production plant in Boxmeer, the Netherlands.[19]

Perhaps the most critical conclusion in retrospect was our observation that the standards of evidence for an effective inspection were high. This was a qualitative problem since unambiguous evidence of non-compliance would be difficult to acquire, but indicators of such activity could be identified given the potential dual-use nature of many biological agents and much of the related equipment such as fermenters, freeze driers, centrifuges etc, inspectors would need evidence from all aspects of a site under investigation if they were to write a report that provided a fully informed account of what they had inspected and discovered.[20] Sampling as ever remained a sensitive topic in view of the potential risk to commercially sensitive information – an anxiety common to the CWC – and in nuclear disarmament verification and the CTBT where sampling could reveal details of isotopic ratios of materials used in weapons. For this reason we concluded that portable candidate BW agent identification kits for both inspectors and sites were needed, but that was going to require further study and development.

A reality check?

As I mentioned above, there was an important footnote to the Evans Medical PCI, which also helped to shape UK thinking and to validate the conclusions and lessons identified during the four BTWC PCIs. In September 1992 the UK, the US and Russian Federation had signed a Joint Statement on Biological Weapons, the primary purpose of which was to enable the Russians to demonstrate that the old offensive BW programme from Soviet days had indeed been closed down and its facilities and personnel redirected to peaceful biological purposes. The genesis of this statement went back to 1989 following the defection of a senior Soviet scientist from an organization called Biopreparat that was the civil cover for a large-scale offensive BW programme. Vladimir Pasechnik defected to the UK and brought considerable detail of this programme, which resulted in high level messages from the UK Prime Minister and US President to President Gorbachev. A series of UK-US expert visits to Biopreparat facilities then ensued, which in turn led to the 1992 joint statement that allowed for a further round of visits to both military and non-military biological facilities. However, this time the visits were to be reciprocal i.e. outward visits to Russian sites, followed by Russian visits to US and UK facilities. Reciprocity proved to be the ultimate undoing of the joint statement, but that story is for another day. What concerns us here is that the Russians were entitled to visit three US non-military biological sites, with one to the UK in the first round. Each side had to make a statement as to why they had selected the site which they could choose at random and notify the host state the week before the planned visit. This was usually a Friday for a visit the following week. Although we had alerted and briefed several UK biological sites that we thought might be candidates and had briefed the ABPI in the preceding weeks, we had no legal authority to compel any company to host a Russian visit. Most said however that they would be willing to do so, which was a relief. We could have used the powers in the Biological Weapons Act 1974, but that would have been an extreme measure and we would certainly have needed Ministerial clearance for such a thing. We only considered such an option fleetingly. So on the Friday heading back to London after the conclusion of PCI4 it was with some trepidation as we waited to see which site the Russians had chosen. When I returned to the FCO in King Charles Street in mid-afternoon it turned out that I would be heading back to Runcorn as the Russians had selected Evans Medical. This was a little surprising, but when we thought about it, Evans Medical had declared that they made anthrax vaccine under the BTWC CBM Form G. However, as we had found out, Evans only formulated the vaccine that had been made at CAMR Porton Down. The Russians confirmed that this was one of their main reasons for choosing this site. I was asked to lead the home team the following week with support this time from the MOD and Porton experts who had been involved in the outbound visits – Peter Smith, Keith Croft, and David Kelly. We also had Suzette de Banzie as our technical interpreter and hired a freelance Russian linguist to serve as the second interpreter. A couple of US experts from the Arms Control and Disarmament Agency and State Department also joined us. The plan then was to host the Russians in the FCO on the Monday and travel up from Euston Station to Runcorn in the afternoon, with the visit running from the Tuesday to the Thursday. The meeting in the FCO, chaired by Timothy Daunt – Assistant Under-Secretary (Defence), was to hear the Russians make their statement of concern and for us to rebut their arguments and outline the plans for the visit. Whilst this was going on Peter Smith and Keith Croft travelled up to the site to help with the preparations and advise the site on what to expect from the Russians. When we arrived at the site ready for the opening briefing on Tuesday I had interesting observations from two of the senior managers that we had worked with the week before. One of them said that deep down he had been secretly hoping that the Russians would choose Evans as he had enjoyed our exercise, finding it an interesting intellectual exercise; the other said with a twinkle in his eye, 'you bastards, you have set us up!' It was certainly a big advantage for me having been the inspection team leader the week before as I had a good appreciation of what the site did and its layout. In his opening site briefing for the Russians Tony Colegate stated that whilst he was offended that anyone should think that he was somehow connected to biological weapons when his sole motivation was public health and saving lives, he would set that aside and concentrate on demonstrating that everything at Evans was solely connected to making human vaccines. Peter Smith had encouraged him to speak along these lines.

Once the visit was underway a couple of things struck me about the Russian approach. First, they did not request access to any records or documentation whatsoever. This did not stop them later making an outrageous claim that documents reviewed during their visit had shown

British government funding for BW activities. Second, they were obviously looking for things that they associated with a military facility, and they were interested in seeing whether the site possessed hardened power supplies to the plant that would enable it to function in wartime. There was even a request to dig up the car park so they could examine the electrical power cables; I said no. Evans only insisted on one significant managed access measure, and that was that we would develop all film overnight and then check the photographs for any commercial sensitivities prior to release to the Russians. Oleg Ignatiev, leader of the Russian team, was not happy about this, but that was the deal if he wanted to retain photographs of the visit. As it happened we did not need to sensor or redact any of the photographs. Evans actually took the film to Boots the Chemist for overnight development. One other aspect of photography caused me a slight problem; Evans did not allow any photographs of the animal house or of the animals being held there. As noted above, the Animals (Scientific Procedures) Act 1986 placed strict controls on access to experimental animals. Moreover, physical security was at a premium given the threat from animal rights extremists. I explained all this to Ignatiev, and we gave him a copy of the Act. Evans did not want any external photographs of the plant either, and this was more problematic and difficult to defend. However, the essential argument I made was that the Russians now had an inside view of the site layout and especially now knew where the animal house was in relation to the public road. The whole idea of animal rights activists was completely new to the Russians, but Ignatiev saw the point. There was one other incident that highlighted the vital importance of making sure that all briefings, statements and information are correct, otherwise there was a risk that you might inadvertently raise some suspicions. We were outside one of the main large storage areas where health and safety rules required the wearing of hard hats. Ignatiev had wanted to enter immediately, and I told him he would have to wait, at which point two Evans employees were seen walking across the shop floor sans hard hats, which Ignatiev was quick to point out with an impish grin. The Evans senior escort in the group was embarrassed, we could only apologise and state that the staff were in breach of company rules. Fortunately, there were no more such inconsistencies during the visit. Evans were able to show the Russians everything that they requested, and no commercial proprietary information was divulged by the company in doing so. In fact, one of the company representatives noted that the PCI4 team that I had led the previous week had been much more intrusive, which was an important lesson that helped shape our overall assessment on the practicalities and utilities of BTWC challenge inspections.

Practice visits

The focus of the PCI programme had been on short notice challenge inspections. The CWC had routine inspections to check the annual declarations of specified civil chemical plants, but it was quite clear to us from an early stage that similar inspections would not really work in biological context. The comparative ease and speed of production of significant quantities of biological warfare agents precludes an approach based on material balances. Significant quantities of biological warfare agents could be produced in a matter of days in the same fermenters used to produce pharmaceuticals or vaccines. It would thus be fatuous to draw reassurance from setting limits on the quantities of agent held by a State Party. Similarly, it would not be practicable to account for all the growth media used at a facility, although there may be circumstances when the fate of large excesses of media requires explanation, for example during the UNSCOM investigations into the Iraqi offensive BW programme. Overall, whilst quantitative statements have a limited role as part of national transparency, a quantitative investigative approach would only rarely be useful in questions of compliance. It is thus not appropriate to think in terms of 'routine inspections' as understood in the CWC, Conventional Forces in Europe and INF Treaties for example. A BW inspection or visit, in contrast, requires a more qualitative approach. In practice this means that inspectors must make an evaluation of a broad range of interrelated factors such as the scale of specific facilities and the explanations provided for their use. Judgement needs to be formed on whether the facilities and activities are consistent with their stated purpose, with descriptions of the development of the site and with the BTWC itself.[21] There can be a fine line between an objective and a subjective assessment, which is precisely what worries some states about BTWC on-site inspections. Insights and transparency as well as understanding the regulatory framework governing biological activities in individual states parties would be key in any overall compliance regime, it would not be a case of simply checking the accuracy of a declaration.

Unfortunately, visits proved to be one of the most contentious issues in the BTWC Protocol negotiations with a broad range of views from those adamantly opposed to those who wanted to see something akin to the CWC industry verification regime with a strict checking of site production declarations. Different permutations were certainly possible, but not necessarily negotiable in the disputatious and fractious Ad Hoc Group, so this was one reason to conduct further trials to see what might be feasible. The UK was involved with two such trials: a joint venture with Brazil at the Instituto Butantan in São Paulo, which made vaccines and sera, in 1996 and a national exercise at GlaxoSmith Kline's Medicines Research facility in Stevenage in 1997.[22]

The initial idea for a joint UK-Brazil exercise came from our Brazilian colleague – Roque Monteleone Neto, who was an official in the Brazilian Ministry of Health and had been the Brazilian expert during the VEREX meetings. One of the issues in what had now become known as non-challenge visits or NCVs centred on Article X related assistance visits where the primary purpose would be to provide technical and scientific advice to the host facility.[23] Not surprisingly this was of most interest to non-aligned states. We did not rule it out, but combining the concept with information/transparency objectives would be difficult and possibly contradictory. Roque certainly wanted to address the assistance dimension, so we suggested that we should split the visit into two parts: the first part would focus on transparency and a site declaration whilst the latter part would consist of briefings on how the UK's Health and Safety Executive went about ensuring safety at biological and pharmaceutical facilities. For this purpose we brought Dr Alison Spalding, an HSE Biologicals Unit inspector. The visiting team would be led by a UK expert from Porton Down – Steve Eley – and a Brazilian arms control expert from the Foreign Ministry. Roque and I served on the control staff. Dr Lorna Miller assisted in advising the home team. We agreed that we would present a joint working paper to the BTWC Ad Hoc Group setting out the conclusions from the visit. The joint practice NCV had three main objectives: to examine the practicalities and issues involved in non-challenge visits, including the role of declarations; to test the utility of VEREX on-site measures except for medical examination. Sampling and identification would only be performed if agreed and as appropriate; and to explore opportunities to address Article X cooperation.[24]

The exercise proceeded much as we expected with similar sorts of lessons emerging through the exercise that we had seen in the UK and in the Netherlands. In fact, there was one incident, which underscored the importance of giving accurate information in the briefings, and that seemingly bizarre explanations can sometimes be the truth. In the Q&A session following the detailed briefing on the site's activities and facilities Steve Eley had asked the site director whether the site worked with non-human primates. A categoric no was the answer. On a subsequent walking tour of the site Steve spotted some open air primate cages as we turned the corner on our route; he stopped and pointed them out, and then I spotted some Macaques in the trees. This was going to take some explaining. The site director duly explained that there was no current work on non-human primates, but there had been some plans to do so several years previously, so the facilities were built, and a colony of monkeys acquired. However, there was a change of mind and plans, but apparently the Macaques liked the facility and stayed, so they were kept. However, they were not part of any scientific or medical research programme. Had the visiting team pressed the point, the site could have demonstrated this with some relevant documentation. In fact had this been a challenge or investigation scenario the inspectors would, or certainly should, have done so.

The degree of access provided to all vaccine and sera production areas, personnel and documentation enabled the inspectors to obtain a good understanding of the site's activities. A key conclusion was that the measures used by the inspectors would also have been deployed had this visit been a challenge inspection. The objective and tools remain the same regardless of the scenario: to obtain an understanding of the activities of the site through the combined use of the VEREX on-site measures such as visual observation, auditing and interviews. Even with a brief period of time available for on-site activities as was the case here, it was still sufficient for the inspectors to acquire a much better appreciation of the nature and scope of the site's activities without detriment to any commercial concerns, or undue inconvenience to the facility personnel. This achieved two things: first, it helped place the site declaration into its proper context; and, second, the information acquired from both declaration and site visit together added significantly to transparency thereby increasing confidence that declared activities were what they claimed to be.[25] We also saw that a separate part of the process on assistance worked well, and the Q&A session between site personnel and the HSE expert appear to have been useful to the hosts.

GlaxoSmithKline, Stevenage

In the following year we decided to look again at the mechanics of how a non-challenge visit, which now had evolved into random or clarification visits, might function at a site where perhaps only a relatively small proportion might be declarable under the emerging declaration provisions then under negotiation in the Ad Hoc Group. We used a simulated declaration format in the practice visit, which asked for information on the following:

(a) the triggered function that led to the declaration, in this case the pilot plant function of the facility;

(b) any associated scientific or technical functions at the facility, to be considered as functions that were integrated with the triggered function and essential to its aims and objectives and/or to its day to day operation. Examples suggested were parts of the facility that dealt with operating records, medical records, quality control tests, health and safety or regulatory aspects of the triggered function.[26]

This time I played the role of visiting team leader with Dr Lorna Miller and Karl Rodrigues from the Department of Trade and Industry (DTI) CWC National Authority playing in the home team along with company experts, and this time we invested a fair bit of time in site preparation and briefing of site personnel, a process which included a preparatory meeting one week before the visit itself. In the first round of practice compliance visits we had seen just how important site preparation was, both for ensuring the smooth conduct of the inspection, and in reassuring industry that such inspections could be managed without compromising commercial confidentiality or causing undue disruption to day-to-day activities. We also saw the importance of interviews once again; five site personnel were interviewed, and the information gleaned from them helped the visiting team to understand the relationships between the pilot plant and the various research programmes elsewhere on the site. It also struck me that a fair bit of time was needed to prepare for these interviews, and that mostly open questions would be much better than closed questions in eliciting information and insights about site activities. There was one feature of the pilot plant that raised some questions in the minds of the visiting team; there was a 1,000 litre fermenter that did not seem to be used, and accounting for this proved to be a challenge for the hosts. It seemed that the original plans had envisaged a larger production capability than the company actually needed in its research programme. This struck me as an expensive mistake, but capacities in excess of current needs would be an alarm bell to inspectors. This highlighted that simply identifying key equipment was not enough, it is how the equipment is used, its context and accounting for that use that is important, especially in any challenge or investigation into a non-compliance concern. We had of course seen a similar problem in Brazil with the abandoned non-human primate research programme.

We derived seven main conclusions from the visit. First, no commercial proprietary information was divulged, which was a result of careful preparatory work by the company, facilitated by the detailed briefing and advice given by the home team a week before the visit, and due to the use of managed access techniques throughout. Second, given the substantial staff time (an estimated thirty-five to fifty staff days in this case – including some essential senior management time) taken up in preparing and hosting the visit, the company representatives would much prefer that there should be no on-site activities other than challenge inspections. However, they acknowledged that the burden should not be intolerable for such a site if visits were operated in the same manner as in the exercise, that is a two day visit by a three person team. Third, the exercise confirmed the potential utility of visits as a means of increasing the understanding of information in a facility declaration and how it related to specific activities in a declared area and elsewhere on a site; and of resolving any ambiguity or anomaly. The visit was not designed to provide significant insights into site activities having no scientific or technical links with the declared activities and did not do so. Fourth, although the visiting team eventually acquired some understanding of the way in which this largely research facility operated, it was nonetheless a time consuming and at times difficult task. This is likely to be the norm at facilities that do not operate quality systems such as ISO 9000, whereas at manufacturing facilities more formalized record keeping may be expected, which would facilitate the visiting team's task. Even in this research context the visiting team did gain insights into the commercial and regulatory rationales reflected in the physical attributes and operating modalities of the declared activities. This would be useful in informing an inspectorate about operational trends in UK industrial facilities. Fifth, there was a range of opinions among the company representatives on whether visits offered any advantage for industry. Some staff felt that the effort expended in preparing and hosting a visit outweighs any benefit that might accrue. We thought too that further work on visit modalities might be useful in this regard. However, there was an acceptance of the view that, should visits be included in a future verification regime under the BTWC, this would be because of a need to strengthen global security through increased transparency. Sixth, the constraints chosen for this exercise (similar ones could well apply in a future Protocol) in respect of the small size of the visiting team and the short time allowed for the visit, and the resulting limitation in the possible degree of scrutiny of site activities as a whole, it was suggested that such procedures should only address transparency objectives and should not be used to determine the compliance of the facility or the site with the BTWC. Seventh, overall, the results indicated that although the transparency benefits from a single visit in isolation may be limited, the accumulation of experience over several years would prove of greater value.[27]

Conclusions

With the benefit of hindsight, the UK's BTWC practice compliance inspections and practice visit exercises were innovative and provided a good deal of insight and solutions for the Protocol negotiations, and they certainly helped to shape in a modest way the draft Protocol text that was produced by the Ad Hoc Group Chairman Tibor Tóth in March 2001.[28] In particular, the Articles and Annexes dealing with visits and investigations echo many of the lessons from the UK programmes. The CWC's managed access provisions also shaped the BTWC Protocol's verification provisions. The contemporaneous experiences with trilateral visits and UNSCOM BW missions had also been influential in shaping British attitudes and policies to BTWC verification. Indeed the lessons from these 'real' inspections, especially on interviews and document reviews, helped reinforce and validate the emerging conclusions in the PCI programme. It would be possible to collect and document enough facts to show that a state was likely non-compliant with the BTWC, or at the very least force them to deny access, repeatedly evade direct questions, fail to give honest answers and generally refuse to cooperate with an inspection team. Such an outcome tells its own story. Sadly, the Protocol was not to be as the US not only rejected the Chairman's draft text in July 2001, but the whole arms control approach to the problem of biological warfare. Many states parties were to hide behind that position despite their demands to resume negotiations on a Protocol.[29] That put paid to any discussion of BTWC verification and the role of on-site inspections for the next twenty years.

Chapter 4

Chemical Weapons 1994–2004
Preparing for entry into force and training inspectors

Introduction

The text of the Chemical Weapons Convention was agreed in Geneva at the CD in September 1992 and opened for signature in Paris in January 1993. The Convention's entry into force provisions required sixty-five states to sign and ratify it. Negotiators had felt that a significant number of states should sign up before such a far reaching and ambitious treaty could enter into force. Indeed, the UK had suggested that the figure should be sixty.[1] It could not enter into force in any case less than two years after its opening, this was because time would be needed to build the embryonic Organisation for the Prohibition of Chemical Weapons (OPCW), including recruitment and training of future inspectors and other Provisional Technical Secretariat personnel so that the OPCW would be ready to begin work as soon the CWC entered into force. As things turned out it would be slightly over four years later in April 1997 when the sixty-fifth ratification (Hungary) was deposited with the UN Secretary General. Since the UK had fought hard to secure the challenge inspection provisions, and even though these ended up not being as extensive as we would have wished, they would still serve as an important deterrent to non-compliance. Perhaps the fear factor might also reduce over time and challenge inspections might be seen as a more routine verification measure, much in the same way as the Stockholm Document on confidence building in Europe's quota of challenge inspections had done in 1986. The Soviet Union had quite happily accepted these and they were no longer seen as an exceptional measure. It was UK policy to make sure proper preparations were made to ensure that if a challenge inspection were ever launched against a British facility, we would be able to demonstrate compliance with the CWC whilst protecting national security information unrelated to CW. The original PCI programme and managed access follow-up work had shown that we could do that, but there was now a major turnover in personnel with the consequent requirement to train facility staff and escorts and to exercise the policies and procedures that were being put in place for handling a challenge inspection. The MOD branch responsible for mounting out-bound arms control inspections and hosting in-bound inspections was Military Operations 4 (MO4), part of the Directorate of Military Operations (DMO). DMO had already established a new Joint Arms Control Implementation Group (JACIG) based at the time at RAF Scampton (home of the WWII 617 Squadron – the Dambusters). JACIG was a tri-service unit with officers and NCOs from the Army, RAF, and Royal Navy, though it was mostly Army and RAF personnel. JACIG were responsible for the Stockholm Document and were also going to manage the future Conventional Forces in Europe Treaty. DMO had agreed that it would also provide the escorts for any in bound CWC challenge inspection at a military facility. For these reasons MO4, supported by the FCO and wider arms control policy community in the MOD decided to embark on a new programme of two inspections per year to train personnel and test facilities' abilities to cope with a challenge inspection. As one of the survivors from the original programme still in post I was asked this time round to be the Chief Inspector, and in later exercises I would move up to be one of the joint exercise controllers. These exercises were also in time used to help train the OPCW inspectorate as well as overseas experts, something which led to practice challenge inspection exercises in Germany, the Netherlands, Switzerland and Sweden. This chapter therefore looks at how these exercises helped build up British expertise, insights and provided opportunities to train the OPCW on how to conduct an effective challenge inspection. However, before proceeding to a discussion of these exercises, there was on important unresolved matter from 1992 that ought to be addressed first.

Clandestine sampling

Although the US had originally proposed anywhere, anytime challenge inspection, it soon changed its policy once the Soviet Union accepted the concept as recounted in chapter 2. The basic problem was that the US could not live with this level of intrusion at its own secret military, nuclear and intelligence related facilities. I had been told by one US official, though I am not sure how true this story is, that during one of the INF Treaty short-notice inspections in the US, someone realized just as the Soviet inspectors were about to arrive that there was a secret defence 'black programme' also at the site in question. It was quickly dismantled and flown out of the area. A black programme was a heavily compartmented top secret project that is not publicly avowed. In a separate discussion between MOD security experts and the US Department of Energy, it also became clear that one of the other main US security anxieties from challenge inspections was the risk posed to nuclear and special access programmes from clandestine sampling. This would be where an inspector managed to remove surreptitiously sensitive materials from a defence programme and then pass the sample to a hostile intelligence service for exploitation. All this helped to explain why the US felt it needed so many hours -108 – to prepare sites before inspection. It also explains why there is the ridiculous perimeter negotiating provisions in the CWC's Verification Annex Part X. In the UK we believed that prior preparation and plans, frequent exercises, effective escorting, and application of managed access was the better route to protect highly classified information. We were invited to send a team of UK verification and security experts in May 1992 to a series of 'walk-through, talk-through visits' to US Department of Energy sites – Sandia National Laboratory, Los Alamos National Laboratory, and the Y-12 Plant at Oak Ridge. I was asked go along to brief on the outcome of our managed access follow-up work at defence and civil nuclear sites. During the visit we compared and contrasted UK and US approaches on how we would go about handling a CWC challenge inspection at a range of locations inside the US labs. We had been invited to request some locations at the three facilities in addition to those shown to us by our US DOE hosts. We learned a lot and there were three specific lessons that we took away from our visit.

First, during our visit to the TA55 plutonium facility at Los Alamos we were in one of the laboratories, which had a series of contained glove boxes housing various bit and pieces of equipment. We asked if there was anything classified on display and if so, what exactly was there, so we could then discuss how to deal with any such items. There was no classified information in view as we walked round the glove boxes. We then asked what if the visit were an international inspectorate, which included a Pakistani inspector. That would be different, exactly how was not explained by our US hosts though they did refer to a level of classification that did not exist in the UK – Unclassified Nuclear Information (UCNI). It seemed that the Americans would not want to divulge even this generic type of information to international inspectors. I found that hard to fathom, but it seemed the worry was in part linked to our old friend 'aggregation' in that a wide range of seemingly innocuous scraps of unclassified information when reassembled and interpreted by a knowledgeable person might then reveal something of a much higher classification. If there was a worry about nationals from a non-NPT aspiring or actual nuclear weapon states such as Pakistan or India, then the draft CWC would allow a state party to reject any inspector for both routine inspections and challenge inspections, or even just challenge.[2] This was precisely the sort of scenario that had led to this provision. We suggested to our hosts that these provisions would solve their problem. However, an inspector could not be rejected once a state party had been notified of an inspection.

When we visited the Y-12, facility at Oak Ridge Tennessee we had a 'walk-through, talk through' around the building used to disassemble the secondary components of retired US thermonuclear weapons, with a particular focus on the weapons' radiation cases.[3] When in the building there were clearly a lot of disassembled radiation cases lying on the workshop floor. Dr Alwyn Davies from ACSA (N) in the MOD nudged me to point out an interesting looking object on one of the lathes – I knew what it was and thought that this probably was the sort of thing that ought to be shrouded or kept out of sight during an inspection. At this point our hosts noticed our curiosity and began to move rapidly towards the object and started to screen it by opening their jackets and standing in front of it. All this did was to excite the attention of the other four UK experts on the visit who were not nuclear experts and had therefore completely missed the significance of the object. This episode embarrassed our hosts as we were clearly not meant to see this object. However, we certainly took an important lesson away from this vignette on how *not* to manage access. Hiding things in plain sight can work, but drawing attention to something that most inspectors would not have noticed in the first place is most definitely not the thing to do. Admittedly this was a 'walk-through, talk through' and was designed to highlight this sort of issue. Our approach in a real inspection would have been for the host to enter the area before the inspectors to check that nothing classified was on display and to ensure that the necessary preparations had been made. Ideally this would only take a few minutes – anything longer would risk raising inspectors' suspicions. Shrouding is best kept to the minimum, using materials that blend in with their environment wherever possible. I was to see how not to do this in a future US hosted challenge inspection exercise at Fort Sill, but that was four years into the future.

Perhaps the main concern from our US hosts throughout our tour was the risk posed by clandestine sampling, especially at nuclear related sites. It would not just be a question of isotopic ratios of the fissile and thermonuclear materials used in weapons – though a lot of that had already been declassified and in the public domain, but other non-nuclear materials used in weapons and their purpose. There would of course be other defence related materials that had nothing to do with nuclear weapons, but still highly classified such as coatings for stealth aircraft. The US worried that an ill-intentioned inspector working for a hostile intelligence agency might obtain samples of potentially sensitive materials and extract them unseen for later exploitation by a capable analytical laboratory. We saw the risk, but felt it was manageable, particularly if there had been careful preparation and rigorous escorting coupled with managed access measures. In addition, clandestine sampling presupposed that some important obstacles could be overcome by a hostile intelligence agency, and much would depend too on the capabilities of such an agency. First, it would need to have a trained inspector already working for it in the Technical Secretariat inspectorate; second, this inspector would have to be selected for the challenge inspection in the first place, which was by no means a given unless it had also suborned the Director-General or other senior managers; third, that inspector would then have to be deployed into the area of the facility where such materials might be present in the environment – presupposing that it was known exactly where on the site that might be; fourth, the inspector would then have to collect some samples unobserved by the escorts and facility personnel; fifth, they would then have to remove the samples undetected and transfer them to his controllers; and sixth, the analytical laboratory would ideally need to know what it was looking for and be able to interpret the results accurately, and then effectively exploit the results. In the nuclear context much would depend on the experience and sophistication of the nuclear weapon state in question.

On our return to the UK, we decided that one way of reassuring the US and validating the soundness of our own approach would be to mount a challenge inspection exercise at AWE Aldermaston with clandestine sampling as one of its main features. MOD Security were in the lead for this exercise, which helped convince AWE to play along. We quickly agreed the parameters of the exercise, which would also be videoed, to ensure that the key objectives would be met. The exercise was scheduled for August 1992. The escorts would be provided by JACIG, the Joint Arms Control Implementation Group; we would have a small inspection team of five, one of whom was given a collection brief by Alwyn Davies and myself of the sorts of things he might look to collect undetected and where he might do so. We decided with AWE's agreement to focus on a radioactive area (A45) and a non-radioactive area (South-East Corner, where high explosive work had been done along with production of some non-radioactive materials). Importantly the JACIG escorts were not told the true purpose of the exercise, but briefed to manage the inspection team escort as they would normally do and to note anything that they thought was unusual, but not to intervene during exercise play if they did. I led the five-person inspection team and we ran the scenario that an inspection sub-team had selected South East Corner and A45 on day two of the inspection after a site brief and windshield tour. The clandestine sampler was instructed to hand any samples he might have collected to Alwyn Davies before he crossed the clean-dirty line at A45 in case he had managed to collect something radioactive, we did not want the alarms going off as he went through the detectors at the barrier. Had that happened the building would have had to be shut down and an enquiry set up to investigate the incident. All samples would be analysed to see what had been found and whether any of the results divulged anything highly classified. We then ran the exercise in role play with South East Corner inspected in the morning, and A45 inspected in the afternoon. A key part of the safety as well as managed access strategy for A45 was to require all inspectors to wear Tyvek over suits and protective shoe coverings. Access to laboratories would be limited to two inspectors with one escort each in addition to the senior JACIG escort officer and site representatives. A key part of the thinking here was that it is much easier to keep a close eye on two inspectors in a small group than a larger number; furthermore, no inspection equipment was allowed in and host supplied notepaper and pencils were provided. The inspection activities were played as if they were real, and finished at about 1600 for the hot-wash up.

The two main points to emerge from the wash-up were that clandestine sampler had indeed managed to collect some samples from both areas of the site; for example, he wore a pair of glasses (which he did not require for his eyesight) and had casually placed this on some surfaces. Unfortunately for him the JACIG escorts had twigged that something was not quite right about this 'inspector;' for example, when the rest of us were in a huddle discussing next steps and questions, he had moved off slightly with his attention elsewhere. This highlighted the value of well-trained escorts who knew the sorts of things and behaviours to look for as well as having clear instructions on how to herd the inspectors safely and securely around the site. Had this been a real inspection the escorts would have intervened and put paid to the clandestine sampler's dastardly plans. We had to wait some weeks before the analytical results became available, and these revealed that nothing classified had been compromised; in the case of the samples from South East Corner a long list of compounds and elements were found, but none of these caused AWE any security concerns. The same applied for the samples from A45. Now we had to share our overall results with the Americans, which we did at a briefing at the Department of Energy in January 1993. I am not sure that we fully convinced them, but we did not hear much more about the risk of clandestine sampling thereafter.

RAF Honington (again) and CBDE Porton Down 1994

As noted above, the MOD decided that it would be important to prepare against the eventuality that a challenge inspection might be launched against the UK. This process would validate the Standing Instruction on Arms Control and its Annex on CWC Challenge Inspections; it would also train and maintain JACIG personnel and their capabilities as well as checking the effectiveness of site reception plans, especially those for the more sensitive sites such as nuclear weapon related establishments. The original plan was to run two exercises a year with the codename Longhole, and at this stage entry into force was still two years away – a fact not apparent at the time. I initially thought Longhole was Long Haul, which would have been more appropriate. This new PCI programme represented a substantial commitment, and as there were only a few of us left from the original PCI programme still in post and available I served as the Chief Inspector in these exercises as well as to design and draft the exercise scenarios. Since we wanted to stress test the system, the exercise scenarios were carefully crafted to ensure that the inspection team would seek access to, and information about, the most sensitive parts of the sites selected to host the exercises. We wanted to see how the managed access plans stood up to intrusive inspection. First up in the programme for 1994 was RAF Honington, last 'inspected' in October 1989. One of the first challenges was dealing with the turnover in staff given the rotation through normal service postings. This manifested itself in RAF Strike Command refusing to accept that an inspection exercise of this nature could be conducted at a nuclear weapons storage site. When it was pointed out that we had already held such an exercise, so we did not see what the problem was, Strike Command responded that there was no record of such an event at their headquarters at High Wycombe. I dug out a copy of the original PCI report that had been prepared by DACU and MO4 sent it to Strike Command. That ended the debate and we were set for the exercise in October 1994. This episode highlighted a recurring problem, not just for the UK; namely retention of expertise and corporate memory in institutions, which is why regular training and exercises were so essential for maintaining and improving capabilities for on-site inspections. As time went by, I was the only one left in the UK with long term experience of previous exercises and the lessons learned. This in part explains why a lot of the time over the coming years we ended up relearning old lessons. However, we also added to the stock of experience, which helped counter the reinvention of the wheel and these lessons were embodied in periodic revisions to the MOD's Standing Instruction on Arms Control.

As in 1989 the key action took place in the SSA, which stored WE177 gravity bombs. Once again managed access was to the fore as the inspection team negotiated access to the storage igloos and their contents. Initially Honington only wanted to stage one igloo with inert training WE177s, but exercise control argued that we needed to have live weapons as part of the game – a point conceded. The principal problem for the inspection team was to reassure ourselves that the weapons seen on their transport trolley did not have a chemical warfare agent fill; that was going to be difficult since strict safety and security measures prevented any unauthorized equipment or procedures in the vicinity of a live weapon. We started with a suggestion that we should access the plant room controlling the temperature and humidity inside the igloo to see whether there were any air filtering systems containing activated charcoal that one might expect if CW were being stored. Now of course that would not be definitive as states who were a bit more cavalier about safety might not have bothered as UNSCOM had seen during its investigation of the Iraqi CW programme in 1992. In any case we found no such systems, but asked if we could take one of the filters for sampling. The initial answer was no, but we eventually negotiated a couple of environmental samples from the plant room.

Although we had notional inspection equipment such as a portable x-ray system, we were not allowed to bring this into the SSA and certainly not allowed to put it anywhere near a weapon. No one on the home team recalled the solution that had been developed in 1989 where a gamma spectrometer could be offered by the hosts to show that the weapon had features consistent with known characteristics of a nuclear weapon system. We suggested to our escorts that perhaps we could take a swab sample from the weapon casing for sampling; they then broke off into a small huddle to discuss our request with the RAF personnel in charge of the SSA. All we could hear from this group was a periodic loud 'No' from the responsible Squadron Leader. At this point even Squadron Leader Jim Squelch from MO4 who was the exercise director whispered to me that this was a nonsense since when he was a pilot on a nuclear capable squadron if hydraulic fluid or oil spilled onto the weapon, the ground crew just wiped it off with some ordinary blue paper towels. So, there should have been no objection to our request. In the end we would not have been able to confirm that the SSA contained no chemical weapons since we had not been given sufficient access or information to help demonstrate the fact. This was disappointing given the fact that we had worked out that a validated gamma spectrometer could have been used to show that the weapons were not CW filled and could also be done without compromising critical nuclear warhead design information. However, there seemed to be continuing sensitivities about this, which I could never really understand given that it was well established that highly enriched uranium and plutonium were used in weapons. Such sensitivities continued into the UK's future work on nuclear disarmament verification, which is discussed in Chapter 6. However, as already noted the problem presented for CWC inspectors by the WE177s disappeared when the last remaining weapons were all withdrawn from service in April 1998.

Next up in December 1994 was CBDE Porton Down. We had not looked at Porton during the original PCI programme since we felt that it would not be too difficult to demonstrate compliance at this facility. However, given that the CWC would hopefully be entering into force soon, the view now was that Porton might well be a likely target given its history and the large range where offensive trials had taken place in the past. There were also two former explosive test chambers from the days of the UK's offensive

CW and BW programmes, which although derelict and unused might well attract attention. Furthermore, there was also the presence of the UK's biodefence programme on the same site, which would add to the difficulties on ensuring access. Work with experimental animals, as we have seen in the BTWC inspections programme, would pose its own set of access issues. For these reasons this was why the scenario that I prepared also included production of toxins for offensive purposes. The CWC included two toxins in its Schedule 1, but toxins were also covered by the Convention's General Purpose Criterion so the prohibitions applied to all toxins unless being used for a permitted purpose in appropriate types and quantities. This would enable inspectors in the exercise to press legitimately on the biological side of Porton's activities.

There were two incidents during this exercise that highlighted the value of carefully developed managed access strategies and the ability of inspectors to unearth potentially suspect things that the host might have overlooked in its preparations, and which would take some explaining. The first of these concerned access to the biological laboratories since only designated vaccinated personnel were allowed in for health and safety reasons and there were no windows from the corridor or even externally that would permit inspectors at least a visual observation of their contents. These occupied a significant amount of floor space and given the scenario noncompliance concern over toxin production, inspectors could not ignore the labs. The site's proposed solution was to send one of the local experts (Richard Manchee whom we last met at Pfizer's site at Sandwich) into the lab with a video camera to film the layout and contents of the lab, and to ensure that it was contemporaneous footage he took a copy of a dated newspaper in with him. The hosts offered us a choice of two brand new video tapes. As chief inspector I also told him what he should film; we had also been briefed on the nature of the research work that was done in the lab. We were also able to interview one of the designated scientists who worked in the lab. These measures in combination provided some reassurance that there was no illegal CW activity taking place, or had taken place in the lab. In the post exercise wash-up, we also suggested that floor plans, utility piping and installation diagrams and lab log books could be offered too as additional ways of helping to demonstrate compliance. Given the advances in miniaturised cameras and real-time transmission, inspectors could now view a controlled access space in real time rather than having to review a video tape at a later point.

On leaving the biology building I noticed that there were four large ISO containers in a row opposite the building across the street. Cleary these needed to be inspected, so we asked for access and were allowed to choose one of them. Keys were duly produced after a short interval and on opening the selected container there in front of us lay what looked like a thirty litre fermenter. Now given the part of the non-compliance scenario that alleged illegal toxin production, this looked like potentially incriminating evidence. Perhaps a key piece of equipment was hastily dumped here out of the way with the hope that inspectors might not bother about these non-descript ISO containers. This discovery was clearly going to need some explaining and inspector questions started to flow: what was this fermenter doing here? How long had it been here? Where had it come from? When was it last used and where were its associated records? What had it been used to produce? What programme did it belong to? Which scientists had used it? The container was notionally sealed as we would also want to return to take some environmental samples from the fermenter and its surroundings. Meanwhile the other inspection sub-team was busy looking at the old explosive test chambers, which were relics of the former UK offensive programmes. That they were still extant was of interest and the inspectors wanted to be sure that they were truly derelict and incapable of functioning as originally intended. We eventually received plausible evidence based explanations for the fermenter in the ISO container, it had been part of a former research programme and was being stored unserviceable pending a decision on whether to retain or dispose of it. The explosive test chambers were on inspection clearly no longer operable, but it was one of the recommendations from the exercise that these should be demolished before the CWC entered into force. Porton took this advice, though there were probably plans in place to do so anyway. Our inspection perhaps accelerated matters.

One of the objectives of these exercises, as noted above, was to validate the MOD's Standing Instruction on Arms Control and its Annex on policy guidance and advice for the conduct of challenge inspections. Key lessons from these two exercises, and all subsequent practice challenge inspections, were embodied in revisions to these instructions; for example, on the content of the opening site brief and the conduct of the windshield tour. During the Porton exercise the inspection team had been shown around the site in two separate mini buses, not in itself an issue, but the commentary and site descriptions provided by the site escorts on comparison by the inspectors back in their working areas were different. This raised potentially awkward questions for the host as they would need to explain the discrepancies. In future, there should be one single prepared script.

RNAD Coulport and Fort Halstead

In the first of the exercises in 1995 we headed to RNAD Coulport on Loch Long, Scotland; this was the depot for Trident missiles and warheads for the UK's nuclear deterrent as well as torpedoes for the submarine fleet and as such was certainly going to present some acute problems over managed access given the serious sensitivities present at this location. Not least of these was the UK's policy of neither confirming nor denying the presence of nuclear weapons at any specific location or time – NCND. This led to some early headaches in this inspection since it hobbled the ability of JACIG and site escorts to demonstrate compliance. It led to some tortuous uses of the English language: Chief Inspector (me): 'What is the purpose of Building X?' Site escort: 'Er. The processing of non-chemical items.' Once on site it was clear to knowledgeable inspectors that given the context of this site – the loading and unloading of armed Trident D-5 missiles on to the Vanguard class nuclear submarines – the structure in question was very probably used to handle nuclear warheads. Even though there had been several House of Commons Defence Select Committee reports on the Trident programme and the delays in the major construction work at Coulport, our escorts were initially coy about the nuclear purpose of the site. Eventually after some prompting by me the JACIG Senior Escort Officer admitted that for the purposes of the inspection only, he was now authorized to state that the site did in fact have a nuclear purpose. The process building was clearly going to be a priority inspection target since the alleged non-compliance concern related to the presence of warheads filled with CW agent. Two inspectors were allowed access, and as was customary at such places no equipment was allowed and strict explosive safety regulations were in force. We noted several storage bays, some of which were empty whilst others contained what looked like large white oil drum like objects. These were in fact Secure Transport Containers (STICs) for Trident warheads. I had seen the same STICs at AWE Burghfield. Given their content, these were not going to be opened since the shape of the re-entry body carried a high classification at that time. We asked for a swab sample of the container, but were going to need some reassurance that the content was not a CW filled warhead. So what next? Our hosts initially would not offer anything, so we stated that if this was all the access provided the inspection report would likely state that the UK had failed to demonstrate compliance with the CWC given the significance of the storage containers to the scenario's non-compliance concern. I suggested that perhaps the use of a Geiger counter might help. One of the processes created by the Standing Instruction was the convening of a CWC In-Bound Challenge Inspections Committee, which would meet in London during an inspection to provide policy advice and guidance to the JACIG Senior Escort Officer if a major impasse should arise during the inspection that could not be resolved on the spot. The Committee had a standing membership drawn from various branches of the MOD and FCO as well as CBDE Porton Down; it was chaired by the Head of MO 4 – usually a Colonel rank post. Other experts could be called to help as required. It was most definitely not a long handled screw driver trying to second guess the JACIG escorts on the ground. That would only add delays and confusion when speed and clarity were needed on the ground to manage the challenge inspection effectively. Instead the sort of impasse that we had reached at Coulport was precisely the situation where the Committee had a role to play, and as it happened we were exercising the Committee as part of the Coulport inspection. As things transpired this was the one and only time that the Committee was convened in London during the inspection exercises conducted between 1995 and 2004. On this occasion the Committee agreed to the proposal that a Geiger counter could be used to measure an indicative level of radiation that would help show that the STICs contained a nuclear rather than chemical content. We played this out with only the Chief Inspector being allowed to observe the measurements performed by one of the local escorts using the site's own equipment. We worked on the assumption that suitable checks had been made to satisfy the inspection team that the Geiger counter was indeed genuine and could be relied upon to give accurate and not spoofed results. (Though we did not play this out it could have been taken to a local hospital to measure radiation sources used for medical purposes. The idea that we had back in 1989 at RAF Honington to take the equipment to Sellafield to measure nuclear material under IAEA safeguards to confirm reliability and functionality would have been impracticable in an inspection lasting eighty-four hours unless both sides agreed to extend the duration, but then again this sort of thing would be exactly when an extension would be needed.) This approach worked in the context of this exercise, but as before more work would be needed on precisely how the UK would deal with this problem – demonstrating that a nuclear weapon was not a chemical weapon. This would entail looking at inspection equipment and confirming it would be safe to use in the presence of a nuclear weapon and the conditions under which it might be used. Such work would also need to consider what equipment the UK itself could offer, such as a gamma ray spectrometer or neutron counter. Changes to security guidelines and policies would also be required. These were amongst the most important lessons from the Coulport PCI.

Before leaving Coulport we had one more incident that turned out to be funny at the time, but also showed the importance of timely and full cooperation by the hosts with inspector requests. We had some time remaining in the exercise after the managed access vignette in the warhead processing building, so we decided to pick some additional buildings for inspection and one large building down by the loch side near the loading jetty attracted our attention. Although it did not have any features that would suggest the safe storge of chemical or even conventional munitions, it could be the sort of place used in an emergency to hide things from the inspectors' prying eyes. It had two large doors – much bigger than the two metre door limitation that applied in the Conventional Forces in Europe Treaty's on-site inspection provisions. (Inspectors were not allowed access to buildings with doors smaller than two metres.)The first problem was the availability of the keys – the owner of the keys was on his way home to Helensburgh, which was not really a plausible tale since surely all keys for buildings on such a site would be held and secured centrally. Eventually keys were found to open one of the doors to reveal what was essentially a large double garage capable of holding two large load carrying vehicles. The building was empty save for a small ISO container sitting in the middle of the garage floor. Needless to say we asked for this to be opened and once again availability of keys was an issue. After about ten minutes keys were found. Once open the ISO container revealed that it was storing of all things a single canvas backed chair of the sort you might expect in a school. It was not even worth an environmental sample. We did speculate as to the purpose of the solitary chair, perhaps used for interrogation training. However, what this demonstrated was the site's willingness to cooperate and its readiness to ensure that the inspection team could have the access it had requested. A key point for the development of policy guidance was that whenever possible comprehensive access should be provided where there are clearly no security sensitivities that would require application of more complex managed access measures.

Fort Halstead, near Sevenoaks, was a site of great historical significance originally built in the late nineteenth century as part of a network of fortifications across the south of England against the possibility of a French invasion. Second, it was home to the UK's nuclear weapons research programme under the anodyne disguise of High Explosive Research before it moved to Aldermaston in 1950.[4] Later it would become part of the Royal Armament Research and Development Establishment, but by the time we held Longhole 2/95 in spring 1995 it was now part of the Defence Evaluation and Research Agency (DERA) or Defence Experts Retrain as Accountants as many caught up in organizational change of defence establishments called it.[5] Fort Halstead contained many features of likely interest for CW inspectors, so the exercise scenario made use of them to ensure that the inspection team would press on the sensitive and difficult buildings and areas. There were a wide range of laboratories, including the Forensic Explosives Laboratory, explosive storage buildings of various sizes, a burning ground as well as several large warehouses. As ever there were a few issues that helped us to develop policy guidance on managed access as well as the pressing need to ensure that all explanations across the site were consistent as well as accurate. This exercise led to one of the longest, if not the longest, managed access negotiations in both the 1989-90 and 1994-2004 PCI programmes. Prior to that we had three incidents that had already sowed some seeds of suspicion in the inspectors' minds, especially since the non-compliance concern in the exercise scenario focussed on the development of chemical weapons. The first of these concerned the discovery of some defective Chemical Agent Monitors (CAMs) in one of the electronic labs, which came as surprise as we had been assured that there was nothing to do with CW on the site. If this was the case what were the CAMs doing here? The second issue related to apparent inconsistent application of health and safety policy between buildings, which suggested that there might be lower standards in one building which the inspection team had identified as a possible concern. The third issue arose in one of the end of on-site inspection activity meetings between inspectors and the home team. These provided an opportunity to present up-dated inspection plans for the following day, raise new questions and information requests that had emerged during the day's inspection activities. In this inspection the JACIG escort team was led by Lieutenant Colonel Colin Winter of the

Royal Highland Fusiliers, who like me hailed from Glasgow, so there was an empathy between us, something that should not be underestimated as being useful in facilitating an effective inspection. In any case I had raised a series of questions earlier in the inspection, responses to which were still outstanding, so it was time to press the home team for answers. A little to my surprise Lieutenant Colonel Winter turned to the home team and said, 'Yes, the esteemed Chief Inspector is quite right. Where are the answers to his questions?' I like the esteemed bit. The delay in providing requested information after a while might start to look suspicious, particularly if there were links to observations made during the inspection of buildings and activities. On this occasion the home team were struggling to find the right people with the documents or answers in an expeditious manner. In future it would be essential to ensure that the home team had the necessary staffing and secretarial support in a central control post to collect collate and check the responses.

My deputy on this inspection was Major Hamish Killip of the Royal Engineers. Hamish had been involved in BTWC trilateral inspections in Russia and UNSCOM CBW missions in Iraq and thus a highly experienced and effective inspector. Hamish's sub-team had run into difficulty when the hosts would not provide sufficient access to one of the explosive storage houses. I was called over to see if the escorts might be more accommodating if the Chief Inspector was present. Things did not turn out that way. In fact we were being refused any access at all, and given what had already happened earlier in the inspection over access and information issues this building assumed a key importance. The non-compliance concern of clandestine CW development now looked as if it might have some basis as here was an explosive storage area certainly capable of hiding small but contextually significant quantities of chemical warfare agent and/or munitions. Our hosts had clearly items of ordnance in here that they did not wish us to see. There then followed a protracted discussion when we tried to elicit at least some details with a series of questions to the senior site representative that went something like this:

Q1.   Is this building storing UK land service ordnance?
A.   I can neither confirm or deny that.

Q2.   Are we talking large calibre or small arms here?
A.   I can neither confirm or deny that.

Q3. Does this building contain artillery projectiles?
A. I can neither confirm or deny that.

Q4. Are we talking about air delivered munitions?
A. I can neither confirm or deny that.

Q5. Does the concern relate to guided weapons?
A. I can neither confirm or deny that.

Q6. Naval ordnance?
A. I can neither confirm or deny that.

Q7. Perhaps you might be able to summarise in general terms the explosive natures stored here?
A. That would not be possible.

Q8. Perhaps then there are experimental or weapons under development here, in which case we could discuss shrouding arrangements and environmental sampling?
A. I can neither confirm or deny that.

And so things continued until it became quite clear that we were not going to be given any access despite me making clear that our hosts had failed to demonstrate compliance, and that this non-cooperation would be highlighted in the inspection report that we would present at the end of the day. It turned out that the storage building was full of foreign military ordnance for exploitation purposes, and it was going to be too difficult to disguise this via managed access measures in the time available. A key post inspection action point therefore was to think how such things could be better stored and dispersed around the storage buildings to make them easier to hide in plain sight along with the rest of the explosives stored on site. However, there was one positive development in this exercise on how to manage access to sensitive lists of research projects and their reports, which was sufficient to enable the inspectors to see that there were no CW related development projects being conducted or had recently been conducted. This would become a model for elsewhere; we requested randomly selected months and could see redacted summaries of the listed projects and could cross check the document reference numbers on the computer screen with hard copies of the front pages of the selected report. Overall even the problems encountered in the Fort Halstead exercise helped the UK further refine and improve its procedures and highlighted some new lessons that we needed to learn if we were ever to face a real challenge inspection. Some years later we made a training film for MOD facilities on how to prepare for and host a challenge inspection, and back we went to Fort Halstead to re-enact elements from the earlier exercises.

RAF Valley and the first OPCW practice challenge inspection

The OPCW Provisional Technical Secretariat (PTS) had trained hard to build up a cadre of inspectors ready to mount the first routine inspections at declared chemical weapons storage and production facilities as well as Schedule 1, 2 and 3 sites. Some modest attention was given to challenge inspection and I helped design a complex table-top exercise along with Ralf Trapp and Maurizio Barbeschi of the PTS that would run over two days to highlight the issues and methodology required for an effective challenge. As the UK had learned by doing we saw great advantage in offering the OPCW TS after the CWC had entered into force an opportunity to send an inspection team to one of our defence sites to participate in a PCI. Our offer was eagerly accepted and a date set in February 1998 for the TS to inspect RAF Valley in Anglesey. We would provide a JACIG and National Authority escort team along with experts (including me) to serve in a joint UK-OPCW control staff. RAF Valley is where fast jet pilots are trained on Hawk aircraft prior to posting to front line squadrons in the RAF; there was also a Search and Rescue (SAR) Sea King Squadron on the base. Although the inspectors would fly into Manchester airport, their equipment would be trucked from The Hague direct to RAF Valley. In total it weighed some four tonnes and included a portable analytical laboratory and a neutron activation monitor to check on the elemental composition of sealed containers such as munitions. (See Chapter 2.)

The mechanics of the exercise were much the same as we had pioneered in the original PCI programme – detailed scenario, opening brief by the station commander, followed by Q&A, then a windshield tour followed by the inspectors returning to their working area to prepare their inspection plan for presentation to the JACIG Senior Escort Officer. In the safety brief it was made clear that mobile phones were not permitted, at which point the phone of one of the OPCW TS control staff members rang out. One thing quickly became apparent and that was the inspectors worked rather slowly –

too slowly in fact and we started to wonder when they would emerge from their office with their initial plan. Of course this was their first time on a challenge inspection exercise, but a leisurely pace was far from ideal in an inspection that was limited to eighty-four consecutive hours unless both sides agreed an extension. This might matter less in small compact sites, but in a much larger area such as an airfield with many diverse buildings and other structures spread out over roughly three square kilometres time is of the essence. As part of the exercise scenario we had prepared some mock CW munitions for the inspectors to find, and then use their non-destructive evaluation equipment to determine the fill. The 'munitions' in question were training rounds for air-to-ground missiles and some gravity bombs, which had been painted grey – the appropriate body colour in NATO ammunition marking regulations for munitions containing a CW fill. We also brought some old demilitarised CW munitions dating from WWII from Porton Down, which were left in an office building. Unfortunately, we had not fully developed the scenario to explain why these items were on site. In the case of the supposed in-service rounds the local escort in charge of the explosive storage area was not sure whether he should be letting the inspectors into the storage shed containing the offending items. In retrospect we should have shrouded them. The inspectors noted the 'CW' munitions, but did not ask any questions of the site or JACIG escorts; this was odd to my mind as they missed an opportunity. Instead, they simply reported back to the Chief Inspector once they had completed their part of the inspection plan for the matter to be raised at a plenary meeting at the end of the day. I felt they ought to have raised the matter immediately with the escorts and asked that the offending articles be moved under seal or escort to an ammunition processing building for closer examination with their non-destructive evaluation equipment. I also had to improvise quickly an explanation for the demilitarised CW munitions found in one of the offices: they were props for an Explosive Ordnance Disposal training course that had recently been held. Old pre-1945 CW munitions were periodically discovered, especially on old firing ranges, so part of the course had been devoted to munition recognition, hence the sectioned pieces found by the inspectors. These items were waiting for collection for return to Porton Down. The Chief Inspector however kept pressing the point about chemical weapons being discovered and insisted upon a full explanation. The matter was only finally resolved when Dr Jim Haley from Porton Down carried one of the demilitarised munitions into the plenary meeting room and dropped it on the table declaring, 'There Chief Inspector, there's your chemical weapon,' from where it started to roll ominously towards the lap of the Chief Inspector. Fortunately it stopped just in time, and there the matter rested: case closed. It was all most of us could do to keep a straight face.

The home team agreed that the grey bodied CW munitions could be transferred to a processing building for evaluation. However, the inspectors had real trouble in setting up their neutron activation analysis equipment, it was far from clear from the operating instructions how the thing should be wired up. This was hardly surprising since it had only recently been acquired and the operators were not fully familiar with it, or had had sufficient training on it so that the equipment could be up and ready to use rapidly. Therefore, more time was wasted, which made it a struggle for the team to fulfil all its tasks within the allotted time in the inspection exercise.

In addition, the OPCW TS had brought along a small portable laboratory equipped with a gas chromatograph-mass spectrometer (GC-MS). Although the CWC had provisions for the creation of a network of designated laboratories for off-site analysis,[6] it also allowed for the option of on-site analysis, which could prove of more immediate value to inspectors as it could provide information that could be followed-up during the inspection. However, this would be contingent on environmental samples having been taken early in the inspection given the time needed by the inspectors running the lab to prepare and analyse a sample. Capacity would thus be limited to a handful of well-chosen samples, something that we had learned back at PCI5 in 1990. There would be no capability for dealing with biological samples on-site such as bloods. Furthermore, another rate limiting factor was the then OPCW TS concept of operations for sample collection. An inspection team would first identify a potential sampling location and report back to the Chief Inspector and then submit a formal sampling request to the escorts, which if approved meant that a sub-team would return to the point of interest. Since there might well be a toxic hazard, this meant that the two inspectors tasked with the sample collection had to suit up in full CW protective mask, suits, gloves and boots. This of course all took more time. Looking to the future we certainly believed that the whole process would need to be speeded up quite considerably, and that full NBC gear might not always be necessary. Perhaps a more dynamic hazard assessment might be useful. Regarding potential toxic hazards that might suggest some non-compliant activities, the Chief Inspector noted a dead crow lying by the path between the OPCW mobile lab, which had been given its own secure building, when he paid the lab a visit to see how it was progressing. He clearly wondered whether the deceased crow had been exposed to a nerve agent because he raised the matter at the next plenary meeting between the inspectors and home team. What was the UK's explanation for the dead crow? My good friend Lieutenant Colonel Colin Winter was the JACIG Senior Escort Officer once again. His instant reply was, 'Ah Nature is very cruel.' That disarmed the question, but there is a serious point here in that if inspectors found large numbers of dead wild or domestic animals, this would certainly be worth investigating in the context of a challenge inspection. In 1968 Utah state officials and veterinarians had been called to investigate reports of thousands of alleged dead sheep in Skull Valley, northeast of Dugway Proving Ground, on 14 March. Dugway was a US Army test and evaluation centre, and it transpired that there had been three open-air nerve agent events on 13 March, one of which was a test involving an F-4 fighter aircraft operating two TMU-28B spray tanks, each holding 160 gallons of VX.[7]

Overall the exercise at RAF Valley had been a valuable one, certainly for the UK since it was clear that the OPCW TS had some way to go in building up an effective operational capability for challenge inspection, but it was still early days as the organization was still less than a year old. Further continuing training and exercises were clearly going to be needed, and over the years that is what the TS did as it worked hard to build and maintain a capability for both challenge inspections and investigation of alleged use. The UK would play a modest part in this work by providing training opportunities for TS personnel to participate in our national CWC practice challenge inspections and related exercises in subsequent years. I was also invited to participate in several exercises hosted by other state parties to help train the OPCW TS, most notably in Switzerland, Germany, Italy and the Netherlands (twice – one at a military site 2002, the other at a civil chemical plant in 2007).[8] One of the serious constraining factors here was the tenure policy adopted by the OPCW States Parties whereby the normal term of office for TS staff was seven years. Just as individuals started to become accomplished and good at conducting challenge inspections, they had to leave. Moreover, the TS found it difficult to manage staffing levels transitions, which meant that frequently large numbers of well-trained and experienced staff left at the same time, so the build-up of effective operational capabilities had to start again. A less charitable mind might suppose that the tenure policy and its adverse impact on effectiveness suited some state parties just fine.

Working with the US

It is often assumed that the UK and US always work in close harmony, sharing common views and approaches to the problems encountered in arms control and disarmament matters. Whilst this is true on many occasions, there have been instances of a difference of opinion. In a special relationship one can always be candid in private, but even then there is always an anxiety about not unduly upsetting the Americans. UK CWC verification experts did not agree with the US approach to challenge inspection, both during the Convention's negotiations and after entry into force. Much of the difference centred on the Verification Annex's Part X provisions on perimeter negotiations, a point which was touched upon earlier. The US read the CWC to mean that they could take the full 108 hours for the perimeter negotiations before they had to let inspectors onto the inspected site; they wanted this time to help prepare the site for inspection. In contrast, our view was that as soon as the inspectors accepted the alternative perimeter, then the inspected state party was required to let inspectors cross it and begin their inspection. The Convention's language was clear on this point. To make matters worse the US approach to conducting a challenge inspection was completely different from our own as we were about to find out.

It had been our policy since PCI 3 to invite a US observer to our exercises: first we had Lieutenant Colonel Guy Lovelace from the Office of the Secretary of Defense (OSD) and for the remaining exercises Lieutenant Colonel Jim Bushong, from the same office. Both officers were part of the US delegation to the CD CWC negotiations at various times. The same practice followed in the post 1994 exercises and as part of the 1996 exercise at Base Ammunition Depot Kineton we had a reciprocal agreement with the US Army to exchange observers at our exercises that year. The US had taken an interesting approach to their exercise in that it was going to be a genuine no-notice inspection for the facility concerned. TRADOC – Training and Doctrine Command – had decided that one of its seven facilities would be chosen using the same time lines that applied in the CWC. The chosen site was Fort Sill, Lawton Oklahoma, base of the US Army Field Artillery School as well as the Marine Corps Field Artillery; it was also one of the four locations for US Army Basic Combat Training. Fort Sill was massive, covering some 380 square kilometres, and had been established in 1869. I was to join the US inspection team whilst Dr John Bartlett from Porton would be an observer.

The exercise started at Washington Dulles Airport where the US On-site Inspection Agency (OSIA) had its base; this was a US designated point of entry for CWC inspections and was used for in-bound Soviet/Russian inspectors under the INF Treaty and START. POE procedures would take place here, including a meticulous equipment check before moving onto the inspection site. The US would x-ray inspection equipment and check every item before agreeing that it could be used in the inspection; a real OPCW team could bring upwards of four tonnes worth as we had seen at RAF Valley, so checking all of this in the time allowed by the Verification Annex would be a big ask. The UK approach was to take a more selective approach, and we certainly had no plans to x-ray any of the approved equipment brought in by the inspectors. It seemed the US approach was in part shaped by their experience with Soviet inspectors and a strict legal mindset to what was and was not allowed; this was going to be manifested in the way the US OSIA escort team composed of US military personnel from the Army, Air Force, Navy and Marine Corps would manage the inspection once we arrived at Fort Sill. In this concept of operations there was to be no flexibility and a rigid adherence to the agreed inspection plan regardless of whether it made sense on the ground or not. One key lesson that we had grasped early on was that pragmatic flexibility by the escorts was the key and a rigid approach would likely only annoy inspectors at best and make them suspicious at worse.

One factor that helped determine the by-the-book US approach to escorting inspectors was shaped by its experience with Soviet Union's attitude during out-bound US inspections at Soviet facilities. This meant that OSIA would take an overly defensive approach mirroring how its inspectors were treated in Russia. Add to that a rigid system of command evident in the US military in which even majors, who were usually sub-team leaders, had to follow the plan strictly and not deviate from it under any circumstances. An abiding fear seemed to be that to do so would set a dangerous precedent. The inspection team was presented with a requirement that six hours' notice had to be provided for any building that it wished to inspect; a similar regime applied to any vehicle crossing the perimeter, which was a bit daft as well as utterly unworkable as US Inter-state Highway 44 from Texas to Kansas cut through the base. Fort Sill also contained a declared site under the INF Treaty – a missile repair facility, and it was one of the first budlings to be inspected; I was allocated to the sub-team sent to check it out. Almost everything in this building was shrouded, ranging from empty oil drums to table-football games in the crew room, every single notice board was shrouded too – all in bright red cloth, which was the colour of the US Army Artillery. All this did was to heighten suspicion and a sense of bewilderment as it drew more attention to features and contents than would normally be the case if a more limited approach had been taken and a more neutral colour used for the shrouding material. Things became even more restricted when I asked one of the building personnel as we walked from the ground floor to the first floor if he could summarise the general purpose of the work done in the building. At which point the OSIA escort intervened and insisted that this was an 'interview', and that we would have to make a formal written request to the senior home team leadership for their consideration. In UK inspections we had always asked local personnel some general questions as we conducted our work, and this was invariably helpful and saved time for both sides. The US escorts were in contrast only interested in following their rigid escort policy, which had been preset regardless of the situation that might be encountered on the ground. The notification period for access to buildings was also a nonsense as the Geronimo Museum was also in the Fort's grounds, and I could pay a few dollars and have immediate access. Moreover, at that time Fort Sill was an open base where it was possible to drive around the site, with access only controlled to specific areas such as ammunition storage areas. This made the six hour notice requirement somewhat questionable, but the rationale behind it we learned later was to treat everything the same thereby concealing the more sensitive buildings. Time was also needed to put in place the sort of over the top shrouding that we had encountered in the missile repair facility. All this made negotiations protracted and consequently it became difficult to complete an effective inspection in the time available. We had seen a similar sort of grudging behaviour during the UK-Soviet exchange visits between CDE Porton Down and the main Soviet CW facility at Shikhany in 1988. Sampling was also another bone of contention. The US Senate in its infinite wisdom when giving its advice and consent to the ratification of the CWC had insisted on Condition 18 whereby no sample could be removed from the continental US for analysis in a foreign laboratory.[9] Such a condition is in clear contradiction with the provisions of the CWC's Verification Annex, which states that samples can be sent off-site to the network of OPCW designated laboratories. In this exercise the inspection team did not have its own mobile lab, instead the US OSIA escort team had brought its own from Edgewood Arsenal and insisted that all samples permitted would be analysed by US experts, although inspectors could observe the process.

There were a couple of incidents in this inspection that showed what could be unearthed even with the overly restrictive approach adopted by the OSIA escorts. Both were incidents that were suggestive of non-compliance. As we entered one compound that appeared to be a depository of waste and scrap materials, we spotted near the entrance what appeared to be 155 mm projectiles lying in a heap amongst other debris. More to the point they were grey and had two green role band markers – standard NATO ammunition regulations for nerve agent filled ordnance. It turned out that they were plastic and served as training aids, for recognition purposes for artillerymen and EOD teams. We were allowed to photograph two of these provided one inspector held them up with one hand to show that they were not real. I got to hold them up. Now at one level this was not surprising since the US did possess a CW stockpile and it would be some years before it would be destroyed as required by the CWC.[10] Training personnel in the safe handling of such a stockpile would still be needed. However, what was odd here was that when pressed on the matter our hosts were evasive, and things only became more difficult when we also found a cupboard full of these training shapes including projectiles marked up with red role bands, which designated a riot control agent fill. The CWC prohibited the use of RCAs as a method of warfare, and 105 mm projectiles are hardly suited for domestic law enforcement. We even found in a class room some old firing tables used by artillery officers to calculate the optimum usage of chemical warfare agent on specific targets over specified ranges. All this made our hosts even more evasive and despite pressing, the inspection team never received a detailed explanation for the existence of these training aids. Since part of the non-compliance concern in the exercise had alleged training in the use of CW, this was even more suspicious. The key learning point here was this problem could have been much reduced in its impact had the presence and purposes of CW marked training shapes been acknowledged and explained in the opening brief. At Fort Sill it was the conjunction of a such a constrained and grudging attitude to access, information and sampling coupled with the discovery of the training shapes that heightened rather than reduced inspectors' concerns. Much of what goes on in a challenge inspection is about the psychology of the process, not just the careful observation of discrete activities and objects.

The CWC's Article X paragraph 11 (a) requires an inspected state party to demonstrate its compliance, and for this to be achieved a forthcoming posture, transparency and cooperation are essential ingredients. Indeed, the CWC's Verification Annex Part II paragraph sixty-two requires the inspection team to comment on the inspected state party's cooperation in their final report. And the sort of experience encountered at Fort Sill was exactly why the UK had been such a strong proponent of this provision during the Convention's negotiations. As Arthur Wesley, later the Duke of Wellington, remarked after his first military experience during the abortive British expedition to the Netherlands in 1794, at least one learned, 'what one ought not to do, and that is always something.' [11] The US clearly had not drawn the proper conclusions.

RAF Molesworth 1998

The CWC's Verification Annex Part II allowed for a scenario in which an inspected site operated by one state was located on the territory of another state party; specific rights were outlined for what is called the host state party in such cases. Essentially these were responsibilities for ensuring that an inspection team could enter its territory and be expeditiously transferred to the site in question. A Host State Party is obliged to facilitate the inspection of those facilities or areas and provide for the necessary support to enable the inspection team to carry out its tasks in a timely and effective manner. With this scenario in mind the UK and US had negotiated, admittedly with some difficulty, a Memorandum of Understanding on challenge inspections at US bases in the UK and UK equivalent areas in the US. This MOU laid out the procedures such as notification and POE arrangements as well as how the actual inspection itself would be managed. A major concern, given the US approach to challenge inspection as we had seen at Fort Sill, was that the UK would be cited as the inspected state party, which carried the obligation to demonstrate compliance, but the site was operated and controlled by the US and virtually all the assets on the site belonged to the US. We had to be sure that the US approach and policies would not compromise UK interests whilst being ever mindful of the need to protect US national security concerns at the same time. There was also the small matter of UK national sovereignty bound up in this; bases were made available for the US under the terms of the NATO Status of Forces Agreement and the UK

Visiting Forces Act 1952. So for example, if an inspection team wanted to collect environmental or air samples from within ten metres of the base perimeter boundary as allowed by Part X of the Verification Annex, the UK escort team could allow this as such activity would be taking place on British sovereign territory and under its control. For all these reasons and more the US decided to conduct a practice challenge inspection at RAF Molesworth and this would enable the UK to deploy its National Authority, JACIG, Porton Down and MOD experts as part of the home team. They would lead the simulated POE procedures and look out for UK interests during the inspection itself as per the MOU. RAF Molesworth was a former GLCM base, though it had only been active for a short period prior to the signature of the INF Treaty in 1987. Nevertheless, it still had the infrastructure necessary to support flights of cruise missiles in place. By the time of the exercise in August 1998 Molesworth was home to three US Major Command branch sites: the United States European Command Joint Intelligence Operations Center, Europe Analytic Center (JAC), and United States Africa Command. It was not a flying station, the main runway had long since been demolished, and there were no explosive storage areas. On the face of it this ought to have been an easy site on which to demonstrate compliance.

The US escort team of OSIA experts and a legion of other DOD, Arms Control and Disarmament Agency and State Department advisers stuck to the rigid policy playbook on challenge inspection. They insisted on 108 hours over the perimeter negotiation, but the inspectors led by Jim Kress (ex US army and OPCW PTS) and me as the token Brit, called their bluff by immediately accepting the US proposed alternative perimeter very shortly after it was proposed. Under the CWC's Verification Annex Part X the alternative perimeter must be proposed not later than twenty-four hours after the team's arrival at the Point of Entry. We had been offered a tour of the alternative perimeter, which ended up back at the RAF Molesworth's main gate, and on arrival there we said we accepted the alternative and would now like to cross the perimeter to begin the inspection. There then followed a stand-up argument over the correct interpretation of the CWC; the optics of this looked bad, and as was pointed out afterwards had this been a real inspection, no doubt the world's press would be camped outside the main gate and this apparent obstruction of an inspection team would be beamed across the planet. This too after we had seen Iraqi obstruction of UNSCOM inspectors over the previous seven years. The US approach seemed to us to be the exact opposite of what was needed to demonstrate compliance; indeed Martin Rudduck, Head of the UK National Authority remarked that the US home team included a raft of State Department lawyers trying to find reasons why the US should not accede to the inspectors' requests. When I had been on the Fort Sill exercise one of the senior US OSIA officials had told me that, 'inspectors were not on a fucking tour.' So you get the flavour; the US approach at the time was adversarial rather than cooperative.[12] This approach put me in mind of Shakespeare's Richard III, 'I'm not in a giving vein today.'

Once on-site there was more of the same; for example, we had agreed an inspection plan which laid out the sequence of activities for two sub-teams. The US home team senior management insisted that this sequence should be followed; however, once our inspection activities began it appeared to me that in one particular sector it would have been more sensible to change the set sequence of buildings and structures inspections. This was too much for the Major in charge of our sub-group; he would have to take it on advisement from senior management whether we could depart from the preordained route. The building in question turned out to be a small security post – a glorified sentry box, which had not been obvious from the site map provided; it would take a few minutes to eliminate this from our list as it would avoid having to double back to check it out. An officer of Major rank ought to have had the discretion to authorize this on the spot, but the fear of creating a precedent that devious inspectors would later exploit was no doubt one of the reasons as well as a rigid insistence on the need to treat all buildings the same regardless of their true sensitivities. Much the same happened when we went off to inspect one of the large former GLCM bunkers, which had been built to house the mobile transport erector launchers. This now seemed to be full of large brown boxes stacked almost from floor to ceiling – looking a bit like an IKEA warehouse. 'What do you store in these boxes?' I asked. 'Flat packed furniture' came the reply from the local site escort who had had to seek permission from the OSIA escort first. 'In which case we would need have a few of these opened to confirm that please.' I replied. But once again the response was that request would need to be submitted in writing to the senior management team who would 'take it under advisement.' More time wasting and needless delay over something that ought to have been easily dealt with in minutes. Worse was to come. As a nuclear weapons storage area in its previous existence there was a large observation tower in the centre of the GLCM compound as part of the standard security arrangements for such places. We had asked whether we could climb to the top in order to have a good overview of the site to check that we had not missed anything of potential interest. The US senior management team checked with the UK National Authority that this was acceptable to the UK as inspectors might then see something in the countryside around the base. It was fine for the UK. As one of my US colleagues in the inspection team later remarked over dinner, this was a bit like the scene in Dr Strangelove where the US President wants to let the Russian Ambassador into the War Room. Flabbergasted, General Buck Turgidson, Chairman of the Joint Chiefs of Staff (played so memorably by George C. Scott) says, 'Are you aware of what a serious breach of security that would be. He'll see everything. He'll see the big board.' [13] Worries about seeing the 'big board' were more of a concern at Molesworth than demonstrating compliance as quickly and effectively as possible.

US paranoia over escorting inspectors everywhere even extended to the local hotel which we were using as a working area and for plenary meetings, something that only added to the time taken to do anything. Now the hotel was located outside the wire and not in an area under US control, but OSIA still insisted that inspectors be escorted from the meeting room to the toilets. We ought to have pushed back on this and asked the UK National Authority to intervene as technically under the CWC it was their responsibility to manage the inspectors until they crossed the perimeter of the inspected site.

Some ten years later at an exercise at RAF Mildenhall, which had similar aims, we encountered similar issues. This time we played a British enclave within the US controlled areas, and in the exercise play this was the only area of the whole base that was inspected by the surrogate inspection team of which I was a member. Once again too much time was spent arguing over perimeters and inspection team requests. So much so that the expert playing the Chief Inspector – Don Claggett (ex ACDA, OPCW PTS and TS and State Department) remarked that the inspectors, 'were in danger of getting callouses on our butt' given the amount of time we had spent sitting around. We were able to submit an initial inspection plan almost as soon as the final perimeter had been confirmed as we had used the detailed site map to identify areas of interest and priority for two sub-teams. Even this took our hosts by surprise and one even felt that it was not appropriate to have submitted such a plan so quickly. At least this time the US had not dragged the perimeter negotiations out over 108 hours.

In the post-exercise wash-up discussions and reporting the UK had pointed out that this US style of challenge inspection was self-defeating as it helped create suspicions where none ought to exist in the first place and ran a real risk that an inspection report would not provide sufficient facts to convince the Executive Council that there was no case to answer. If we saw such behaviour from Russia, Iran or China in a challenge inspection that we had requested, for example, we would only have our own compliance concerns amplified not assuaged. Many of our US colleagues saw this over the years, but the basic policy and mindset remained the same. As time went by UK experts became only more and more convinced that our approach was the better one – national security and commercial confidentiality could be protected and compliance with the CWC could be demonstrated at the same time.

Working with Switzerland, Sweden, Germany, The Netherlands and Italy

The UK was the pioneer of practice challenge inspections during the CWC negotiations and was perhaps the only state party (other than the US) that continued to exercise regularly to validate its own procedures and train its personnel. Other states' parties were interested in learning from the British experience as they built up their own national capabilities, so this led to invitations to send a UK inspection team to exercises first in Switzerland in 1997 and then in the following year to Sweden. Both offered many learning opportunities, not just for our hosts but also the UK as they added to our body of experience. Once gain both exercises provided examples of what not to do as per Arthur Wesley, especially the Swiss exercise which was held in an area that included Spiez NBC Laboratory, the Wimmis rocket propellent plant and an underground explosives storage facility housed inside a mountain. The Senior Swiss military escort officer from the Federal Ministry of Defence was my direct counterpart as I led a small British team of experts from Porton Down, JACIG and the MOD. This proved to be a classic case of not heeding advice from expert subordinates, which led my Swiss colleague to dig himself more and more into trouble and thereby only amplify concerns rather than dispel them. Once again this experience highlights the crucial part that psychology plays in a challenge inspection.

Things started to go wrong for our hosts in a site briefing. The non-compliance concern in the exercise inspection mandate had alleged that there were underground facilities being used to store chemical weapons, so we were on the lookout for any such place within the requested perimeter which captured quite a large area of ground, in the middle of which was a large mountain flanked by roads, a river and railway line. We were briefed on Spiez NBC laboratory and the WIMMIS plant, but there was no reference to any other military or defence related facilities or structures within the perimeter. I pressed the point: 'can you confirm that there are no facilities or buildings belonging to the Federal Swiss MOD?' I was assured that there were none. We were then offered an overflight of the inspection area. This was to be in an Alouette four seater helicopter, which was well suited to ground observation with its large glass canopy. There was room for two inspectors, so I took the front port seat next to the pilot and my MOD colleague sat in the back starboard passenger seat with a Swiss escort in the remaining berth. We agreed that I would concentrate my observations forward and port, while my MOD colleague would focus on the starboard. The key was to find anything that looked like the entrance to an underground facility. The area was heavily forested, so that made picking out any secret entrance a challenge. We did not manage to spot anything that looked the part, even from about 1,000 feet. The view of the Alps and Lake Thun was rather grand though. However, I had spotted what looked to be a small cluster of explosive storage buildings on a track leading off from what appeared to be a main road. These had not been mentioned, so once back on the ground we asked to visit them. I asked why these evidently military buildings had not been mentioned, and no satisfactory answer was forthcoming. We were able to enter them and to my surprise we found several 155 mm artillery projectiles. After this we continued the search for the underground storage site, which we knew had to be nearby. As we walked along the side of the main road skirting the western side of the mountain we noticed what appeared to be a gun emplacement in the woods built into the hillside– it seemed to have two embrasures, one for a large calibre gun and a smaller one perhaps for a machine gun. Given the dishonest statements we had heard thus far we thought that we should look inside as there was likely a magazine for ammunition storage. Our Swiss senior escort officer insisted that the bunker was empty and that there was no need to go in. I said that we still needed to confirm this in view of the non-compliance concern. In the larger of the two chambers there seemed to be a large object lying on the ground, on closer look it was the gun barrel for a 75 mm gun, possibly even 105 mm. It was difficult to see in the dark as there was no electric power, or so we were told. I pointed this out to our escort who denied it was a gun barrel. There was a pattern emerging here. We noted our discoveries and the responses and pressed on with the inspection as time was running out in the exercise to find the underground storage facility. Further down the roadway we could see a narrow gauge rack railway heading up the hillside to what looked to be an entrance into the mountain. This must be the place, so we suggested that we ought to use the rack railway to reach the top. 'Unfortunately, Chief Inspector the railway isn't working, so we'll have to walk.' And so we did at a brisk pace to make sure there was minimal further delay. Once at the top the Swiss escort leader said that they were now going to apply managed access and only one inspector with no equipment would be allowed in to the facility. There was little choice but to agree. In future the OPCW TS would have a two person rule so that all inspection activity would require two inspectors for both safety and validation reasons. Once inside it was clear that access would be extremely limited and I was not even permitted access to any of the explosive storage areas, so had no way of confirming the nature of the stores held there. It was argued that this was for safety reasons. It seemed, as I was to learn later, that there had been a fatal accident in another Swiss underground storge site, the cause of which had never been determined. (This was at Mitholz in 1947 when 3,000 tonnes of ammunition the army had stored in the mountain overlooking the village exploded. Nine people were killed and the village was destroyed.) This made the authorities nervous about letting anyone into underground ammunition storage facilities. Inspectors always need to be careful to avoid ascribing the same safety standards that might apply in their own country, they might be different but not necessarily weaker. This is why it is important to have some understanding of the regulatory framework that applies in state parties and how it is applied – there could well be differences. Despite pointing out that such a denial would not look good in the inspection report, especially in view of the catalogue of misleading and incorrect information already provided, the Swiss escorts did not change their decision. Lies would perhaps be too strong a word. The Swiss were not able to demonstrate compliance with the CWC and left the main concern in the inspection mandate – the nature of the underground storage facility – unaddressed. When I came out of the facility to join the rest of the inspection team I was told that no sooner had I disappeared inside the mountain, when a technician came out and used the rack railway to go down the mountain side. So the line that it was inoperative was another falsehood.

Some of the key lessons here for how to escort an inspection team reinforced what was at least UK best practice – one of the most important was that answers to inspector questions should never be guessed or assumed as that will only very likely store up trouble later in the inspection as we saw here. If uncertain, the ideal response from the escort is to be honest and admit that there is a need to check or gather the information before responding orally or in writing. The nature of the question or issue must also be carefully recorded (which was one of the roles of the JACIG escorts) to prevent later misunderstandings, incomplete or incorrect responses. This must be done as expeditiously as possible. The Swiss experience was the complete antithesis of the US approach with decision making vested in a single person unlike the rigid control and inflexibility of OSIA policy that we saw in action at Fort Sill, RAF Molesworth and RAF Mildenhall. A Swedish armed forces observer who was also on the Swiss exercise left thinking that the Sweden ought to run its own exercise to test its own readiness levels. He was obviously impressed with the service provided by UK experts so we were invited the following year to send an inspection team to Sweden. This time the UK team included Lieutenant Colonel Colin Winter who came as JACIG's representative and he appeared at the airport dressed in deerstalker, cape and tweeds and carrying his cromach[14] – appropriate garb I suppose for an inspector. Colin, as part of his duties as a flight leader at JACIG, had arranged for a special bottling of a Speyside single malt whisky called 'The Inspector's Choice' and this was available for those in the know at one of the whisky shop duty frees at Heathrow. Colin used to provide bottles for in-bound inspection teams from Russia and Eastern Europe on CFE and other inspections as part of the overall cooperative approach – but only at the end of the inspections. The inspection scenario on this occasion was jointly prepared between the UK and Sweden, and the site that they had allocated for the PCI was something else – a naval dockyard inside a mountain with very few of its facilities above ground. Muskö was just south of Stockholm and contained dry docks, ammunition stores, a hospital, a communications centre, accommodation in numerous chambers and tunnels connected by some twenty kilometres of underground roads. The ammunition stores were outside the scope of the exercise, which was unfortunate. All in all the whole place looked like the set of a James Bond film; 'You Only Live Twice' sprang to mind.

There were no echoes of the Swiss exercise the previous year; the Swedish observer had clearly been paying attention. The major issue for the inspection team on this occasion was the Swedish application of managed access measures, which made it very difficult to work out where all the air and ventilation shafts went to and where they broke the surface. Our aim was to see whether there was any chemical pilot plant hidden in one of the tunnels; we asked for a full diagram showing all utilities and ducts for the tunnels, but this was not forthcoming. In the end it was possible to agree on a sampling strategy, which would have allowed us access to one shaft from one of the main work areas chosen at random. This was only played notionally, but it was far from clear whether this would have provided sufficient convincing evidence. The greatest challenge was trying to be sure that we had mapped all the tunnels and chambers even with the provision of maps by our hosts. Avoiding disorientation was a major problem underground: a key question was had we seen all of it? However, everything else seen in the dry docks and tunnels was fully consistent with Muskö being what it was claimed to be – namely a naval dockyard, and overall our Swedish hosts cooperated with the inspection team. In the context of this exercise the explosive storage and processing areas were not part of the game, but had they been excluded for real then any inspection team clearly would be unable to gather sufficient facts to help the Executive Council to determine whether non-compliance had occurred. Many years later Per Runn, a Swedish CWC expert from FOI at Umeä – the Swedish equivalent of Porton Down and who later went on to work for the OPCW TS' Verification Division, told me that when they were conducting a recce for the exercise they found an illicit spirit still at the end of one of the little used tunnels. So there was a pilot plant of sorts after all.

The Netherlands – Coevorden 2002

The idea for this exercise originated in one of the annual UK PCIs at the Royal Artillery training range at Larkhill; as usual we had invited the OPCW TS to send three of its inspectors to take part. UK only exercises carried the codeword Longhole, whilst one involving overseas experts was known as a Macavity. The basic objectives of these exercises were to train UK National Authority, JACIG and site representatives, validate the Standing Instruction on Arms Control and present the OPCW with a realistic challenge inspection training opportunity as well as sharing inspection experience with other states parties.[15] Larkhill did not present any difficult national security issues, which was one reason it was selected for a Macavity. It was also difficult to create artificial security sensitivities unless these were very carefully designed and carried a credible context and history, which would then give the escorts something to negotiate with and to develop plausible managed access strategies to protect the secrets. As we had seen as far back as PCI2 at RNAD Crombie and elsewhere just covering a pile of empty ammunition boxes with a tarpaulin and asserting it was to protect national security was insufficient. UK policy for hosting a challenge inspection was to demonstrate compliance as quickly as possible and cooperate as fully as possible with the inspection team consistent with protecting national security information. We therefore wanted to see escorts play these roles in exercises exactly as we expected them to behave in a real challenge inspection. Paul Schulte, the originator of the managed access concept, was now back in the MOD arms control branch, but this time as its head. Paul was also the UK Commissioner on UNSCOM/UNMOVIC and came to the Larkhall exercise to observe proceedings. He told me that he thought the exercise did not really prepare the OPCW TS inspectors for the more likely scenario of an obstructive state party, echoing the sort of behaviour that had bedevilled UNSCOM operations in Iraq. Things were too easy. This was true to an extent, but first steps still required the TS to learn to walk before it could run. In other words given the seven year rule and staff turnover, new inspectors had to learn the basics first in a friendly environment. I said to Paul that we could certainly look to designing a more rigorous test for TS inspectors. Thus was born the concept of a challenge inspection in a non-cooperative environment, and since optically it might be better to find another state party to host such an exercise rather than UK, I thought that our Dutch colleagues could be persuaded to provide a facility. Indeed in the early days of the PTS a training exercise had been held at the Woensdrecht airbase in the former GLCM compound in which I had participated. When approached with this idea both the TS and Dutch were very keen and the Dutch suggested that we use Coevorden, a NATO mobilisation base – a store of prepositioned military equipment and munitions – near the German border as there would be less disruption at such a place compared to an operational flying station such as Woensdrecht. The UK produced the first draft of the scenario in conjunction with the TS and Dutch. We would also provide some key experts to play the leader of the Inspected State Party, the RSO and a couple of technical advisers (one on CW and one on ammunition) along with two experts for the control team – me and Clive Rowland from the MOD. The expert we had in mind for the leader of the ISP side was someone well versed in how to obstruct and delay an inspection team – Rod Godfrey, ex British Army Major and MOD had worked as an inspector for UNSCOM and UNMOVIC and had seen first-hand how the Iraqis had sought to obstruct their missions over the years. He would understand the brief that his main task in this exercise was to obstruct and annoy the inspectors, but with a smile. All very much in the mode of the 1932 Marx Brothers film 'Horse Feathers' in which Groucho sings a song to the assembled professors and students, 'Whatever it is I'm against it.' Dr David Kelly would play the RSO. Our Dutch colleagues would provide all the other escorts and site personnel. Arend Meerburg, from the Dutch MFA and an arms control expert who had taken part in the CWC negotiations and was also serving at this time as the Task Leader for the draft OSI Operational Manual in the CTBTO's Preparatory Commission, would play the hard line deputy to Rod. This was to prove an interesting dynamic as the exercise developed.

The intention was to make the inspection team work for its access and to work out solutions and possible alternative strategies that might help them gain some access and information out of the non-cooperative state party. We quickly saw that Rod was rather too adept at his role and the OPCW Chief Inspector (Henry Arvidsson – an ex UNSCOM inspector) tried too hard to secure all of his aims; result impasse at first on the perimeter negotiations and then over the acceptability of the inspection team's initial plan. Neither side would give an inch, but if this posture continued the inspectors would not escape the meeting room and start their inspection of the site. On the one hand this was certainly providing the inspectors with a tough assignment, which was part of the exercise's objectives. However, we needed to see some activity on the ground, so this was the time for the control staff to intervene to break the impasse and tell the two sides to assume that the inspection plan had now been agreed. This process continued once on site with the escorts being difficult and obstructive every step of the way and finding reasons for rejecting the inspectors' requests. So once again we had to ask Rod to ease off a little. At this point Arend Meerburg made clear (in role play of course) that he was not happy with the decision by the leader of the ISP team to start making concessions: muttering words such as treason and surrender. When we were all in the canteen just after lunch Arend stormed in accompanied by two very large Dutch military policemen wearing white crash helmets with the visors down shouting whilst pointing to Rod, 'There he is, there he is, arrest the traitor.' At this point Rod could see what was happening and started to get out of his seat, but he was still grabbed by the MPs and dragged out of the canteen pleading his innocence. Everyone looked on in stunned silence. A few moments after they had left the canteen, we could hear a shot being fired. The inspection team cheered loudly as their nemesis bit the dust. The 'shot' was a blank and Rod and the MPs returned safely to the canteen to a round of well-earned applause.

In terms of lessons for the TS and how they might deal with comparable levels of non-cooperation in a real inspection, it seemed that the best tactic would be to accept under protest the levels of access offered, saying something like: 'We doubt whether this will address our questions or the non-compliance concerns in the inspection mandate, but let us see where this gets us. We reserve our right to return to this matter.' It would be essential for the subsequent deliberations in the Executive Council for the inspectors to show in their final report that they had made every effort to collect all the necessary facts. They would also need to catalogue and describe every obstruction and lack of cooperation from the ISP. If things were so bad and it proved impossible to conduct an effective inspection the chief inspector, in close consultation with the Director General, could always threaten to call off the inspection. But this would very much be the last resort in extreme circumstances. The UK had long since thought that one of the key values of the challenge inspection regime would be that it could expose and highlight obstruction that quite likely betokened attempts to conceal non-compliance. Coevorden showed that such an outcome could well be possible, and it was essential that inspectors were trained on how to deal with it. The TS would not look at this again in an exercise until 2015.

Rieti, Italy, 2015[16]

The OPCW Fact Finding Missions operating in Syria post 2012 encountered persistent non-cooperative and non-permissive environments. In addition to a surly Syrian government, inspectors had to operate in a war zone, which placed extra safety and security burdens on them. In order to train the latest batch of new inspectors the TS with the cooperation of the Italian NBC Joint Defense School, which is based at the Verdirosi Barracks in Rieti, staged a training exercise designed to replicate a hostile environment for the trainees. This entailed armed guards everywhere and large numbers of them too; the Italian Lieutenant Colonel serving as the head of the fictious establishment played his part to the tee as the hostile and aggressive military type who was unhappy at hosting international inspectors. My colleague Clive Rowland from the MOD was asked to play the Head of the National Authority and he was as uncooperative as the Lieutenant Colonel. I played the RSO. After a slow start and failing to find some key incriminating evidence planted by the exercise control staff and one of the female inspectors getting locked in the toilets – a new take on managed access, the team gradually found their feet and coped with the pressure applied throughout the inspection. As ever the key to success was to be thorough and quick, a leisurely approach would not work in these circumstances. As the team got closer to the incriminating facts, the control staff had a cunning plan to bring the exercise to a close. During a plenary meeting I just happened to be standing by one of the doors when someone quietly whispered that I ought to stand to one side. As I did so the base commander, by now highly irate and excitable and in an Oscar winning performance, launched into a tirade against the inspectors, and demanded that they get off his base at which point all the doors burst open and a dozen or more armed soldiers stormed in and pointed their guns at the inspectors. 'You have two hours to leave. Get out.' At which point the National Authority could only meekly agree, though he too made clear that he shared the sentiments. When we were developing our initial ideas and concepts for challenge inspection in 1988-1990 we had assumed that there could well be non-cooperation, and that this could be exposed in the final inspection report. We had also come to the view that challenge inspection should ideally be routine as it had become under the 1986 Stockholm Document. However, what was clear now after experiences in Iraq under UNSCOM and UNMOVIC and more recently in Syria, inspectors would be much more likely to be exposed to hostile and non-permissive environments in cases where the state party in question was indeed in breach of its CWC obligations. Exercises such as Rieti would now need to be standard preparation for all future OPCW inspectors as non-cooperative and non-permissive environments were likely to be the norm in challenge inspections and investigations of alleged use.

UK Macavity exercises 1996-2015

The original MOD plan had been to conduct two practice challenge inspections each year, but a combination of budget cuts and the continuing absence of a real challenge inspection being requested reduced this to one per year. In these years we used quite a diverse range of sites, Aberporth (a missile test range on the Welsh coast), AWE Burghfield, Princess Royal Barracks Gütersloh (Germany), Devonport Naval Dockyard, Royal School of Artillery Larkhill, RNAS Culdrose, RAF Stafford (where I spotted a ballistic casing for one of Britain's early nuclear weapons – the Yellow Sun Mark II lurking in a storage hanger), Marchwood Military Port, the University of Surrey's School of Chemistry and Chemical Engineering, Dstl Porton Down and RAF Honington. We also arranged several smaller more focussed exercises aimed primarily as OPCW TS training events focussed on managed access and interviewing; these took place at Gosport – naval ordnance depot, Kineton and RAF Honington. I was also able to participate as the Requesting State Observer in three large OPCW challenge inspection exercises hosted by Germany at the Luftwaffe air base at Pfedersfeld, at a large multi-purpose civil chemical plant in Delft, the Netherlands, and at an explosive and small arms manufacturing facility at Altdorf in Switzerland. And not even being driven around with my own personal escort and driver in a black Mercedes Benz at Altdorf changed my mind about the utility of RSOs. In all the other exercises I served on the control staff having graduated through all the roles from inspector, chief inspector, escort, head of the home team, RSO and co-exercise director. These CWC exercises were supplemented to an extent by the practice Ottawa Convention Fact Finding Missions that the MOD also ran for several years. Although the banned items were anti-personal landmines, we quickly saw that the inspection mechanics and processes were very similar to a CWC challenge inspection; for instance, the importance of detailed briefings, windshield tours, initial inspection plans, the critical importance of a central control point to log all inspection movements and questions, escorting and negotiation, managed access and interviewing. Many of the Standing Instruction on Arms Control measures were directly transferable. I served in these exercises too either as head of the National Authority or control staff. These practice FFMs took place at mostly ammunition storage depots, so we were back at RNAD Crombie, Kineton, Longtown and its satellite storage areas at Eastriggs and Glen Douglas in Scotland. We did the latter three in a single exercise since an

Ottawa Convention FFM is not confined to a defined inspection site as is the case in the CWC. We also went to two new sites, RAF Wittering and RNAD Plymouth at Ernesettle. The lessons from these exercises chimed and reinforced those from the CWC PCIs; for example, at RAF Wittering we saw the importance of dealing effectively with lodger units that are present within an inspection site, but subject to a different military command chain or even in the private sector. All of this needed to be factored into site reception plans.

The remainder of this chapter will highlight some of the more memorable incidents in the UK's CWC PCIs, especially those that brought to light a new lesson or issue that had not been seen before, or was a variant of an old song. The first of these concerned the PCI at HMNB Devonport. One of the reasons for this PCI was that thus far we had never conducted an exercise at a naval port, and that access to ships alongside could be problematic as the Royal Navy was perhaps the least enthusiastic about arms control. A further reason for the exercise concerned how the dockyard was managed: it was essentially split between Devonport Management Limited (DML), a private company responsible for the ship repair side of the base with the dockyard being one of the Royal Navy's two main bases, the other being Portsmouth. Devonport's buildings, facilities and structures were split between the Navy and DML. It is also the Royal Navy's only nuclear repair and refuelling facility as well as being the largest naval base in western Europe. Given the site's complexity, this PCI set a record for the number of written questions and requests put to the escort team during a UK exercise – well over eighty, including a request for a hydrographic survey of the sea bed in the vicinity of the dockyard since part of the non-compliance concern had alleged hasty disposal of chemical munitions. Access to ships had seemed to some problematic, so when I requested access to a destroyer alongside in order to inspect its ready-issue ammunition lockers on deck and the deep hold magazine below the waterline, eyebrows were raised. Furthermore, the ship in question was preparing to depart for a sea training exercise and a short-notice inspection would be disruptive to say the least and could even delay departure. Fortunately Flag Officer Sea Training, who was consulted about our inspection request agreed; apparently he thought this would present an extra unscheduled problem for the crew to solve under pressure, so he actually welcomed the suggestion. So on board we went to start with the ready issue magazines on deck. The first one I asked to be opened was readily agreed, but they could not immediately find the key. Moments later a matelot appeared with a large key and proceeded to put it into the lock; the key snapped in two leaving the head in the lock and the stem in the hands of an embarrassed sailor. 'We are going to need this open, so what are you going to do about this?' 'We'll get it open, don't worry' said the Lieutenant Commander escorting us. This was an occasion for the invaluable notional seals that we always carried, so we could continue the inspection and return when the ship's crew were ready to open it. Meantime, we continued down to the main magazine and confirmed that the bulk of the ordnance stored there was for the ship's main gun; there were various smaller natures, but nothing to excite the interest of a CW inspector. The items shown tallied with the inventory that we reviewed. Elsewhere on the ship when reviewing records we found papers that referenced the handling of chemical weapons, which clearly raised a question for follow-up. It seemed that this was an out-of-date manual that had not been revised; the context did not make clear enough that the guidance was what to do about chemical weapons encountered in a combat zone. One of the post-exercise recommendations was that anything in a military manual or instruction or guidance document that mentioned chemical weapons should be reviewed to ensure that the context was made clear, that the UK itself did not possess CW and that all military activities must be in compliance with the CWC. I do not know whether this was ever done. Meanwhile up on deck, the ready-issue locker was ready for opening; it contained anti-aircraft and small arms ammunition as one might expect.

In theory all buildings on Devonport were allocated to either DML or the Navy, but we managed to find the one building that nobody claimed to own, it was on no one's inventory and no one knew what it contained. Fortunately it was relatively small, and not at all capable of storing ammunition safely given its proximity to other occupied buildings or in any bulk; it could, however, be storing chemicals of CW interest. Eventually, a key was found from somewhere so we could inspect the contents, and behold it did contain a wide range of innocuous chemicals. The one item of CW interest was isopropyl alcohol, which is used in the last stage in the manufacture of sarin. It has other legitimate uses of course, such as a cleaning agent, and in this case the small quantities found were certainly consistent with this purpose. I use IPA to clean the track on my model railway. Devonport is an historic site, being a home of the Royal Navy since the late seventeenth century, which meant that were many buildings extant from previous centuries. One of which was a ropery from the eighteenth century, part of which was used as a temporary prisoner of war camp for French sailors during the Napoleonic Wars. A relic of this period was a working drop gallows (fortunately all locked up), which wins the prize for by far the most bizarre thing we ever found during a PCI.

We had conducted as noted above a PCI at Porton Down in 1994, so by 2002 it was time that we went back – in part there had been new extensive construction on the site as well as a new management structure. The site threw up similar challenges to 1994: that there were both chemical and biological defence activities on the site, work with experimental animals and a large open air range. One of the issues this time round was making sure that the MOD and other customers for the work being done at Porton were content that their project details could be shared with inspection teams as necessary. Therefore explaining the management structure and how work was funded turned out to be one of the key problems for the home team to overcome. Furthermore, collating the information needed to respond to inspectors' questions in a timely manner proved difficult on this occasion, notwithstanding the fact the need for this was a long established lesson from previous exercises. Unfortunately it was more a lesson identified rather than learned. Dealing with highly compartmentalised secret projects was challenging too; however, Porton could still show quite easily that the scale of operations on the site was entirely consistent with a defensive CW programme and that there were no facilities for the manufacture of bulk quantities of chemical warfare agent or for the filling on such agent into munitions. Although, one of the allegations levelled in the exercise scenario was that the site was engaged in the development of chemical weapons and this was harder to counter, nonetheless the scale and content of the research programmes that the inspectors showed an interest in could be demonstrated to have no offensive intent. Once again the passage of time was a problem in that many of those involved in the 1994 exercise were no longer around, so corporate memory once again was a bit of an issue. We had seen this already at RAF Honington between 1989 and 1994. This problem can be countered to an extent by making sure that preparation plans are kept up-to-date in light of changing circumstances and key personnel and periodically exercised; if left to gather dust at the back of cupboards their utility is much diminished, and it would be much harder to cope on the day of a future practice or real challenge inspection.

AWE Burghfield

When the MOD were trying to convince Aldermaston to host one of the initial PCIs back in 1989, there had been a fair degree of reluctance as we saw in Chapter 2. However, by the early 2000s that attitude had changed so that the initiative for a further practice challenge inspection came from Aldermaston's contingency planning and site security experts. Therefore when we needed a volunteer to host the annual exercise, we had to look no further than Berkshire. This was important because most of the sites used since Coulport had very few real security sensitivities on them and it was difficult to find genuine cases where we could test extensive managed access measures in a realistic setting. As we had seen at places such as PRB Gütersloh, you cannot really invent plausible artificial contexts; a pile of empty ammunition boxes does not cut the mustard if you pardon the pun. This time there would be plenty of genuine opportunities to test out managed access, and to reinforce the point we agreed that we would use AWE Burghfield where UK nuclear weapons are assembled and disassembled. By this time there was only one UK type of warhead – the Holbrook warhead for Trident – in service as the WE177s had long since been withdrawn and dismantled. We had of course visited Burghfield before as part of the managed access follow-up work in November 1990, but that had been over twenty years ago and there were only two experts from that visit still in post – Alwyn Davies of ACSA (N), MOD and me. Given the nature of Burghfield, the exercise in 2003 was going to be a UK eyes only exercise. I asked my ACDRU colleague Andrew Barlow to play the role of the Requesting State Observer, a part he played rather too well. A good deal of the site had fallen into disuse as many buildings no longer had a role to play in supporting the UK nuclear weapons programme. The areas of main security concern were the 'gravel gerties,' the buildings where weapons were assembled or dismantled, the lithium salts laboratory, weapons storage and a few of the warehouses where classified non-nuclear weapon components were stored. One of the key approaches that we had developed in the initial PCI programme was that prior to admitting inspectors to a building or area containing sensitive information a couple of the escorts would enter first to make sure the area was ready to receive the inspectors; for example, classified items had been put away, computers logged off and any necessary shrouding was in place. On this occasion Dr Alwyn Davies was serving as the final checker of one of the assembly bays and as a control staff member I accompanied him. We found several things that should not have been left out – for instance supporting 'furniture' that held weapon components and if left on display could have revealed size and geometry; these were very easily put away in cupboards beneath the work benches; same with some of the tooling. The space was now clear for the inspection team to enter, all they would see would be some sort of workshop with no features associated with chemistry or chemical weapons present. Even if the inspectors asked what was inside the workbench cupboards, one could have been opened on a randomly selective basis provided the objects inside were either back in their storage cradles or carefully shrouded. There would have been a very much bigger challenge if a live weapon had been present in various states of dismantlement, but even this would not have presented an impossible situation. Inspectors could be told to wait until all sensitive objects had been either put away and/or suitable shrouding was put in place and the area made safe. They could monitor the area to make sure nothing came out prior to their access. And as we saw back at RNAD Coulport in 1996 dealing with a live weapon in its transport container would not have presented insurmountable problems. Inspectors and site experts assisted by a CWC technical adviser from Porton Down found a jointly agreed way of addressing a sampling request problem. There were many storage drums containing lithium compounds, the isotopic composition was highly classified, which the inspection team wanted to sample in their mobile laboratory. Essentially the hosts would take the sample under inspector supervision and then jointly prepare the sample for the GC-MS in the mobile laboratory. The GC-MS would be operated in closed mode so that only chemicals of CW relevance could be looked for; the hosts would retain the column from the GC-MS after the analysis. The exercise showed once again that with careful planning, escorting, and technical advice an intrusive challenge inspection at one of the UK's most sensitive defence sites could be handled with confidence: CWC compliance could be demonstrated and national security could be protected.

Requesting State Observers (RSO)

I ended up playing the RSO in several exercises in the UK and overseas; it was a difficult role to play. During the CWC negotiations the original US proposal had been that an observer from the requesting state party would accompany the OPCW TS inspection team. Such an observer could brief the inspection team in detail on the original request and make sure that the team inspected those parts of the challenged site of greatest concern. Although initially appealing, it soon became clear that not every state in the CD shared this view, and the observer was seen as a threat. The final compromise in the negotiations was that accepting an RSO would be discretionary, and that the requested state party, should it accept an observer, would only be obliged to permit access to the final perimeter. Anything beyond that would also be discretionary, so it would be perfectly within the CWC to keep the RSO outside the inspected site. However, the RSO would be entitled to brief the inspection team and have updates on the progress of the inspection from the ITL. We had always viewed the RSO on an in-bound inspection as much more of a security threat than the inspection team, and even in the initial PCI programme Robin Waters as the RSO was given much less access to buildings even though he shared the same working space as the IT; for example, at AWE Aldermaston he was not allowed into any of the buildings. Once it became clear that accepting an RSO was going to be voluntary, it struck me that the sorts of states that the UK might be challenging – Iran and Russia for instance – would be highly unlikely to accept an observer. Iran's attitude to the RSO in the CTBT Preparatory Commission's Working Group B work on the OSI operational manual left one in little doubt of Tehran's negative view. So the question arose why should the UK put itself at a disadvantage by accepting one?

In the second round of PCIs the RSO was given much less access to the site and generally left confined to an office under escort for the bulk of the exercise; for example at RAF Honington and RNAD Coulport I had to brief the RSOs (both experts drawn from the MOD's central staff) periodically about what the inspection team had been doing. My escorts asked me to keep the detail general. This in part made it difficult in future exercises to find volunteers willing to spend the bulk of their time confined to barracks as it were. One way round that was to have one member of the control staff play the RSO as needed, which was not satisfactory either as the players were never quite sure whether I was RSO or Control staff. Even changing the colour of my exercise role armband did not really help. In our exercises we tried to find ways to spice up the role of the RSO and give the escorts something extra to worry about. Such wheezes include convening press conferences to complain about the lack of access or information and to make allegations that the inspection was clearly worthless as the observer was unable to check whether it was being conducted effectively and efficiently. On another occasion we listed two RSOs in the inspection notification.

The two RSOs started at the PCI we conducted at PRB Gütersloh, Germany. One of the main reasons for this exercise was to test the recently concluded UK-Germany MOU on challenge inspections at British military bases in Germany. The intent was similar to the UK-US MOU as it was to facilitate the role of host state party and inspected state party by setting out their responsibilities. In order to see whether our German colleagues in the Federal Verification Office (JACIG equivalent) were on the ball we sent a notification of the intent to inspect to their office in real time, simulating the role of the TS. The notification had to include the name of the RSO, so I added the name Colonel Mustard accompanied by his ADC Major Denis Bloodnok.[17] After the PCI with the TS at RAF Valley where the RSO drip fed information to the inspectors throughout the inspection, which was considered very unhelpful as it disrupted planning and added a degree of continuing uncertainty, the TS concluded that in future they would insist that any information should be provided up front at the opening briefing. We adopted the same approach in our PCIs, so at Gütersloh I took the opportunity to brief the ITL in private after the main site brief to the inspectors, accompanied by the faithful Major Bloodnok played by Jim Haley from Porton. We had just started when there was a knock on the door and a somewhat sheepish German Verification Agency officer put his head round the door and pointed out that two RSOs were not permitted by the CWC and that one would not be allowed any further access and would have to leave the country. Found out. Later in the exercise, as again part of strategy to make the RSO role a nuisance for the escorts, I approached the JACIG Senior Escort Leader – a Royal Marines Lieutenant Colonel – stating that I wished to defect – claiming that I feared for my life. I was told that arrangements would be made, but in the meantime it would be best if I returned to the plenary meeting room to await developments. Shortly afterwards the Colonel returned with two red capped military police men and pointing at me shouted: 'There's the man – there's the security threat. Remove him.' At which point I started to get out of my seat before being grabbed, but was then put under arrest and frog marched out of the room much to the astonishment of many of the other exercise players who had no idea what was going on, and even initially thought this was all for real. The colonel, two MPs and I stood outside for a few minutes, before returning to a round of applause. It turned out that JACIG already had a standard procedure to follow in the event that an inspector wished to defect, which was of course done notionally as there was no point in setting alarm bells ringing unnecessarily. All of this experience, along with my further adventures as an RSO in other exercises in Germany, Switzerland and the Netherlands was instrumental in shaping a new British approach to handling an RSO in the event of a real challenge inspection in the UK. The Standing Instruction was amended to note that the general approach would be to accept an RSO, but at especially sensitive sites such as AWE Aldermaston, access would be limited to the minimum access allowed for by the CWC's Verification Annex Part X i.e. no access within the final perimeter. Everywhere else access would be at the discretion of the commanding officer and National Authority.

Conclusion

Despite all the effort that went into the design and conduct of these exercises, there were no real challenge inspections in the first twenty-three years of the CWC. So perhaps all the time and energy that we devoted to developing concepts and procedures for inspectors and hosts were wasted. However, if we view challenge primarily as a deterrent, which had been the original UK concept in the early 1980s, then it is at least arguable that the existence of the CWC's Article IX and Part X of the Verification Annex may have had a role to play in keeping non-compliance to a minimum. For a deterrent to be effective it must be perceived as being so. In the case of OPCW inspectors, constant preparation, training and the knowledge that it possess an effective capability is part of this, and the TS regularly reported to CWC states parties on its preparations to conduct a challenge inspection. The UK's input to this with exercises and training courses was significant. Making sure that you can cope with an in-bound inspection gives confidence to states parties that their own sensitives can be protected whilst being able to demonstrate compliance. Domestically it is clear that constant preparation and training are essential if a national capability to handle a challenge effectively is to remain. The passage of time, rotation of staff, changes in site purposes and design, changing weapon systems all add to the challenge. Interest wanes and after 2004 the UK ceased conducting annual full-scale exercises, partly on costs grounds and partly since there had been no challenge inspections. The institutional memory dulls too. However, circumstances can easily

The CTBTO's Geoprobe sitting at the Base of Operations during IFE14. (Author)

Inspection Field Teams and their equipment waiting to depart for the Inspection Area during IFE14. (Author)

Left: The author hard at work in the Evaluation Team work Tent at the Base Of Operations during IFE14. (Author)

Middle: CTBTO Inspection Team Equipment Transportation Pods set up as a field store at the Base of Operations during IFE14. (Author)

Bottom: A general view of the Base of Operations at IFE14. (Author)

Inspection Team and Head of the Inspected State Party team during IFE14 arguing about some point or other. (Author)

Right: Inspection team members preparing Equipment at the Base of Operations for field use during IFE14. (Author)

Below: Another general view of the BOO at IFE14. The Evaluation Team work tent is nearest the camera. (Author)

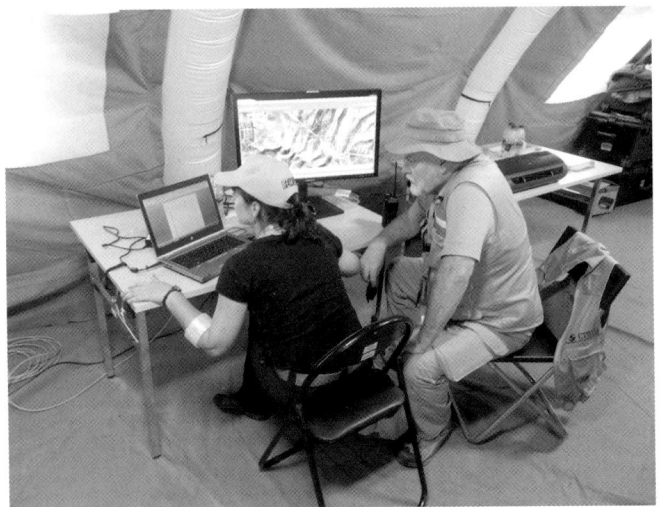

Inspection Team members reviewing Inspection Field Team plans in one of the working area tents during IFE14. (Author)

Preparing equipment for sub-soil gas sampling during IFE14. (Author)

Inspectors having a hard time from a non-cooperative inspected state party during the CWC challenge inspection training exercise at Rieti in 2015. (Author)

CWC inspectors waiting patiently for access during the Rieti exercise in 2015. (Author)

Inspector and Escorts fully kitted out in NBC protective gear during the Rieti CWC exercise in 2015. (Author)

Armed escorts burst into the plenary meeting room in order to invite the inspection team to leave promptly during the Rieti exercise. (Author)

CTBTO inspection team members preparing to install a seismic after shock monitor during IFE08. (CTBTO Public Information www.ctbto.org)

CTBTO Inspectors installing an after- shock seismometer during IFE08. (CTBTO Public Information www.ctbto.org)

What were we thinking? Taking a swab sample from a rail tank wagon during the UK-German practice challenge inspection at Pfedersfeld in 1990. The author is standing taking notes. In the future OPCW inspectors would normally dress in full protective clothing for such a task. (Author's collection)

Tense negotiations during IFE08 – the author left listens to the Inspection Team Leader making his points. (CTBTO Public Information www.ctbto.org)

Finalizing details of the next stage of the inspection during IFE08. (CTBTO Public Information www.ctbto.org)

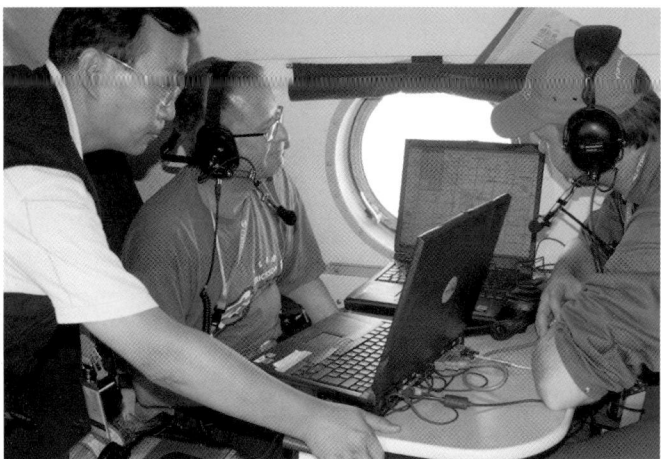

Left: Inspectors during an additional overflight during IFE08. (CTBTO Public Information www.ctbto.org)

Below: The Base of Operations at IFE08 – the Inspection Team Area is at the top of the picture. My main working area was the long tent in the centre of the camp. (CTBTO Public Information www.ctbto.org)

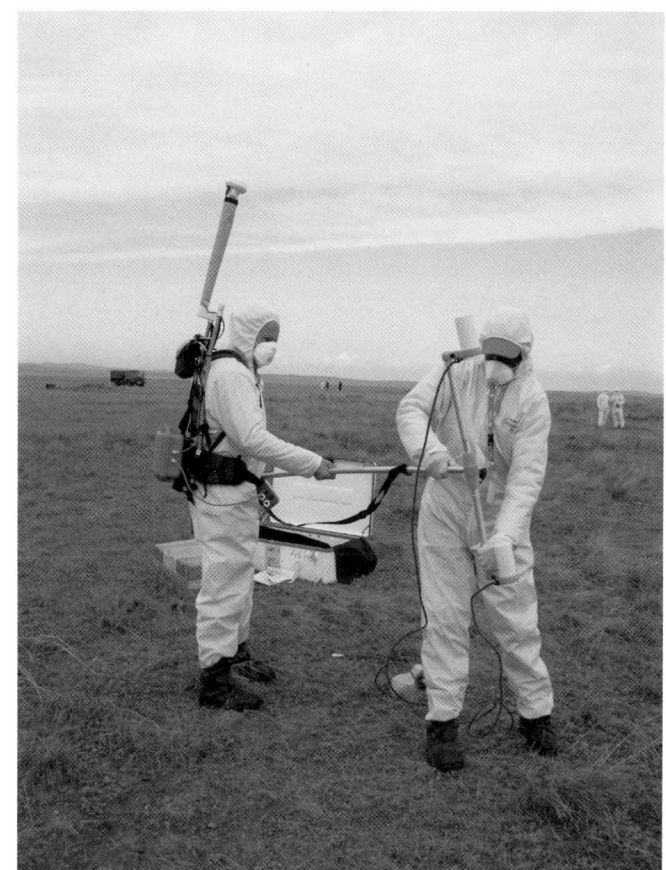

Right: Inspectors preparing a magnetometer for a survey of a selected grid of the inspection area. (CTBTO Public Information www.ctbto.org)

Below: Inspector conducting a magnetometer survey during IFE08. (CTBTO Public Information www.ctbto.org)

Inspectors preparing for sub-soil gas sampling looking for traces of argon-37 during IFE08. (CTBTO Public Information www.ctbto.org)

Sub-soil gas sample being collected during IFE08. (CTBTO Public Information www.ctbto.org)

This is the emplacement tower for the planned UK underground Nuclear Test Icecap in Area 1 at the Nevada Test Site in 1993. This test never took place as the US decided to have a moratorium on nuclear testing in 1992. This shows the scale and level of instrumentation required for a test, which is why the preparations for IFE08's scenario fell a little short, even for a clandestine test – a derelict caravan, shallow trench and small tent were not credible. The IFE08 experience showed the challenges in creating a credible scenario, one that was fully addressed in IFE14. (Footage provided by Nevada National Security Site Nevada Field Office, Nuclear Testing Archive)

It's very technical. Inspectors, in Tyvek suits, and home team experts prepare to take some verification measurements during the Letterpress exercise. The 'weapon' is behind the author who is looking on with his evaluation hat on. (Ministry of Defence)

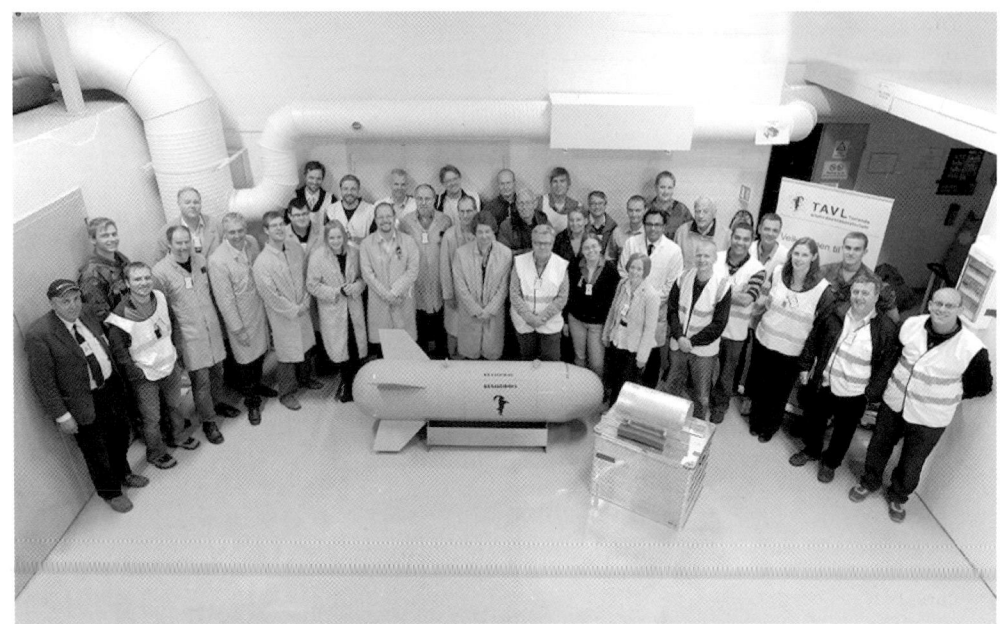

Group photograph of all the participants at the end of the UK-Norway exercise in 2009. (Norwegian Defence Research Establishment)

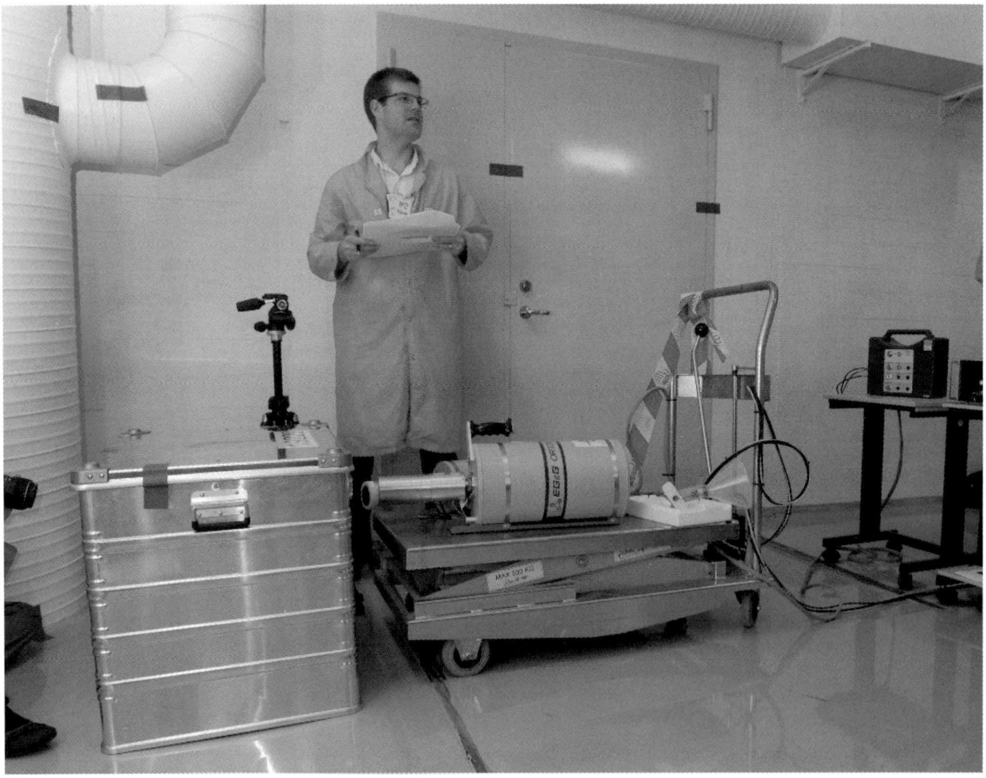

The Information Barrier being set up for use during the UK-Norway Initiative exercise. (Norwegian Defence Research Establishment)

The Information Barrier being used to confirm the presence of the 'fissile material' removed from the Odin Weapon. (Norwegian Defence Research Establishment)

More measurements during the UK-Norway Initiative, this time with a neutron counter. (Norwegian Defence Research Establishment)

The WE177A inert training round along with a WE155 transport container at RAF Honington ready for verification measurements during the Letterpress exercise. (Author)

A WE155 secure transport container used for road or air movement for the WE177. In this picture the container is ready to be towed to the next stage of the Letterpress verification exercise. (Author)

Nuclear warhead transport containers being moved as part of the Letterpress exercise in 2017. (Ministry of Defence)

One of the original explosive storage bunkers in the Supplementary Storage Area at RAF Honington, which was a key facility in the original CWC Practice Challenge Inspection programme and then later used as the location for the Letterpress exercise. (Ministry of Defence)

The 'B5' in one of the explosive storage bunkers in RAF Honington's SSA. B5 was the exercise designation for the nuclear weapon being subject to verification measures in the Letterpress exercise. (Ministry of Defence)

An overdressed group of inspectors setting off on their next task at RAF Honington during the Letterpress exercise (Ministry of Defence)

A row of explosive storage bunkers at RAF Honington originally designed to house the UK's WE177 tactical nuclear bombs. This was the sight that greeted UK CW inspectors in the exercises held in 1989 and again in 1994. We also used Honington for training exercises for the OPCW Technical Secretariat, and for the Letterpress nuclear disarmament verification exercise in 2017. (Ministry of Defence)

change and you can readily be caught out and have to reestablish old skills and lessons, often in a hurry.

The exercises were always fun things to do; there was always something new to learn and it was intellectually stimulating to work out ways of squaring some complex circles. It seemed to me at the time, and certainly looking back, that we could always find a way of enabling sufficient access for inspectors at sensitive sites, and that on most sites there were hardly any major sensitivities at all. Furthermore, it was also apparent that many of the lessons and experiences from the CWC PCIs would likely be relevant in nuclear arms control. Following the demise of the BTWC Protocol in 2001 I was asked to turn my attention to on-site inspections in the CTBT where efforts were underway to develop an on-site inspection manual and build an operational OSI capability for the day the CTBT would enter into force. This would open a whole new set of opportunities for field exercises on an even grander and more ambitious scale than even the largest of the CWC PCIs. Time to turn to this in the next chapter.

Chapter 5

The CTBT, on-site inspection and the Integrated Field Exercise 2008 (IFE08)

Introduction

The first proposal for a treaty banning all nuclear tests came in 1954 when Indian Prime Minister Pandit Nehru called for an end to all tests. Until this point all nuclear tests had taken place in the atmosphere, and there were growing concerns about the health and environmental effects. The key issue for the UK and US, apart from trying to balance the needs of arms control with the development of nuclear weapons was how might such a treaty be verified. Atmospheric monitoring was comparably straightforward; however, the identification of underground tests was another matter. Although the 1957 Geneva Experts Conference had posited a global system of monitoring stations that might be created to monitor a comprehensive ban, the core problem of discriminating between an earthquake and possible underground nuclear test was a demanding one.[1] This was especially true in highly active seismic areas such as the Soviet Union. The only way to be sure was by an on-site inspection (OSI), which could identify the tell-tale signs such as the presence of certain radioactive isotopes that leaked out to the surface.[2] Following the Geneva Experts Conference the UK, US and USSR began the Conference on the Discontinuance of Nuclear Weapon Tests in Geneva in November 1958. As things transpired one of the major bones of contention concerned on-site inspection: the UK and US saw it as essential while the Soviet Union saw it as a form of espionage. Even limiting a treaty verification regime to a system of inspection quotas, even down to a handful, was still too much for the Soviet Union to stomach. Without provisions for effective OSIs a Treaty would never receive the US

Senate's advice and consent for its ratification. One last attempt was made in July 1963 to conclude a CTBT, but Soviet leader Khrushchev peremptorily rejected any treaty with OSIs. Instead the three powers opted for a Partial Test Ban Treaty that banned tests in all locations expect underground.[3]

Although OSI had been central to the Western Powers' position, relatively little if any practical work seems to have been done by either the UK or US on how a CTBT OSI regime would work in practice. For this reason it is useful to look at the information contained in the British state papers from the early 1960s alongside reports of the US Vela Uniform test ban treaty verification effort, which ran sixteen separate projects to look at OSI practicalities of various techniques between 1960 and 1962. These were the first concerted attempt to address CTBT OSI issues.[4] The sixteen techniques were clustered under three headings:

- airborne survey – conventional aerial photography, airborne high-precision stereophotogrammetry; airborne magnetometer; airborne spectral reconnaissance system; airborne scintillometer;
- surface survey – visual inspection, changes in solid-state characteristics of minerals and rocks; monitoring of aftershocks, radon release from surface; gamma-ray surveys; soil density changes; reflectance changes from vegetation damage; induced earth currents in proximity of explosion cavity; and,
- subsurface surveys – visual inspection of mine tunnels; gamma-ray logging; geochemical surveys using shallow bore-holes and seismic profiling.

Of the techniques examined by 1962, the US programme tentatively concluded that ten had utility under the conditions existing at the Gnome underground nuclear test that had taken place on 10 December 1961 in New Mexico and at the Nevada Test Site locale of the Antler nuclear test on 15 September 1961. Promising techniques included visual and photographic reconnaissance, changes in solid-state characteristics of certain minerals, gamma ray surveys and after-shock monitoring. Problems still existed with deeply buried explosions, polar areas, and regions of shallow water cover.[5] However, according to a 1963 Congressional testimony of Theodore A. George, Vela Uniform did not entail any integration of the inspection techniques, since the United States considered this too expensive to test under realistic field conditions at that time. Integrated application of on-site inspection techniques would not start until the 2000s, which will be the main subject matter of this chapter. But meanwhile back in the 1960s Harold Macmillan (British Prime Minister) wanted to make progress on a test ban and relied heavily on two key senior scientific experts to advise him on detection, identification and discrimination of underground seismic events; the requirements for effective verification set against these challenges and the risks involved in Soviet cheating under a test ban treaty. On 15 May 1963, Sir William Penney (former Director of the Atomic Weapons Research Establishment Aldermaston, but now deputy-chairman of the UK Atomic Energy Authority in 1963) and Sir Solly Zukerman (Chief Scientific Adviser to the Ministry of Defence) sent the Prime Minister a memorandum on the test ban. This was in response to a series of questions that Macmillan had posed on 9 May 1963, and here is what they said on OSI:

'Whatever the reasons may be for insisting on on-site inspection, it is difficult to see how an inspection could serve any useful purpose unless some thorough inspection was carried out in the suspected area. Procedurally, any seismic event chosen for inspection would have to satisfy certain instrumental criteria, in respect of location and depth of focus, as determined from seismic records obtained at several seismic stations. On present technical evidence, we cannot assume exact location of a seismic event by long-range detection to within a radius of less than ten kilometres, i.e. an area of about 300 square kilometres. In exceptionally favourable circumstances, or if good and reliable records were obtained from the seismic stations of the country where the event occurred, this area might be reduced to about 200 square kilometres; but in very unfavourable cases, it might be increased several times.

If a suspected area of even the smallest size is to be effectively inspected, in the quickest possible time by a reasonably small group of inspectors, it is very important to have low level aerial inspection as a first approach to reducing and pin-pointing the most suspicious area. During this phase, photographic, magnetic and radioactive survey techniques would be used. Thereafter, very thorough ground inspection of the reduced area would be required to tabulate evidence of on-site activity and results characteristic of underground nuclear testing. For this purpose an inspection team would require portable seismographs, radioactive detectors, portable equipment for analysis of material samples collected in the area, and photographic equipment. Unless the suspected test had caused radioactive debris to escape above the surface, there would be no means, other than drilling, of obtaining final evidence necessary to establish the nuclear origin of an explosion. It is conceivable that detailed ground inspection might produce a justifiable need for drilling, but this should be requested only if the inspection had already provided positive grounds for doing so. In any case, a major difficulty would be to know exactly where to drill; and actual drilling for radioactive debris would not be lightly embarked upon in view of uncertainty, time and expense. Hence, we would suggest that the drilling stage in an inspection operation should not be pursued as a routine matter, but only after showing a well-founded suspicion produced by the inspection itself.' Penney and Zuckerman went on to note that, 'having examined all relevant technical factors in the detection and identification of seismic events, we conclude ... So long as it is technically necessary to establish the cause of a seismic event, detailed visual on-site inspection will be necessary in selected cases and that over an area of at least 200 square kilometres.' [6]

How did these UK perceptions and assessments in 1963 sit with the contemporaneous Vela Uniform projects? The underlying concepts appear to have been the same, which should not be too surprising on two counts. First, a technical appreciation of the problems facing on-site inspection in a CTBT considering the then available verification technologies and scientific knowledge of underground nuclear test observables could hardly fail to come to broadly similar conclusions. Second, given the very close UK-US collaboration on test ban treaty issues and negotiations between 1958 and 1963, technical exchanges between experts occurred frequently with shared perceptions often emerging as a result. [7] According to the 1963 testimony of Dr Charles C. Bates, the US Vela Uniform programme built its OSI techniques projects around the concept that an on-site inspection would normally employ three phases. Phase I would involve the use of large-scale investigation techniques primarily suitable for use in a properly equipped aircraft. The purpose of these techniques would be to reduce very quickly the geographic area of forty to two hundred square miles in which the suspicious seismic events might have occurred to a more workable size such as square mile or so, for the surface inspection team to inspect in detail. Phase II would consist of a series of rigorously applied visual and geophysical inspection techniques aimed at identifying the most likely area or areas for drilling or, as the case may be, for positively identifying the suspicious event as having been nonnuclear in origin without the necessity for drilling. Phase III would consist of drilling at the site of the supposed explosion cavity and obtaining sufficient evidence from either gas or core samples to establish without a doubt that a nuclear test ban violation had taken place.[8] So there was a fair amount of theoretical convergence about how a CTBT OSI ought to be conducted.

There was no further detailed consideration of CTBT OSI issues in the immediate years following conclusion of the Partial Test Ban Treaty in July 1963 as far as one can tell, certainly in the UK. We must wait some fourteen years until the Tripartite Test Ban Treaty negotiations began in July 1977 with the UK, US and USSR once again trying to conclude a CTBT.[9] However, as in the 1950s and early 1960s agreement on verification proved to be a major stumbling block with provisions for on-site inspection still proving highly contentious. The USSR insisted that OSIs should be voluntary, and although the US initially wanted mandatory provisions they went along with the UK view in the end that provided the detailed OSI provisions were laid out in detail in the treaty so that further time would not be wasted arguing about the provisions before an inspection team could set foot on Soviet territory. The longer the interval between an inspection request being made and the time taken to reach the inspection area, the greater the chance that perishable observables such as aftershocks and radionuclides would become harder to detect or disappear altogether. Although OSI was a highly contentious topic, it was not the prime reason why the tripartite negotiations ultimately failed. Other more pressing matters such as the need to maintain nuclear weapons stockpile reliability and safety, the duration of a treaty and the role to be played by National Seismic Stations in the Separate Verification Arrangement ensured failure of the negotiations[10], which were suspended sine die in 1980. In any case neither the UK or US had conduced any practical work on how an OSI regime would operate on the ground. Fast forward sixteen years and a CTBT was finally concluded after a short two year negotiation in Geneva. The end of the Cold War and by this time the much wider acceptance of verification meant that the CTBT contained extensive provisions on OSI in its Article IV and in Part II of its Protocol – a text that ran to some thirty pages. The Treaty created a Preparatory Commission and Provisional Technical Secretariat (PTS) to build up its verification regime so that it would be ready to function as soon as the Treaty entered into force. The two main tasks concerning OSI were to develop an operational manual and build up an operational capability of well trained and equipped inspectors armed with all the necessary guidance needed for an effective inspection. The first task was the responsibility of the state signatories, which proved to be a major mistake as that provided an opportunity for those less enamoured of effective OSIs to delay and obstruct the process, whilst the second task would devolve primarily to the PTS with guidance from the Preparatory Commission. Theoretical studies would now no longer suffice, some real and extensive field work would be needed to see how a CTBT OSI operational capability could be made to work. This is where I became involved again in CTBT matters.

The Draft Operational Manual and the OSI Major Programme

One of the key tasks remitted to the Preparatory Commission was the development of the Treaty's verification regime, which consists of the International Monitoring System (IMS) – a global network of 337 primary seismic, auxiliary seismic, radionuclide, infrasound and hydroacoustic stations and RN laboratories; the International Data Centre – to process and report on the information collected by the IMS; and on-site inspection (OSI). I represented the UK in Working Group B on Verification OSI related issues from February 2002 until May 2020. This included working on the draft of an OSI Operational Manual, whose aim was to provide detailed guidance for future inspectors and state party representatives. This was a painfully slow process and by the time I retired at the end of May 2020 we still had not finished the task, though we were close to doing so. In mitigation in the latter years there were only about four or six hour sessions a year devoted to the manual in Working Group B. Indeed WGB itself had been reduced from three sessions a year of eight weeks down to two sessions of four weeks. The issues were technically complex and when this is overlaid with the inevitable political differences with some states like Iran obstructing progress and constantly trying to undermine the effectiveness of the draft manual, the progress was only ever going to be incremental. Moreover, OSI was usually the neglected child in the CTBTO with the bulk of the resources and staffing going into the building of the IMS, which was a much bigger task. It was out of this situation that the idea for a large scale OSI exercise emerged following the Starr Report in 2004 into the overall operation of the PTS.[11] This report had highlighted that the PTS Divisions were not as fully integrated as they could be, and in a real OSI all the Divisions would have a role to play, it would not just be down to the small OSI Division. The Starr Report recommended therefore that a 'near full- scale OSI' should be conducted to help build up integration and OSI capabilities. Until this point there had been various Directed Exercises and equipment evaluations, as well as a small Field Exercise at the former Soviet nuclear test site at Semipalatinsk in Kazakhstan in 2002. However, something much more ambitious in scope and scale was now required, but the size of the challenge did cause some anxieties in the OSI Division. Given its small staff relative to the rest of the PTS – roughly about twenty to twenty-five people – such an exercise seemed beyond them without additional resources and contributions in kind from the states signatories. There was also some arcane theology – there could not be a mock or practice inspection until after entry into force of the Treaty. Despite this, the reality remained that what would be required would essentially be a practice OSI. A full CTBT OSI could last up to 130 days involving more than forty surrogate inspectors to allow for rotations and the application of all the approved inspection technologies as laid down in Part II of the Treaty Protocol. To help matters along the UK presented a national working paper to WGB, which I had drafted, suggesting that we could look at various ways of running an effective exercise, primarily by condensing the time frame and the numbers of personnel needed and testing the equipment that the PTS already had or might be able to borrow from states signatories or as contributions in-kind. In response to the call for a near full scale exercise, the OSI Division came up with what it called an Integrated Field Exercise (IFE) in which the approved inspection technologies, or as many of them that would be ready in time, could be tested in an integrated fashion with an inspection team deployed to an area of 1,000km^2 as per the Treaty. However, even this sort of exercise would require additional funding beyond the usual budgetary costings as well as contributions in kind of equipment and national experts. WGB approved the plan, so the target was to complete all the preparations in order to conduct an exercise over three weeks in late summer/early autumn 2008. A host state party would be needed who could offer 1,000km^2 as well as other logistical support to sustain such an exercise. Volunteers were called for and Kazakhstan won the bid by offering up Semipalatinsk, the former Soviet nuclear test site. This would have plenty of observables – craters, boreholes, infrastructure – for inspectors to find and characterise, but we would also need to develop a scientifically credible scenario to apply to this large stage. Simulating the signatures of an underground test would not be easy. I hoped to have some role to play in this exercise since if you were not there your ability to influence subsequent drafting of the OSI operational manual and development of OSI capabilities under the Preparatory Commission's Major Task 3 would be much diminished. Unfortunately the FCO felt at the time that I was needed for my other duties on BTWC and CWC matters and I could not be spared for a three-four week absence even though I would normally be away at WGB in Vienna for two. (There was a slight overlap in the planned schedule.) As it transpired my Israeli colleague Itzhak Lederman who had been scheduled to play the role of the head of the inspected state party (Itzhak was also leading the Scenario Task Force team) had to pull out for medical reasons. Boris Kvok, the Russian head of the OSI Division, then asked me if I could take his place as ISP representative and member of the exercise control staff. This time the FCO agreed that I should accept.

The logistical requirements for the exercise IFE08 were considerable. Remoteness of the site was only one part of the challenge. In the work on the OSI manual and development of operational concepts for an OSI we had seen that there would be a need for a Base of Operations (BOO) at which the inspection team would both live and work. In a real OSI we would not be near hotels and other amenities; we might well need to be as self-sufficient as possible with support from the ISP. This meant creating a camp complete with working tents, equipment storage areas, meeting tents, mobile laboratories, catering and ablution facilities for forty inspectors. In fact more space would be needed for an exercise as we would have experts playing the role of ISP, an external evaluation team, control team, observers, media as well as a parallel camp containing our Kazakh hosts. They would provide the drivers, escorts, catering and other support staff. In short, at its peak we would have well over 200 individuals on the camp site. Getting there was going to be time consuming – there were too many of us to fly and the cheapest option was to take the train from the simulated

Point of Entry at Almaty to Semey (the Kazakhs changed the name from Semipalatinsk). This involved a twenty-four hour train trip across some dramatic landscapes – one of the highlights of the exercise in fact. Once at Semey it was then a three hour journey to Kurchatov – a closed city in Soviet days and one that had been created especially as the scientific and logistical support centre for the test site. From there it was a further three hours by pot holed roads and dirt tracks of varying qualities to the site selected for the Base of Operations (BOO). As we left Kurchatov the landscape was billiard table smooth as far as the eye could see in all directions to the horizon. The BOO was located just outside the 'Polygon', which was the Soviet name for the test site and reflected the shape of the test site's boundaries.

I was dual hatted for this exercise – the head of the ISP team and member of the small control staff whose task was to see that the exercise was meeting its objectives and for the overall safety of the participants. However, the ISP team was a small one; Graham Cooper a former FCO colleague (Graham was in fact originally from Porton Down and had been the technical adviser to the UK delegation during the CWC negotiations and Chief Inspector in the 1988-90 PCI programme), Li Hua (a Chinese scientific expert from their delegation to WGB) and two PTS experts – Ivan Kitov (seismic) and Robert Wertgei (RN). Unfortunately, these latter two would only be available for part of the exercise. I quickly made sure that we called a couple of the Kazakh experts into the home team. This was more realistic as they were the ones who for real would provide information about the test site and help organise all the transport for the inspection sub-teams.

The exercise scenario that had been developed for IFE08 posited a compliant one; however, the fictitious state party – Arcania – was on the point of conducting a test. Details of the scenario were deliberately kept secret from all participants expect the control staff and ISP players. Several artifacts had been created to support this scenario and to give the inspection team something to find and characterise; however, this would have some adverse implications for how the exercise would be conducted and for my role as ISP representative. The first signs that not all was well with the scenario came during the drive out to the BOO. As we bounced along in a Soviet era UAZ-452 four wheel drive minibus, which despite its vintage was ideally suited to the terrain, I got the first inkling that something was not quite right. Towards the end of the journey Graham nudged me and nodded his head in the direction of what looked like a small orange caravan some distance away on our right. This was to be the centrepiece of the scenario – a test site in preparation for firing. I would now need to keep the team away from this for as long as possible otherwise the exercise would be blown too early in the time on site.

IFE08 did not deploy the full suite of OSI techniques permitted by the Protocol's paragraph 65, largely because they were not available to the PTS or had not been sufficiently developed. There would be no drilling for samples, multispectral or infrared imagery, resonance seismometry, gravity meters or xenon radioactive gas detectors even though the Swedes had developed a handy piece of equipment for this very purpose. Exactly why this was declined by the PTS was never made clear. There would however be seismic aftershock detection equipment (SAMS), visual observation – including photography, initial and additional overflights and selected geophysical technologies for the continuation period such as magnetometry and ground penetrating radar. There would be laptops and even a colour photocopier for production of mapping. Environmental sampling would also be allowed, though any samples actually collected from the test site had to be switched on return to the BOO with some local dirt collected inside the BOO by the control staff. This apparently was a Russian stipulation, though exactly what we might find after the passage of time since the last underground and atmospheric tests was never clear to me. Samples would be analysed in a mobile laboratory housed in a specially outfitted ISO container provided by AWE Aldermaston as one of the more significant contributions in kind. In the same vein we also had a Chinese experimental Argon-37 radionuclide detector.[12] In addition, there were a large number of modern tents that could be configured for sleeping accommodation or for working purposes, so that entailed a lot of sleeping bags, camp beds, generators, external lighting, tables and chairs, mobile showers and toilets. This amounted to some 150 tonnes of equipment, quite an increase on the four tonnes that the OPCW TS brought to RAF Valley in 1998 for its first PCI. Apart from the AWE mobile laboratory, all of this was delivered to the site in four large ISO containers that had been taken out to Kazakhstan and then trucked out to the Polygon earlier. In a real OSI equipment and inspectors would need to arrive more or less at the same time at the Point of Entry, which is a massive logistical and scheduling challenge. Therefore for IFE08 this was one of the unavoidable exercise artificialities: time compression was another as we were not going to be able to run the full-time lines from the initial inspection period to continuation period, which is twenty-five days in the Treaty, out to the full

131

130 days. However, this did not mean that those activities. equipment and procedures that were being exercised were not useful or would not likely generate many valuable lessons for further development.

The main activity for me as the ISP head was to decide in light of scenario requirements and Kazakh support capacities to agree to the IT's inspection plans. The IT was led by the OSI Division's Chief of the Documentation Section Jun Wang; he and I were to become sparring partners over the next month as we negotiated and argued over all aspects of the inspection. As already noted, I had to keep the IT away from the main managed access locations for as long as possible. In general the idea was to make things tough for the inspection team. Once the IT had completed the initial overflight they identified several areas of interest, including the orange caravan and a large concrete circle, quickly nicknamed the aspirin. I was then asked for an explanation, Unfortunately, the scenario offered no explanation, so I had to make something up – echoes of some of the earlier CWC PCIs where the scenario only went so far and was not backed up with a history or credible context that could be drawn upon in discussions with the inspectors. Scenario credibility was vitally important, all the more so in a CTBT simulated on-site inspection where the sorts of observables and signatures created by an underground nuclear explosion are not easy to replicate or mimic above or below ground. In the case of the 'aspirin' I said it was a new type of reinforced concrete used to cap the former nuclear test boreholes on the test site as the old type used in the 1960s was prone to disintegrate. I learned later that there is in fact a type of concrete known as Reinforced autoclaved aerated concrete, which was cheaper type of building material used between the 1950s and 1990s and is relatively weak and prone to degradation over time. So at least my improvised explanation had some scientific justification.

Health and safety were major challenges in such an environment. The main reason why we were conducting the exercise in late August and early September was that the weather on the steppe would not be extreme, neither too hot or cold, which would have made working and living conditions unpleasant and difficult at the same time. Unfortunately, we were hit by what became known as the curse of CTBTO OSI weather. In fact, the weather turned unseasonably wet and cold. Most of the camp had no effective heating in the accommodation tents – the Kazakhs had wood burning stoves in theirs. At least the light weight sleeping bags were warm. More to the point many of the participants had not brought suitable cold weather gear. I was not one of those. One day the weather became so bad we had to convene an emergency meeting of the control staff to review the situation. We met in what was the warmest part of the CTBTO supplied tented camp site – the one housing the large colour printer, which radiated a welcome heat. Conditions out on the 'Polygon' were becoming hazardous, so much so that there was a concern that even the robust minibuses might become stuck in the muddy tracks. Inspectors were not properly equipped with cold weather gear either, so we decided to suspend the inspection until the weather improved and call the sub-teams back. This was a timely reminder that CTBT OSIs were likely to be subject to extremes of weather, climate, and topography even before an obstructive and argumentative ISP enters the equation. For the future both inspectors and their equipment would need to be able to operate in such conditions. In addition, the control team decided that when the weather improved sufficiently for the vehicles to be used, we would send a foraging party off to Kurchatov to buy supplies of cold weather gear for the participants since the weather forecast for the remainder of our stay was not encouraging. A couple of days later the supplies arrived from Kurchatov, and a bizarre mix of items they were too. The most notable items in the pile from which people were invited to take what they needed were several bright orange long quilted winter jackets emblazoned with the England national football team's badge – the three lions. As a proud Scot I would rather be cold than wear such a thing, but fortunately I was warm enough with what I had.

Catering and ablutions were another daily challenge; if inspectors were not well fed and rested, especially when working long hours as they were in this exercise, their performance and effectiveness would likely diminish over the long duration of a CTBT OSI. The catering tent was not large enough to cater for everyone at the same time, so a first and second sitting system was established. Inspectors went first with everybody else taking the second sitting, which meant for the ISP team, control team, evaluators and other exercise participants we had to wait until 1400 or so for lunch and 1930 for dinner. I had anticipated that I might well be continually hungry on this exercise so came equipped with cereal bars and chocolate as well some stock powder to make a soup like drink. My colleague on the Evaluation Team, Ian Oliver, ex-Parachute Regiment, came armed with British Army compo rations. I had already gone down with a minor case of food poisoning back in Almaty the night before the train journey to Semey. The catering was not really up to the mark and I really doubted that there was sufficient calorific intake for the inspectors, many of whom were doing hard physical work. Fortunately for me I was mostly sedentary in my work/meeting tent. By the end of the exercise we had all lost weight. Clearly what became known as 'Arcania' burgers, small meat patties of indeterminant origin were insufficient. At least there was plenty of good bread and chocolates. Once we were back in Almaty some of us went out to a grill restaurant for a large barbecue, the sight of all that meat was something I will not forget. All this underlines the vital importance of reliable logistical support for an OSI in a remote and inaccessible location.

Ablutions were another challenging area. In our CWC and BTWC PCIs at the end of the day we all retired to a comfortable hotel with our own rooms and en suite facilities, and a welcoming bar and warm fire in which to review the day's proceedings after a good dinner. Although the tents were better than I had expected, we at least had our own private compartments that were zipped off from the rest of the six person tent. Toilet and shower facilities were established in the BOO at the north side of the camp away from the accommodation and working tents. On arrival at the BOO we were instructed in the correct usage of the electric toilets, of which there were about eight. The less said about these the better, suffice it to say they were really only designed for a small family. They were Scandinavian and primarily intended for holiday cottages; they were not designed for a camp of 150. They needed power to incinerate the waste. And no one had thought about a cleaning regime or provision of toilet paper and the paper insert that had to be placed into the pan before use. On the Kazakh side of the camp, they had dug a large latrine trench. Unfortunately this was not deep enough as on one particularly windy day – it was always windy at the BOO – we had the delights of seeing some soiled toilet paper blowing through the camp – a bit like the tumbleweed you would see in Wild West movies. Power for the camp was provided by two generators that the PTS had brought to the site as part of the OSI equipment package. These were second hand but reconditioned German machines. Unfortunately, they did not like the poor quality of the diesel fuel provided by the hosts, so tended to cut out without warning thereby removing power for lighting, laptops, electric kettles, equipment battery chargers, and the shower heaters. The shower tent was adjacent to the generators. There was insufficient fresh water supplies and shower cubicles for large numbers to take their ablutions at the same time, and sometimes the generators were switched off to conserve fuel and to work out what the problem was – blocked filters apparently. So generally the best time to take a shower was late afternoon, and on one occasion I was in the shower and heard the generator cut out, which meant that I had about thirty seconds before the hot water ran cold and there I was covered in soap and shampoo. You can get used to cold showers. There was also supposed to be a separate tent with handbasins, instead we had a solitary kitchen sink unit sitting on a wooden pallet exposed to the elements with a foot pump to provide the cold water from a plastic jerry can. This presented one of the more bizarre sights of the exercise, and was one reason why most people used bottled water to clean their teeth. And those with toothpaste stains on their clothes had obviously forgotten to check which direction the wind was blowing before rinsing.

We did have a bar running out of one of the Kazakh tents, where you could at least buy some bottles of beer and light snacks to supplement your meagre diet. However, as there were no en suite facilities in the accommodation tents, it would not do to overindulge lest a call of nature interrupt your sleep in the middle of the night. In which case you first had to get out of your sleeping bag – the first zip, the second zip was your compartment, the third zip was the inner flap to the tent and fourth zip was the outer tent porch. If it was blowing a gale and pouring rain, then things were all the more uncomfortable. You tended not to bother with the electric toilets, but just walk far enough away from the tents, checking the wind direction first. One individual, who shall remain nameless, thought he might retain an empty beer bottle for nocturnal calls of nature. The tents had a canvas floor that was uneven as it sort of followed the ground contours and you had to store all your gear on it. This individual was seen the following morning with a mop and bucket.

There is a serious point to all of these stories though, thinking about effective catering is likely to be a key consideration in the conduct of a real OSI, especially in cold weather. Morale and effectiveness will decline if the food and accommodation are poor and insufficient. IFE08 had turned into a bit of a survival exercise, which was clearly not the original intent, but was not necessarily a bad thing either as the experience served as an important reminder of the conditions that would need to be planned for. In a real OSI which, by its very nature, is likely to be in a remote location without ready access to facilities, inspectors would have to be prepared for basic conditions, However, they should be made as comfortable as possible. Furthermore, IFE08 also showed that some individuals were better suited temperamentally, psychologically and by experience for the sort of experiences encountered during the exercise. This has implications for inspector selection and training, and has certainly been noted by the PTS OSI Division in its current work.

The daily routine was punctuated by regular meetings between the ISP and the IT leadership, these had begun back at the simulated point of entry at the hotel in Almaty. This had run along very similar lines to a CWC PCI where there were briefings, equipment checks, discussions over escorting, health and safety, logistical and transport arrangements; the IT leader also handed over the Inspection Mandate. At least we did not have to argue over a requested perimeter. There were generally two meetings per day, the evening meeting was perhaps the key one as this was when the IT outlined its revised inspection plan for the coming days, how many sub-teams and their proposed tasks and importantly where in the inspection area they wanted to go. The meeting also reviewed other outstanding inspection team questions and issues, a function of the morning meeting too. We would also hold ad hoc meetings to review specific matters and the ITL and I would have private consultations especially over contentious matters. We also made a point of putting questions and answers in writing to ensure that nothing was missed and to keep careful track of all outstanding points. I created some document formats to do this and colour coded them accordingly: red meant unanswered or still open, green meant response provided, whilst amber meant something was in hand. The basic idea came from the JACIG log book used in the control point in UK exercises and in CFE and Vienna Document inspections, I added the colour coding. Keeping track and on top of all the myriad flows of information, questions and responses was a key lesson from our CWC PCIs, and it applied equally in a CTBT OSI where the volume of information would likely be very much greater and over a longer period of time. In IFE08 I had to use my own personal laptop for all of this as none were provided for ISP use by the PTS. At least I was able to scrounge the use of a printer. Resourcing of the ISP team would be one of the many lessons from IFE08, and would be considered in the preparations for the next IFE in 2014 – see Chapter 7.

The inspectors had, unsurprisingly, observed the orange caravan from their initial overflight, and inevitably it appeared as one of the areas of interest in their proposed inspection plans. I could have kept saying no and declared it a Restricted Access Site in accordance with the Protocol II's provisions, which would allow us to refuse comprehensive access. However, this feature was intended as a prop to enable us to test out the managed access provisions that were in the Protocol and further amplified in the OSI Test Manual prepared specially for IFE08. These had largely been drafted by me with the assistance of Itzhak Lederman. The Initial Draft of the Rolling Text (IDRT) of the manual would have been utterly unusable by inspectors in the IFE08 at almost 900 pages; it was full of squared bracketed text, contradictions, extensive duplication or text that was very similar. Worse still it was also full of damaging text that would make it impossible for inspectors to do their job effectively and efficiently and gave more rights to the ISP that went well beyond the Treaty and Protocol. These bits of text had been largely inserted into the draft by China, Israel, Iran and Russia who were more concerned about keeping inspectors out and in state party rights at the expense of state party obligations. We had to cut the IDRT down to a more manageable and pragmatic size for use in IFE08. This was done over two specially convened expert workshops in Vienna with the aim of creating a 'test manual' for surrogate inspector training and use during IFE08 itself. We were very successful in this, but we did park the relatively small number of highly contested issues; the caveat was that the test manual was only for IFE08 and that IDRT was still the basis of work. Over time we dropped the later part of this caveat; nobody noticed.

To keep the inspectors away from the orange caravan I made up a tale that this part of the inspection area was used by the Arcanian Army as an artillery range where live firing was permissible. There had recently been an exercise, which unfortunately had several blinds (i.e. unexploded projectiles), which were now in the process of being cleared by 11 EOD Regiment. This would take some time, which was the line I took for many days. Of course the unseasonably poor weather had hampered things further. I even typed up a fictious EOD report describing the regiment's activities signed off by its commanding officer, which I then provided to the ITL under cover of a memorandum from me. I also decided that I would need to go and have a closer look at exactly what was out there in the proposed managed access area. The exercise rationale for the managed access area was that Arcania was about to resume testing, and had started to drill a test borehole and prepare a shallow sub-surface cable run to diagnostic trailers; the ground round about the caravan was also supposed to be marked with multiple tyre tracks from heavy vehicles. Once up close this area was a massive disappointment in terms of the original ambitions of the Scenario Task Force; the orange caravan was derelict, the supposed borehole was just a shallow hole with a white one-man tent pitched over it, running out from this was a single shallow trench several metres in length. If this was meant to resemble preparations for an underground nuclear test, then it was a considerable underachievement. Given the remoteness of the site and distance from Vienna it had not been possible for the scenario team to check on preparations: this was to be a key lesson for the next IFE. If we let the inspectors too close to this, they would see through it and the scenario would lose any remaining credibility. Indeed several geophysicists who had arrived for the continuation period were starting to become grumpy about the lack of substantive things to do or find. However, it was now time to allow access under strict managed access conditions, so the take it or leave it option for the ITL was that only he would be allowed into the area, but would have to remain at least 100 metres from the objects, he would be allowed no inspection equipment and could only use a notepad and pencil. We would allow environmental sampling from locations of the ITL's choosing, but these would be collected by me. As a managed access plan it seemed a good way to test the relevant parts of the draft operational test manual, but for real the ITL should have insisted on two inspectors for evidentiary and health and safety reasons. However, the fewer people who saw this scene the better as it would probably only make dissatisfaction with the scenario even stronger. Once out at the site we spent about an hour viewing and discussing the scene before us, and I made up some cock and bull story that this was a sensitive experiment where we had to keep disturbance and viewing to a minimum. The ITL could clearly see that there was an orange van, a tent and some sort of trench, but we did not let him close enough to discern the detail. He requested that several soil samples should be collected from the proximity of the features with which we complied. Wang shouted his directions to me as to where he wanted the samples, left a bit, right a bit etc. For health and safety reasons for the exercise we were both suited up in Tyvek white protective suits, gloves, masks and overshoes. When I first joined the FCO's Arms Control and Disarmament Research Unit in 1985 I never imaged that one day twenty-three years later I would be digging up bits of the Soviet nuclear test site with a small green garden trowel. This experience served as a timely reminder that things change and what seemed inconceivable one moment can be common place the next. We headed back to the BOO and went through the decontamination line before entering the main site. The samples were swapped as per the exercise rules and these went off to the onsite laboratory for analysis with gamma spectrometers. The RN lab was being operated by three AWE experts Kevin Russell, Graham Hughes and Jonny Hartnell; there were two Chinese experts with their Argon-37 detector. The sample results were negative of course.

One of the key operational characteristics of the Chinese Argon-37 detector was that it needed bromine gas to serve as a quench system, and for some reason they had run out of the stuff, which was going to be a problem if we wanted to keep the system running. The control staff had decided to take this problem out of the exercise and try and sort things out somehow with the PTS in Vienna and Kazakh authorities. So as far as I was concerned it was out of the game, or so I thought. In one of the IT-ISP plenary meetings Rainier Arndt, the German Head of the OSI Division's Equipment Section and playing on the inspection team, raised the bromine gas problem and asked whether the ISP could acquire a few litres from a local university or research institute. I waited for one of the control staff members to rule this out of play, but no such ruling came. In which case I decided to play along as it would be a shame to lose the opportunity to make the point. In my response I stated that there were no universities remotely close, and that it was for the TS to supply bromine gas bottles. Dr Arndt then pressed the point and asked about obtaining some from an industrial plant. I said if the TS could source some and send it to the POE, we would endeavour to transport it to the POE. Rainier kept being assertive, perhaps a couple of inspectors could go to a university to collect some bromine, or something like that. It was good to see inspectors pressing the point of course; they should not meekly accept everything that an ISP representative says. This argument went on for what seemed ages, so I decided to feign a loss of temper and stated abruptly, 'Dr Arndt, what part of the word no don't you understand?' That killed the conversation and we moved on to something else. Apparently this statement was rapidly reported around the BOO and at the end of exercise party at Almaty we had a mock awards ceremony for the best and worst of things in IFE08 and my 'Dr Arndt, what part of the word no don't you understand?' won the prize for the best statement. I received a cheap Chinese plastic laser pointer for my efforts. As ever with these sort of stories there is a serious point lurking behind the humour. A CTBT IT needs to come as self-sufficient as possible and should ideally not have equipment, especially critical items, that use expensive and/or difficult to acquire consumables and spare parts given the remote locations in which an OSI is likely to occur.

Visual observation is a key inspection activity expressly permitted by the Protocol; one should never underestimate the value of the Mark I eyeball, especially in an inspector who knows what to look for in the landscape. Photography is also allowed by the Protocol, and we had agreed a revised set of procedures in the OSI Test Manual, which I had drafted in my then capacity as 'Friend of the Task Leader', on how we would handle digital photographic products for any confidentiality concerns by the ISP. The IT took hundreds of digital images from the air and ground, so we had to find the time to review the results jointly. Handling digital media was also likely to be a concern given its ability to be manipulated or readily transmitted off site. We needed strict control of the discs and laptops containing the downloaded images until such times as I in my ISP role had determined any confidentiality issues and what we would do with any such images so classified. The PTS were trying out a new camera with a motorised drive and stable platform, ideal for aerial photography. This meant there were a very large number of images to review; the overwhelming majority were of no conceivable confidentiality concern. But in order to test out the Test Manual procedures for handling any images that were deemed sensitive, I decided that I would classify as highly protective those pictures showing clearly the diameter of test boreholes and the steel casing. Not even the Russians worried about this, but this is one of the artificialities one has occasionally to introduce into a practice inspection in order to test or validate procedures. This request now required saving the images to a separate disc and deleting the ones held on the IT's computers; hard copies were printed off and signed and the classified version along with the printed copies were held under joint sealed storage in the ITL's work tent. We signed and dated the back of the hard copies to show that we both agreed that this was a true image. They would remain under lock and key until the end of the inspection when their fate would be determined. However, when the time came there was no agreement on the disposition of these images; the inspection team wanted to include them in their preliminary findings report and I refused, offering instead an 'unclassified' description of the features in question, but this was unacceptable to the IT. There was also a disagreement over whether they could leave the country, so the matter remained unresolved and the images would stay under sealed joint storage on the territory of the ISP until the matter was addressed by the Executive Council when it considered the final inspection report. That was the control team's way out of the dilemma, and had such an event happened for real the most likely outcome. In any case the IT had more than enough information to produce an accurate sketch for their reporting.

The continuation period of an OSI allowed the use of various geophysical techniques, including airborne deployments for wider area searches. One of the key objectives of this exercise was to test out airborne magnetometry, the main aim of which would be to detect the steel casing used in test boreholes. As already noted the geophysicists in the inspection team were becoming increasingly unimpressed with the scenario as there was nothing of interest for them to find. However, in a real OSI this might well be the case, that the triggering event that led to the OSI request had a natural origin and was nothing to do with an underground test. In IFE08 we were in limbo on a former test site containing plenty of relevant observables with a scenario that was positioned between compliance and non-compliance given Arcania's plan to conduct a test. On reflection we could have done better, and this became clearer when I observed an IT sub-team conduct a geophysical survey of a former Soviet era test borehole. In addition to the main borehole, which was about eight to ten feet in diameter, there were also several much smaller diameter holes, which I assumed were either diagnostic cable channels or the drill back entry holes to recover radioactive samples from the melt puddle in the heart of the underground cavity created by the nuclear test. Instead of creating the staged managed access set complete with derelict orange caravan we might have been better to cover this borehole over with fresh soil and vegetation and then see if the IT could detect it from the air with magnetometry. All this contributed to one of the key sets of lessons for next time, the scenario needed to be scientifically credible and coherent and present a good challenge for the inspection team. As we will see in Chapter 7, a much greater effort was put into scenario design.

Negotiating skills are crucial for any effective inspection as we saw clearly for example at Coevorden. The ITL needs to convince the ISP to provide the access and information the team needs in order to fulfil its mandate; this will be tough ask when the ISP is deliberately obstructive, disorganised and under resourced; or under the sort of strict central control after the US approach that we saw at Fort Sill (see Chapter 4). So as we have already seen in IFE08 I made the inspection team work for its access, but making sure at the same time that we were able to meet as many of the as possible exercise objectives. Gaining a psychological edge was important, so at various stages of our exchanges during the formal plenary meetings I sought to unbalance the ITL and his senior inspection team leaders from each of the disciplines represented in the team. On one occasion when we were arguing about access to part of the inspection area I was insisting on what the inspectors regarded as unreasonable demands that would hamper their ability to do their job. After arguing the point, the ITL and his colleagues stormed out of the meeting claiming that we were being uncooperative. Leaving such meetings in an abrupt manor is never a good idea no matter what the temptation or provocation; you will only have to walk back again at some stage. As we saw at Coevorden, it is better to pocket small victories and insist that the matter remains open for discussion, making clear that ISP cooperation or the lack thereof is going to be a key feature in the final report. Documenting every ISP obstruction, obfuscation, denial, lie, delay and infraction of the Treaty's verification procedures is the better way to proceed. There may well be a point in an inspection when no further progress is possible, but it will be essential to show that all avenues and possibilities had been exhausted first before ending the inspection. Such a decision would also need to have the full support of the Director-General.

External evaluation was also a critical component in the conduct of IFE08; a group of experts led by a US OSI expert Paul Stokes was tasked to review the conduct of the exercise and report on the extent to which the objectives had been met and to comment on the state of OSI development and capabilities in each of the various inspection techniques under test. An external review was important politically in the wider context of WGB as an independent voice would be an important counter balance against a temptation by the PTS to gloss over shortcomings and exaggerate successes. The evaluators directly observed inspection activities in the field or at ISP-ITL meetings – though at times this was grudging by some – took photographs, circulated a questionnaire and conducted interviews with a representative selection of participants.[13] As head of the ISP team I was one of the happy few chosen for interview. I think there is a perception of an evaluator as someone in white lab coat wandering around with a clipboard and pen, tutting as they do so.[14] There was an apprehensiveness too about the process when some were perhaps worried that what was being judged or marked was the individual's performance, actions or behaviour and not the overall process. This was no doubt a contributory factor to the reception of the evaluators' final report by the PTS. The report had laid out a scoring system to mark the level of achievement in each of the key OSI areas, such as radionuclide monitoring or overflights. Inevitably the scoring was generally low such as two or three out of five, though the methodology for arriving at such marks was not clear, and some thought that the figures were just plucked out of thin air. It did not help that the evaluation team was not shown the exercise mandate or even the scenario. However, all this led to a somewhat tense evaluation workshop in Baden, about sixteen miles south of Vienna, in March 2009. I ended up trying to find the middle ground and helped draft the final report for WGB. At some level the disputes were unnecessary as at heart everyone had essentially seen the same things and had largely come to the same or similar conclusions on the state of play on OSI and what needed to be done next. This experience was to have major implications for the next IFE since at least two of us – myself and Ian Oliver, who served on the Evaluation Team – vowed that there would be no repeat of this next time round and both of us would end up in a position to make sure. All will be explained in Chapter 7.

Conclusion

Despite the hardships and frustrations, IFE08 was a great experience; I do not think anyone who was there despite their grumbles and complaints at the time would have missed it. It was a very dramatic illustration of the differences between negotiating or elaborating treaty verification regimes in comfortable places such as Geneva or Vienna and the cold reality of what things are actually like at the coal face. There is an adage that you learn by doing, and this was certainly true during the UK CWC PCIs, so the CTBTO PTS was following the same path. In order to capture the lessons from IFE, a major OSI Workshop was held in Baden in December 2008. This and other post-exercise reviews gathered some 800 lessons that were entered into a new Lessons Learned Data Base, which led to an OSI Action Plan that helped prepare the way for the next large-scale exercise, which was even bigger, in 2014. One of the many positive findings is that notwithstanding the shortcoming and artificialities, such as time compression, the IT still managed to review the inspection area of 1,000km and had identified the exercise anomalies that had been placed for them to find.[15] This was a good foundation on which to build. Moreover, many of the same lessons that we had learned in both the CWC and BTWC PCIs were also identifiable during IFE08. These included the importance of accurate site briefings, well-organised inspection teams, keeping track of documentation, questions and answers, the importance of negotiating technique, effective use of time, equipment fit for purpose, meticulous and detailed reporting, well-designed scenarios matched to exercise objectives, integration of information, judicious use of managed access techniques and prior preparation for ISP sensitive facilities and areas. At one level I was not surprised by any of this, but even so gaining such practical experience of a nuclear weapons related OSI added an extra level of validation that the way the UK had thought about, designed and conducted OSI exercises for arms control and disarmament treaties was the right one. The next stage was how to see how this experience might also apply to nuclear disarmament verification, to which we now turn.

Chapter 6

Nuclear Disarmament Verification

The UK-Norway Initiative and Letterpress 2009–2017

Introduction

Throughout the Cold War the UK, whilst supporting nuclear arms control between the superpowers, was much less keen on any suggestion that its own modest strategic deterrent should be included in any negotiations or agreements. Indeed throughout the Strategic Arms Limitation Talks between the US and USSR between 1969 and 1979 British officials constantly badgered the US to make sure that the Polaris force was excluded from any bilateral deals struck with the Russians.[1] British concerns centred on preventing non-transfer and non-circumvention clauses from being included in a SALT agreement that would undermine or invalidate the 1958 Mutual Defence Agreement or the 1963 Polaris Sales Agreement given their centrality to the continued role of the UK as a viable nuclear weapons state. Such anxieties became acuter still as the UK approached a decision point in the late 1970s and early 1980s on a replacement for Polaris, something which would depend on the US for a new delivery system as well as warhead design information. Whilst these concerns were not articulated publicly, the face of British nuclear arms control policy through the 1960s, 70s, 80s and early 90s was essentially that only if US and Soviet/Russian strategic forces were substantially reduced would the UK wish to look to see how it might contribute to further disarmament measures. Thus in the UK view the primary responsibility for negotiations fell to these two powers.[2] Even this was a conditional posture. We also need to keep in mind that the 1972 SALT Interim Agreement and 1979 Treaty were primarily about controlling launchers, not warheads. The later START agreement constrained the numbers of nuclear warheads allowed for the US and Soviet Union/Russia, but there was no question of warhead dismantlement, let alone international on-site inspection to verify such dismantlement.

As already noted the UK saw verification as a central requirement for any arms control and disarmament treaty. The thinking behind this position was laid out clearly by Foreign Office Minister of State at the FCO in June 1985, and can be seen as a summation of an enduring British approach over the decades. Richard Luce made it clear that the UK was not looking for perfect or one hundred per cent verification. But he was absolutely clear about what verification would be required. Luce underlined the point that the definition of adequate verification would always be a matter for careful political judgment, which must none the less rest upon technical factors. He posed several questions which, in studying the verification provisions of any arms control agreement, needed to be addressed. First, will any undetected evasion of an agreement provide a significant military advantage? Secondly, will significant non-observance of the agreement be detected early enough to allow any necessary counter-measures to be taken? Thirdly, even if the evidence of such non-observance is available, will it be convincing enough to justify such counter-measures? Lastly, if the UK was confident that it could give the right answers to these questions, would it then be possible to deter any temptation to depart from strict compliance with the agreement?[3] We should note here the reference to adequate verification resting on technical factors since this provides the historical background and context to UK work on the considerable challenges that states would face in devising and implementing verification measures in a nuclear disarmament agreement.

The other contextual consideration leading to UK practical work on nuclear disarmament verification in the 2000s was the relationship between progress, or more usually the absence thereof, on nuclear disarmament by the nuclear weapons states and the wider health of the Non-Proliferation Treaty, whose continued good health was an absolutely central part of UK arms control policy. Article VI of this Treaty calls for its state parties to undertake, "to pursue negotiations in good faith on effective measures relating to cessation of the nuclear arms race at an early date and to nuclear disarmament, and on a Treaty on general and complete disarmament under strict and effective international control." Over the years there had been a growing tension between the NWS and NNWS; for example, the

1980 Review Conference failed to produce a consensus Final Declaration largely on account of the failure of the US, USSR and UK to conclude a CTBT. Even the 1995 Review and Extension Conference only manged to agree an indefinite extension of the Treaty, but no other agreement proved possible. By the 2000s the UK looked to find ways of addressing the political pressures facing the NPT and in particular the role of the P5 (UK, US, France, China and Russia), and practical work on nuclear disarmament verification was certainly one promising area for detailed study. The UK and US worked jointly on various exercises and issues looking at how it would be possible to design and implement a verification regime for the dismantlement of nuclear weapons without compromising classified warhead design secrets at the same time. Verification exercises were held at AWE Burghfield – the UK's nuclear weapons assembly and disassembly facility and the Pantex Plant, Texas – the US equivalent, where the technical challenges were investigated and issues identified for further consideration. In the first instance it was of course easier to work with the US on this issue given the longstanding cooperation on nuclear weapons going back to 1958. Work on the practical aspects of verification, as we have seen, dates back to the mid-1950s through to the pioneering efforts on CWC on-site inspection verification described in Chapters 2 and 4 as well as the BTWC work discussed in Chapter 3. Whilst verification research on nuclear disarmament was easier with an allied NWS, joint efforts with a non-nuclear weapon state would raise a whole series of problems, not least of which would be how could you discuss the details without revealing classified warhead design and production details? This is where Norway enters the equation as a NATO state with a strong tradition of supporting arms control and disarmament, for example NORSAR made a significant contribution to the design of the CTBT's IMS.[4] Norwegian interest in exploring the issues of nuclear disarmament verification mirrored UK ideas on examining the problems with a non-nuclear weapon state. The UK-Norway Initiative was thus born.

UK-Norway Initiative

In early 2007, representatives from UK Ministry of Defence, the UK Atomic Weapons Establishment, several Norwegian laboratories and the non-governmental organization VERTIC (Verification Research, Training and Information Centre) began work on the technical verification of nuclear arms control.[5] This was to culminate in a major exercise held in Norway in 2009 in which I took part as one of the inspectors. The UK-Norway Initiative (UKNI) brought together a nuclear and non-nuclear weapon state for the first time to discuss what verification tools and methods could be required to verify nuclear disarmament, also to explore how all states parties to the NPT could contribute and cooperate to this end. The UKNI went on to present its findings through several technical papers and presentations at NPT Preparatory Committees and the 2010 NPT Review Conference.[6]

This initiative, and the Letterpress exercise that followed eight years later, were, unlike the CWC, BTWC and CTBT exercises, not predicated on an absolute ban on a whole class of weapons or activities. The intent was not to see how a challenge inspection type regime might operate looking for clandestine production or storage of prohibited items or evidence of illegal activities such as nuclear testing. In the case of the UK-Norway Initiative the aim was to monitor the declaration of a nuclear weapon that was scheduled for dismantlement, its movement from storage to a disassembly facility and the subsequent disposition of its fissile material in a long-term secure storage in yet another location. The primary aim of the game was to see how and whether the inspectors could maintain an unbroken chain of custody across all stages of this process. Fissile material accountancy was the basis for IAEA safeguards, and whilst warhead declaration was a similar process, the challenges were more acute – especially on the dismantlement of the warhead.

The core element of the framework was a hypothetical Treaty and its associated Verification Procedure, between two hypothetical countries, the Kingdom of Torland, a nuclear weapons state (NWS), and the Republic of Luvania, a non-nuclear weapon state (NNWS). In an initial declaration, Torland stated its intention to dismantle its ten remaining Odin class nuclear weapons (gravity bombs). Torland invited Luvania to verify the dismantlement process for one of these weapons. The Verification Procedure allowed for the Luvanian inspectors to undertake a Familiarization Visit to Torland's Nuclear Weapon Complex, and subsequently to conduct a Monitoring Visit to the same facilities to verify the dismantlement of one Odin class bomb. The dismantlement would be considered complete once the Odin's fissile material pit had been placed in a monitored store. The exercise was designed to have a broad enough scope to provide an overview of the whole dismantlement and verification process.[7]

As a key part of this exercise UK and Norwegian experts had developed two information barriers, both of which could be used to determine whether the declared weapon contained fissile material consistent with known characteristics of a nuclear weapons system.[8] The detector would simply give a 'yes' or 'no' answer indicted by a green or red light, but not reveal any quantitative or qualitative information about the warhead. Such a piece of kit would have been ideal at the RAF Honington, AWE and Coulport CWC PCIs. Information barriers must prevent the disclosure of sensitive measurement data to uncleared personnel and as such are an important concept when considering future inspections, as inspectors would not be given unrestricted access to nuclear warheads. Such access could breach the mutual non-proliferation obligations of the NPT, as well as reveal national security-sensitive information.[9]

For the purposes of the exercise the Norwegians built a weapon ballistic casing to represent an Odin class weapon that was being withdrawn from service; it contained a Cobalt-60 source to mimic fissile material, so this was all about demonstrating proof of principle rather than a complete system that could be used in a real verification setting. As part of the preparation for the main exercise there was also a final reconnaissance visit to look at the four facilities the Norwegians proposed to use as stage for the exercise. The UK would play the role of the NNWS invited by the fictious NWS played by Norway, so we were going to have to make a judgment on the suitability of these sites; all bar one looked good enough for their simulated roles – weapons storage, hot cell and nuclear waste store, but the laboratory suggested for the disassembly bay was not really credible. Fortunately there was another facility at the Norwegian Institute for Energy Research (IFE) that better fitted the bill in terms of size and access, and it even had an overhead crane.

This exercise, given the scenario, was limited to specific areas of the declared facilities coupled with strict limitations on the inspectors: equipment would be provided by the hosts, no personal items such as watches or mobile phones were permitted inside the working areas, protective clothing had to be worn and there was a limited ability to seek additional information. All this was intended to show that access inside nuclear weapons facilities would need to be tightly managed. It struck me as odd that the constraints whilst comparable to those that we had encountered during the UK CWC PCIs at nuclear sites such as Aldermaston, Burghfield, Coulport, Foulness and Honington, seemed much more rigorous and limiting. During the exercise we conducted countless radiation sweeps using gamma and neutron count rate monitors of the various areas before and after the controlled object or Treaty Accountable Item (i.e. the Odin warhead) was moved into and out of them. This was to ensure that no fissile material or isotopes were being removed or added surreptitiously to enable Torland to retain the recovered fissile material for the manufacture of new weapons. We also applied numerous seals and tags, including glitter tags that were then photographed as their application would create a unique pattern, which could then be re-photographed to see whether there had been any tampering. However, these were time consuming to apply and verify, and certainly not user friendly as they relied on the operator making a visual comparison. As such they failed my standard for what is needed in an effective inspection process, which is quick, robust, easy to apply and check. Of course they must also be tamper indicating. If the image comparison process could be automated then that might speed things up. We also submitted a larger number of clarificatory questions to help us in our task, and I kept a log of these using the same format I had developed during IFE08 with the colour coding to indicate whether answers had been provided (green), were pending (amber) or unanswered or unsatisfactory (red).

As part of the exercise the inspectors submitted a report to their hosts shortly after the conclusion of the on-site activities. We made the following observations:

- We were able to deploy all the techniques deemed necessary to sustain an unbroken chain of custody of the item declared by Torland as the Treaty Accountable Item, from start to finish of the inspection.
- The Information Barrier system was successfully deployed four times during the inspection process – the presence of the notional weapons grade plutonium (in reality, radioactive cobalt) was confirmed each time.
- The co-operation from Torland was exemplary.
- As a result of the above, the inspection team was able to confirm with a high degree of confidence that the object declared as the Odin weapon, and its associated containers, moved through the declared dismantlement process.
- Further scientific measurements and documentation indicating provenance could, in future dismantlement processes, provide greater reassurance that the object was the Odin system.[10]

However, there is an important caveat here since none of the verification measures used could confirm that the object presented as an Odin class weapon was as declared. The Information Barrier measurements, along with the documentary evidence, built confidence that things were as they were supposed to be, but were not definitive proof. However, it was not the intention of this exercise to solve this initialisation problem; but, it highlighted the issue as one that would need to be addressed. It seemed to me then, that in any viable and credible nuclear disarmament verification regime far more detail on the physical characteristics of a declared weapon would be required. The CWC's Verification Annex Part IV (2) (g), by way of comparison, requires the declaration of the agent fill and the quantity for each declared chemical weapon along with its size or calibre and the nominal weight of the chemical fill per item. We would need therefore to have the type and nominal quantity of fissile material as well as any thermonuclear fuel present in each weapon along with its dimensions. Other characteristics would be useful too such as weapon serial numbers; for example, the UK WE177 A, B and C all carried five digit unique numbers. The issue of serial numbers came up during the UKNI exercise, but the hosts were reluctant to address the question. Other weapon characteristics such as tritium gas bottles and radiation cases would also be useful to declare. It is hardly state secrets that plutonium, enriched uranium, lithium 6 and 7 and tritium are used in modern nuclear weapons and accounting for these materials must surely be a critical part of any future nuclear disarmament verification regime. One could go further and require declaration of the standard weapons storage and transport containers. Such details would give inspectors more confidence that a nuclear weapon declared as scheduled for dismantlement is what it is claimed to be when they have completed a visual check and taken necessary measurements, including with an information barrier type of detector. UKNI showed that a chain of custody could be established, and that would certainly be an essential component of an overall disarmament regime, but the NWS would have to be prepared to divulge some design information if an overall verification regime were to be truly effective. This was my main lesson from participation in the UKNI. Work would continue in the subsequent years under the UKNI framework to follow-up the lessons learned from the 2009 exercise through workshops and table-top exercises. Such work included further research into managed access of inspectors during warhead dismantlement verification in an exercise in 2020 for example.[11] As for the Information Barriers, these were not yet a deployable system, but the UK and Norway planned to move the system towards the identification of grade as well as material presence; the exercises also highlighted the need for an additional phase of development towards mass threshold measurements. British and Norwegian experts noted that the complexity of the system also increased, and that trend was thought likely to continue as additional functionality was added. Conversations between the engineering and arms control communities would need to continue to ensure that any proposed solutions are simple, cost effective and fit for purpose.[12] Equipment needs to be easy to set up and use, and the production of measurement data available promptly – all of which were key lessons from CWC and CTBT exercises. As it transpired we would not have another large scale field exercise until 2017, but this time round with US and Swedish participation. This was Letterpress, but on this occasion I would be wearing an evaluator's rather than an inspector's hat. And once again we were back at RAF Honington for another historic disarmament verification exercise almost thirty years since PCI 2 back in October 1989. Things move slowly in international arms control.

Letterpress: UK, US, Norway, Sweden – RAF Honington 16-19 October 2017

In 2015 Norway, Sweden, the UK and US agreed upon a new multiyear arms control initiative, referred to as the Quad. This built on the previous experience acquired during the UKNI and UK-US bilateral work to study the challenges associated with monitoring aspects of future nuclear arms control treaties and agreements. Like the UKNI exercises, Letterpress was not a challenge scenario. Letterpress was the unclassified code name for a joint UK, US, Norway and Sweden exercise to examine another aspect of an overarching nuclear disarmament treaty. It had much in common with the 2009 UKNI monitoring visit exercise, but this time round we had multinational teams playing with combined inspection and home teams, control staff and evaluation team – i.e. UK, US, Norwegian and Swedish experts served in each of the teams. Following the example of the CTBTO's IFE14, which will be discussed in the next chapter, the exercise planners decided to include an evaluation team with each member looking at specific aspects of the exercise. My main focus was to look at nuclear weapon related managed access as well as inspector and host state interactions.[13] The evaluation framework for this was not nearly as sophisticated and extensive as the one used for IFE14 (see next chapter), but more than adequate for the highly focused exercise that was Letterpress. Unlike the UKNI we did not have to create a simulated weapon, we used an old WE177A inert training round, a device that weighed and looked the same as a live weapon. We also made use of a standard WE177 transport container – the WE155, which added further realism to proceedings. The former SSA at RAF Honington provided the set and was renamed Notinghon for exercise purposes. The core scenario posited that two NWS had agreed to significant reduction in their weapons stockpiles. They also agreed to include two neighbouring NNWS as part of the inspectorate tasked with confirming the technical aspects of the treaty's monitoring regime. Notinghon was described as an interim storage site where nuclear weapons that had been removed from active service were stored awaiting retirement and dismantlement or refurbishment. The dismantlement site was the location where retired weapons were sent to be dismantled; separate buildings at Honington's SSA served to simulate these facilities.[14] In the real world the last duty of Honington as a live nuclear weapon storage site was to store withdrawn Chevaline warheads prior to their dismantlement at Burghfield.

The main activities in this exercise focussed on establishing a chain of custody for a weapon scheduled for dismantlement as it was moved between storage and dismantlement facilities, but this time a much more significant array of verification equipment was in play and inspectors were allowed to take direct measurements of the weapon to confirm its identity – this was known as attribute measurements and trusting the radiation signature of the trusted template i.e. an already measured and agreed set of weapon characteristics used to confirm that the object in front of the inspectors was indeed a true treaty accountable item. Inspectors were also allowed to take absence measurements of an empty bunker to confirm the lack of a neutron signature. The UK-Norway Initiative Information Barrier (IB) and the US developed Trusted Radiation Identification System (TRIS) were identified as technologies to use in measuring gamma attributes and confirming radiation signature templates, respectively. The important distinction between the IB and TRIS systems is how they confirm the presence of a treaty accountable item (TAI). The UKNI IB evaluates whether the gamma spectrum of an object indicates the presence of a declared attribute of the TAI, in this case the presence of weapons grade plutonium. TRIS determines that the gamma signature of a declared item is similar to a previously measured TAI, within the resolution of the fifteen spectral energy windows measured by TRIS's gamma detector.[15] Adhesive seals, Reflective Particle Tags (RPT), and a Chain of Custody Item Monitor (CoCIM) were used to provide applied unique identifiers signatures to verify the WE155 container's identity during the inspection: the RPT and adhesive seals, being analogue signatures, and the CoCIM, a digital signature. Both the adhesive seals and CoCIM were also designed to indicate unauthorized access to the weapon container. Application of a physical unique identifier to the weapon casing was not allowed on safety grounds. Overall the inspectors were able to confirm the identity of the declared weapon and also sustained a clear chain of custody as it moved from the storage site to dismantlement facility. This represented one of the major differences between the original CWC PCI programme and BTWC exercises.

There were several things that struck me about the conduct and outcome of this exercise, considering the previous work at the UKNI exercise in 2009 and the host of CWC and CTDT inspection exercises conducted over the preceding thirty years. In a nuclear weapons facility it is self-evident that access, safety and security regulations will be tightly controlled, but there were two aspects at Letterpress that seemed to me to be unnecessarily restrictive. Whilst one of the scenario aims was to create a clear sense of control for the inspectors and making clear the restrictive environment in which they were to operate, the requirement to have them fully suited in protective clothing, even to the extent of making them wear gloves taped onto their sleeves was not only unrealistic for a storage facility, but was seriously time consuming as they had to suit up before being allowed access to the storage facilities, then a similar protracted period afterwards to disrobe. In hot weather this would have further impaired the performance of the inspectors, but even in a British autumn operating in such conditions was tiring. None of the host team were similarly garbed, so this was clearly not a safety requirement such as one might expect in radiation areas to be found in buildings A45 and A90 at AWE. If the concern is a security one in that inspectors might be able, even inadvertently, to collect an environmental sample from the working area, what could this possibly reveal to a hostile intelligence agency? If the treaty requirement already states that a declared weapon template would have a certain radiation signature that can be measured, then what is the concern? Modern weapons are sealed units, so it is hardly likely that fissile material particles could be found on the floor and wall of a storage bunker. In PCI2 in 1989 and again in 1994 when the SSA stored live WE177 weapons we were not asked to don such an elaborate suite of protective clothing. The same applied to the nuclear weapon storage areas at RNAD Coulport in 1996. In a disarmament treaty the quantity and isotopic ratios of declared weapons would need to be provided, so going to elaborate lengths to guard against clandestine sampling would seem self-defeating. Moreover, as we saw at the clandestine sampling exercise at AWE Aldermaston in 1992, the likelihood of finding anything meaningful is very low even if some of the inspectors come from a NNWS.

Measurement equipment, seals and tags will be of the utmost importance in any future disarmament treaty for several reasons.[16] First, the equipment must enjoy the full confidence of the states using it; they must have a very high assurance that the measurement results from an information barrier, for example, are authentic, reliable and repeatable. There must also be an extremely low likelihood of false or negative positives. Furthermore, they must have confidence that it will not divulge classified warhead design features or have any hidden capabilities; such equipment must be safe to use in the proximity of live nuclear weapons, it must be robust and easy to use by the inspectors and hosts. The equipment in use in Letterpress was still experimental and clearly required further development work before it could be used in a real inspection; indeed one piece of equipment proved temperamental and was clearly far from being field ready. However, the important point to note here is that inspector confidence levels increase when several different measurement devices all give the same result, or should one fail for whatever reason, then two out of three positive or identical results should suffice for the inspectors to maintain confidence levels. In fact, at Letterpress we had exactly this situation and it was the two out of three positive results that enabled the inspectors to state their confidence that the necessary chain of custody had been maintained through the initial inspection of the declared weapon through to its transfer to the dismantlement facility. When the inspectors were back in their working area reviewing their findings, they were grouped together examining some maps and documents. As one of the evaluators I was looking at how the team reviewed their findings and planned their next activities, but on this occasion I noted some activity taking place outside the window in the distance: the declared weapon was being moved in its transport container from one location to another storage bunker. I quickly took a photograph of the inspectors engrossed in their discussion, not noticing the treaty accountable item seemingly being towed away out of their control in the background. I thought such a photo would prove very useful in future inspector training courses on the need for inspectors to remain vigilant at all times. In terms of the exercise this was actually a controlled move, which the team did know about, but the photo opportunity was too good to miss and it was even used in the exercise debrief to highlight the need for situational awareness at all times during an inspection.

The inspection protocol developed for Letterpress, which drew on START and the CWC's verification procedures, added to the verisimilitude of the proceedings. In the exercise the working assumption was that all inspection equipment brought by (or held on site under secured storage conditions) would be operated by host state experts under supervision of the inspection team. This was in essence a managed access measure, but looking at things dispassionately it is not in practice at all clear what it achieves for the hosts: an elevated sense of safety and security in that they are in control at all times? However, as already noted there is likely to be full disclosure of the workings of all measurement equipment, so the state will know exactly what the equipment can and cannot do. Such items may well have been jointly developed. Inspectors would in any case need to be trained on the equipment and fully conversant with its set up and use. So in such circumstances why should the inspectors themselves not operate the equipment? Escorts would of course be closely involved too, observing each step and even assisting in the process as indeed happens during OPCW routine Schedule 2 inspections when the mobile analytical laboratory is in use. One might add too that the mutual confidence levels that would enable a nuclear disarmament treaty to be signed and implemented in the first place is a very different world from the one in which we live now, or did during the Cold War or even at the time of the exercise in 2017.

Developing and executing an exercise is a major undertaking – even one with a relatively narrow focus such as Letterpress, with many moving parts that require close attention to ensure they continue to all move in the same direction and at the right time.[17] This is undoubtedly true, but careful planning, scenario design, defining of objectives, participant training, design and selection of props – whether that be equipment, objects or documentation, and the stage on which the exercise is performed are all indispensable. Logistics are essential too, especially as in Letterpress a large amount of equipment and props had to be acquired and deployed to the site. Feeding, watering, accommodation and transport of exercise players are as critical as they would be in a real inspection. These need to be right otherwise the value and validity of the lessons learned are much diminished at best or potentially misleading at worst. The meticulous planning that went into Letterpress was rewarded by a very rich seam of lessons that could be used for further research and future exercises.[17] So much of this echoed the experiences of the earlier CWC and BTWC exercises. Since then other states have followed suit and conducted their own exercises – French-German exercises at Jülich in 2019 (I was an advisor during the preparatory work for the first exercise) and 2022, and a United Nations Institute for Disarmament Research and Swiss hosted one at Menzingen in March 2023.[18]

It was certainly strange being back at Honington conducting the sort of exercise and context set in the Letterpress project, especially since we were using as the main prop a WE177A training round. Given all the security and safety concerns over these weapons and the SAA back in 1989, we simply could not have envisaged then how things might change over time. As we stood in a huddle as a small group of inspectors outside one of the storage bunkers on a cold October afternoon working out our next access request none of us would have believed a nuclear disarmament verification exercise with Norwegians and Swedes would play out on the same turf almost thirty years later. There is another element to this story on historical change and the unimaginable becoming possible or even real. Every day the exercise participants were bussed into the site from their respective hotels – inspectors were kept separate from evaluators and home team; and not just to the main gate and guard room, the two buses with their civilian drivers went straight into the SSA to drop off the players. The contrast with 1989 or 1994 could not have been sharper. On the last day once exercise play had concluded inside the SSA we all assembled for a group photograph – all of us resplendent in our colour coded polo shirts (green for the evaluators) with the WE177A training round centre stage. We even invited the bus drivers to join in, and one of them sat astride the WE177 on its trolley waving his cap in the air. I do not know whether this was a conscious homage to Slim Pickens' character Major T. J. 'King' Kong, the B52 pilot who ends up riding a US thermonuclear bomb as it falls out of his plane in the final sequences of Stanley Kubrick's masterpiece 'Dr Strangelove'. Such a scene at RAF Honington would have been downright impossible to imagine in 1989. Progress in arms control and disarmament is generally incremental, with many reverses on the way, but it is the practical work done when things are grim and prospects poor that lays the basis for more rapid progress when the good times return. This is why work on the practicalities and challenges of nuclear disarmament verification, such as that done in the UKNI and Quad, is so important, and has to continue as there is still much to learn and many problems still to resolve.

Chapter 7

The Comprehensive Nuclear Test Ban Treaty

Build-Up Exercises and the Integrated Field Exercise (IFE14) 2012–2014

Introduction

Building a CTBT OSI operational capability is no easy matter given the broad range of technologies, methodologies, procedures, not to mention the logistical and personnel issues involved. This task has not been made any easier given the remote prospects for the Treaty's entry into force. Nevertheless, the Provisional Technical Secretariat and the Preparatory Commission could not afford to stand still: an operational capability cannot be switched on and off like a light bulb. Realistic field exercises would be an essential tool in the development and consolidation of OSI capabilities. IFE08, which was discussed in Chapter 5, generated over 800 lessons for the PTS to digest and act upon. The best way of testing whether progress had been made in addressing the issues thrown up by IFE08 would unavoidably require an IFE: small scale directed exercises and table-top exercises though useful would not be a credible way to measure progress. For these reasons both the OSI Division in the PTS and many key states signatories saw the need for a new and larger IFE. As such exercises take considerable time to plan and prepare, several years were going to be needed for all the necessary arrangements to be made such as finding a suitable host, developing a scenario, and training a new batch of surrogate inspectors. There were two major differences this time round: first the US was back contributing substantively to Preparatory Commission work on OSI, which meant a major inject of intellectual and financial support for the IFE14; the second was the concept of Build-Up exercises (BUEs) to precede the main event. These had originally been conceived by Ian Oliver in the OSI Division and the Executive Secretary Tibor Tóth and would see the four phases of a CTBT OSI played out in a time compressed set of exercises as a dry run or rehearsal before IFE14. These BUEs, as they were known, would include what was described as formative evaluation whereby the evaluation team would provide comments – positive and critical – at the end of each day's play so that improvements could be made in real time. These exercises, the evaluation input and lessons learned would, hopefully, mean that many problems or potential problems could be addressed before IFE14 itself. This would give IFE14 the best chance of success, not least because of the sizeable cost of some $13 million, which did not include all the contributions in kind (experts' time, equipment, and materials for example) provided by the eventual host state and many contributing states signatories, including the UK. The Preparatory Commission agreed that an IFE should take place, and it was proposed by the PTS that there should be three Build-Up Exercises in 2012 and 2013, with the IFE14 taking place at the end of 2014. The stage was set for what would become the highlight of my career working in the FCO and in arms control and disarmament.

External Evaluation

I was invited by Tibor Tóth to lead the external evaluation team, which was going to involve a substantial amount of my time given the preparation, system design, training, conduct and reporting out afterwards. We would need a much more solid methodology and process to ensure that all reporting and judgments were evidence based. This would mean working closely with the Evaluation Section in the Executive Secretary's Office, fortunately that was going to mean Ian Oliver whom we met in Chapter 5. It would also require a good working relationship with the OSI Division if we were to avoid the misunderstandings and divisive arguments from 2008. I felt sure that this would be straightforward given the calibre of the individuals working in the Division, and particularly the two key players Oleg Rozhkov, the OSI Division Director and Gordon MacLeod, the Chief of the Methodology Section and Project Manager for IFE14. However, this would still require considerable effort, tact, patience, and diplomacy to ensure that we could all enjoy a harmonious and productive working relationship, which would make the reporting process easier. Several people were nervous about evaluation, thinking it would be about offering public personal critiques that might be unflattering. Part of this is what I called 'surrogate inspector anxiety syndrome;' a fear that in an exercise there would be something substantial to find in the scenario and they did not find it, thereby making them look inefficient at best and incompetent at worst. Evaluation, however, was about process, procedure, methodology, and equipment, it was most certainly not about an individual's personal performance. If an individual struggled in his/her role this was much more likely to be down to selection and training. This message was to be constantly repeated over the years.

Evaluation would not be about wandering around the exercise with a clipboard and tutting loudly every time something was observed that was not up to expected levels. We needed to have a sound evidence based system for gathering information and using it to generate key findings and recommendations. Initially I had thought about defining a set of OSI capability components, such as negotiating skills or radionuclide detection, each with several expected indicators, such as effective, efficient, and timely that would demonstrate a field operational capability. Drawing partly on this Ian Oliver devised a system of evaluation targets that would be assigned to each evaluator; it would be their job to observe the target in the field during the exercise, conduct interviews, review the relevant documents such as Policy Guidance Documents, Standing Operating Procedures (SOPs), Work Instructions (WINs), interview some of the key players, take photographs of relevant activities; there would also be an overall standard generalised questionnaire circulated to all participants.

In total we eventually created seventeen evaluation targets for the BUEs and IFE14, although not all were in play during BUE 1 and BUE 2, but all of which were defined in connection with the requirements for future OSI operational capability; a further target was defined for exercise planning, preparation, and management. These were all agreed with the OSI Division.[1] The Targets were as follows:

Target 1   Operations, leadership, and Inspection Team Functionality
Target 2   Operations Support Centre
Target 3   Information and communications technology and
            management
Target 4   Operational Security and confidentiality
Target 5   Logistics

Target 6   Health and safety
Target 7   Radionuclide field measurements
Target 8   Radionuclide environmental sampling
Target 9   Radionuclide laboratory analysis
Target 10   Visual observation
Target 11   Multispectral imaging including infrared
Target 12   Seismic Aftershock Monitoring System
Target 13   Active Seismic
Target 14   Ground and aeromagnetic field mapping
Target 15   Electromagnetic and electrical conductivity measurements
Target 16   Ground penetrating radar
Target 17   Gravimetrics
Target 18   Exercise Planning and Management

An information collation plan for the IFE was established to guide individual evaluators of which there were ten with each allocated specific targets. I was responsible for Targets 1 and 18 as well as overall leadership of the team. Ian Oliver and I adopted a holistic approach, which was applied to break down each of the eighteen targets into their constituent components and sub-components and to situate the latter in time and space according to the phase of the inspection in which they occurred – i.e., launch, pre-inspection, inspection, and post-inspection. An Evaluation Information Management System (EIMS) electronic platform was created with a bespoke software package to facilitate this process and essentially converted the paper based system used to evaluate the first BUEs into an electronic format. This was a major technical accomplishment and a massive advance on the paper based approach that I had to use to write the evaluation report for BUE 1. Targeting data were loaded onto the system down to the sub-component level, together with their associated prompts for observations, document reviews and interviews. These were essentiality reminders to go and look at specific activities and processes. As and when the evaluators responded to their prompts, they recorded their observations (initial findings) directly into the EIMS, which stored their comments while assigning linkages for later cross-referencing. The EIMS facilitated the assessment process, which we described as funnelling, whereby the initial findings were presented to the evaluators in such a way as to help them find, analyse, and collate similar entries to compose key findings. These key findings were then presented in a similar way as the raw data to assist the evaluator to compose recommendations on further actions to build or maintain operational capabilities. This was the evidence trail in that, for example, there might be eight or so initial findings on one of the prompts, these would then provide the basis for a Key Finding. A recommendation would follow in those cases where further development or improvement would be required. Throughout this process, the EIMS maintained the linkages and cross-referencing to provide a clear chain of evidence for the detailed evaluator reporting that had shaped the key findings and recommendations. I then assembled these into the overall report. I borrowed the idea of Key Findings and Recommendations from the format of UK House of Commons Select Committee Reports.

We had four overarching high level evaluation questions for us to address at the end of IFE14 for which the EIMS Key Findings and Recommendations would provide the raw material for the overall responses:

Question 1   Did the IFE14 provide a realistic and credible platform on which to test capabilities?

Question 2   What progress has been made in bridging operational capability gaps since IFE08 and the three Build-Up Exercises?

Question 3   What are the capability gaps and areas that require further development and training?

Question 4   What is the current level of preparedness to conduct an OSI using the technologies and techniques exercised during IFE14?

EIMS would ensure that the ultimate judgments and assessments in the answers to these questions were all evidence based and not the result of personal bias or any prejudgment. Now of course the evaluators were all experts in their fields and would have to use their professional expertise, experience, and skills to assess what was in front of them, and then use the structure of the evaluation methodology to compose their key findings and recommendations.

Build-Up Exercise 1: Guntramsdorf 2012

The BUEs were, as already noted, intended to be rehearsals or dry runs for the main event so that problems could be identified early and fixed before the full integrated field exercise in 2014. The idea was that this would likely make the main event more successful. It is also worth noting that the theology of the CTBT approach to exercises for some reason deliberately eschewed the term practice on-site inspection before entry into force of the Treaty. This always struck me as odd since for all intents and purposes what we were doing in IFE08, the three Build-Up Exercises and in IFE14 was a practice inspection. If it looks like a duck, walks like a duck and quacks like a duck, then it is a duck. We did nothing different from what would be done or need to be done post-EIF. We could of course only exercise a compressed version of a full OSI for whole host of reasons, not least of these was cost and the impracticalities of running a realistic and credible exercise over the maximum duration for a CTBT OSI – 130 days. The BUEs divided the four phases of an OSI into three exercises: BUE 1 would address the launch phase over a week, BUE 2 would combine the pre-inspection and post-inspection phases – also over a week, whilst BUE 3, which was the longest of the three at two weeks would focus on the continuation period. In retrospect, it was probably a mistake to conflate the initial period with the post-inspection phase since this required a massive time jump over a very short period. The BUEs were based on the same scenario throughout, which certainly did make sense.

Guntramsdorf, a small village some seventeen and a half miles south of Vienna, was at the time of BUE 1 the home of the CTBTO Equipment Storage and Maintenance Facility (ESMF). This was a temporary rented commercial warehouse that stored the CTBTO's OSI equipment, it also had a maintenance workshop and a few offices that were used for training purposes. This would be the location for BUE 1 and would double up as the Operations Support Centre (OSC), an interdivisional body, that would be created by the Technical Secretariat immediately following a request for an onsite inspection. Its primary task would be to make all the administrative and logistical arrangements to ensure that an inspection team and its equipment was ready to deploy within the time lines established by the Treaty and Protocol and once the Executive Council had given its approval. The OSC would also support the inspectors in the field and arrange their return to Vienna. Now this would be no trivial task and is a good deal more demanding than the comparable arrangements that apply in the CWC's Article IX. Unlike the OPCW TS, the CTBTO has no permanent inspectors of its own; all are nominated by member states, though it is expected that some members of the OSI Division would serve as inspectors too. Although the Treaty states that only forty inspectors can be on the territory of the inspected state party at any time, in practice the CTBTO TS will need to call up many more than just forty. It will need to consider the possibility of a continuation period in which case geophysicists would be needed in the team, it might also have to allow for rotation of personnel if the inspection is a long one. Therefore, there might well need to be perhaps sixty or more inspectors' names on the inspection mandate. These individuals would then need to be called up, flights organised from their home country to Vienna, accommodation booked for them there. Nor is it a simple matter of numbers, there must be an appropriate mix of experts – a team would need to have a broad range of skills as per the inspection technologies allowed for under the Protocol Part II paragraph 69.[2] It is conceivable that depending on the scenario, the TS might need to select more radionuclide experts than passive seismic ones. Politics would require that the inspection team be geographically representative and have a good gender balance too, but much will depend on the nominees submitted by the states' parties. Once in Vienna the inspectors must begin preparation of an initial inspection plan based on the information available in the request and the IDC's analysis of the triggering event plus information about the state already in possession of the TS such as climate and topography. Another key document that would be prepared in parallel is the Inspection Mandate, and this provides the formal authorisation for the IT signed by the Director-General. The juggling act does not stop with this; there is also the dynamic Logistics and Operations Support Plan (LOSP – a term that sounded to me as if it ought to be the name of a military helicopter), which describes inter alia how the team's 150 tonnes or so of equipment will be transported to the Point of Entry in the short time lines established by the Treaty. The LOSP also addresses accommodation, health screening, sourcing of in-country support, and IT travel. In short, BUE 1 was going to address a complex set of dynamic issues moving sometimes in parallel, sometimes not and a lot of interlinked issues too where progress on one was dependent on progress on others. Only the first six of the evaluation targets (plus the last one) were in play during BUE 1, so we deployed a small team of four evaluators at Guntramsdorf.

All the exercise play was confined to the ESMF over two floors with part of the building representing the OSC, which for real would be at the Vienna International Centre, with the rest of the ESMF playing its 'wartime role.' Given the nature of the pre-inspection phase all the action was largely meeting based as a series of briefings, planning and review meetings, phone calls and e-mails and work on lap-tops predominated the action. Speed would be of the essence to ensure completion of all the necessary preparations in the allotted time; one main artificiality is that the exercise was not being run on a 24 hour basis, but a largely normal set of working hours. Whilst none of this made for good spectator sport, the failure of any one of the tasks would mean that the inspectors and their equipment would not get out of the door in time. All this served to underline that in an inspection of the complexity of one called under the CTBT, effective and efficient administrative, organizational, and logistical capabilities are essential. If the pre-inspection phase fails, then there is no OSI and all the high-tech verification equipment from noble gas detectors to gravity meters becomes meaningless.

BUE 1 was in the end a successful exercise in that the four main documents required were all produced in the time available: the initial inspection plan, the inspection mandate, a list of approved equipment ready to be shipped to the Vienna International Airport, and the LOSP. Forty inspectors were identified and air tickets and suitable flights all arranged (though not executed), though in two cases inspectors were flown to Vienna to check that the procedures worked, one from China and one from Mexico. Flying all that way for a day was way above and beyond the call of duty. There were inevitably several aspects of the exercise that could have been improved upon such as the depth and quality of IDC briefings to the initial inspectors in the planning team outlining its analysis of the inspection request. The LOSP could also have carried more detail and a stronger sense that this was going to be a dynamic plan in that it would evolve and change through to the post-inspection phase. Establishing quickly the level of logistical support that the inspected state party would provide was challenging as it affected OSC planning in terms of working out how self-sufficient the inspectors would need to be, and how many field teams the ISP could support once the OSI began. BUE 1 showed clearly just how much effort would be required to launch an on-site inspection. If anyone had any doubts beforehand, then these would have been quickly dispelled. None of these aspects had been played in IFE08. I was the head of the ISP team and received a few emails on the Friday afternoon before departing for Kazakhstan on the Saturday asking for details on the level of logistical support that would be provided by the ISP such as supplies of bottled water and toilet rolls. I simply said details would be provided on arrival at the

POE. Capabilities and planning had evidently moved on since 2008, most notably the new equipment transport containers that were designed to fit into the cargo hold of commercial aircraft.

BUE 2 – Bruckneudorf, September 2012

BUE 2 was a one-week exercise testing the OSI pre- and post-inspection phases, including point of entry activities, set-up of a base of operations, review and signing of a preliminary findings document, disassembly of the BOO, and departure. This was hosted by the Federal Austrian Army's training facility at Bruckneudorf, where the Army had cleared a field for the CTBTO exercise. We ended up in a bit of a dust bowl once all the grass had been removed, which had apparently been an attempt to reduce the risk of Lyme Disease caried by ticks. This was an odd exercise in that it moved from the pre-inspection phase to the post-inspection phase with no intervening inspection activity, and indeed some of the subject matter experts in the IT had no equipment either. I think this made it difficult to create a realistic environment for the participants. The IT had to set up its base of operations (BOO), essentially a tented camp much as we had seen in IFE08, but this time with a much improved layout. All this had to be done before the IT would be ready to begin on-site activities, so things such as reliable power supply would be essential and a working medical tent had to be established. The equipment transport containers had to be checked – only a few were brought by road to simulate the large outload that would have been deployed for real. Hardly had all of this been done, when we all had to switch to the post-inspection phase. As already noted, this seemed to be the weakest part of the scenario, or to be more precise the organization of the BUEs. It was also clear that the few experts playing the Inspected State Party team were under resourced and underequipped, having very few laptops and mobile phones, which made their task harder. Indeed, they had to borrow some kit from my evaluation team as well as the control staff. This would certainly need to improve in time for IFE14 where the ISP team would be playing a central role and would be very much bigger and more capable than the handful of experts that I had in IFE08. There was an early major row between the ISP and Inspection Team Leader over the ISP's intention to restrict access, which prompted the ITL to threaten to call off the inspection unless the policy was withdrawn. An IT has few weapons in its arsenal, and if an ISP wants to be obstructive, obtuse, and offensive, there is little the IT can do about it as we saw in the Coevorden challenge inspection in a non-cooperative environment (Chapter 4). Reminding the ISP that its lack of cooperation will be called out in the final inspection report is perhaps the most important weapon, as indeed is threatening to call off the inspection. However, that is the last option and would certainly need authorisation from the Director-General and only after exhaustive efforts had been made to convince the ISP to see the error of its ways. The IT is there to collect facts and if it is prevented from doing so, then a case for calling a halt arises. As we saw at Coevorden, it can be easy to become sucked into an endless argument within the confines of an office (or in this case a tent) without doing any inspecting; the important thing for the IT is to at least conduct some activity whilst making clear that it is reserving its position and any minimal levels of access are not likely to enable the team to gather all the pertinent facts. So, the concept and issue here at BUE 2 was in essence no different from the one encountered at the CWC PCI at Coevorden.

BUE 2 also included a simulated press conference, in part to test out the CTBTO's media policy in which only the ITL interacts with the TV, radio and press journalists – the fourth estate.[3] The intent was to put the ITL under a bit of pressure; and the surrogate media were suitably aggressive. However, the ITL would only be authorized by the DG to say little and confine statements to a very general and factual nature, steering well clear of any comment on what the inspectors think of the inspection request, the ISP and certainly nothing at all on their emerging and preliminary findings. All requests for information would be referred to Vienna and the CTBTO's own media office. This struck me as all right and proper as inspectors have far more important things to do than deal with the prying media. That said, it would be an important part of future inspector training to make sure that team leaders were given some directions and advice on how to handle the media in high profile events such as an OSI. The UK had looked at the role of the media during our CWC PCIs and Ottawa Convention FFM exercises and seen the clear need for guidance for escorts in the field and the press offices back in London. Indeed, several years later, when designing and helping to run training courses for the United Nations Secretary-General Mechanism (UNSGM) qualified experts, we included a media module that was run by a former BBC news journalist and producer. This entailed coping with being 'door stopped,' face-to face interviews, down-the-line interviews and press conferences. All this just adds to the skills needed by inspection team leaders and senior members. One can be sure that if there is ever a real CTBT OSI it will be a major media event with the world's journalists pressing for exclusives and interviews. Inspectors will need to be prepared. BUE 2 helped show why.

BUE 3 – Veszprém, Hungary, May/June 2013

BUE 3 was a much larger two-week exercise testing the continuation period of the inspection phase, including IT functionality and search logic concepts, equipment use, data collection and analysis and preparation of a preliminary findings document. This was naturally a much more interesting exercise as it involved on-site activity, and would see the focus on geophysical techniques, multispectral infrared for the first time as well as sub-soil gas sampling to look for radioactive noble gases. This time round the inspectors would live in tented accommodation, whilst the rest of us were lodged in a former barrack block. I was given quarters on my own – privilege of rank I suppose as head of the evaluation team. At the end of IFE08 whilst we were staying at Kurchatov I ended up in the dacha used by the director of the Soviet underground tests out on the Polygon. Veszprém is a Hungarian Army training ground, which encompassed heathlands and woods; the BOO was set up a short walk away from the living quarters and this time rather than the irregular pattern of working tents, the BOO was now structured along a main axis with working tents for each of the subject areas as it had been in BUE 2; for example, visual observation, radionuclide, and the ITL's working area set up off this main spine. This was a considerable improvement and by its very structure helped promote integration of the various inspection techniques, which was one of the main aims of BUE 3. I also noted an ammunition depot a short distance away and by my calculation this was possibly too close to a tented BOO – certainly by UK explosive distance regulations. When I pointed this out to the exercise director Gordon MacLeod, he became a bit anxious, but assured me that the Hungarians had said the depot was now empty, so we were in the clear. Health and safety had a high priority in the whole BUE and IFE cycle and great efforts were made to ensure that we all emerged from the exercises unscathed. We even included a fire drill as part of the scenario. And one of the guiding principles was that if anyone saw what they considered to be an unsafe practice, they were to call it out immediately and activity would cease until the problem had been addressed. Hence my query about the ammunition depot.

The exercise scenario used in the two previous BUEs was the same, so by the time we came to BUE 3 we had already conducted the initial period of inspection and certain activities were now presumed to have been completed and the IT was now about to begin the continuation period. As ever with CTBT exercises there had to be quite a bit of time compression. Certain artifacts had been created on the training range, which was now being used to simulate parts of the $1,000km^2$ inspection area. One of these artifacts was to provide a realistic managed access negotiation. The inspectors were using the Inspection Team Functionality (ITF) concept, which was designed to enable the team to prioritize areas of interest inside the Inspection Area depending on what was seen or detected there. It was a planning tool also so that inspectors could generate specific questions to be addressed about each area of interest, and then deploy the most appropriate expertise and equipment in a field team. We had moved well beyond just deploying a Visual Observation sub-team or radionuclide team. Questions and priorities were reviewed by internal meetings of the IT leadership. Many of the field teams over an exercise might be multidisciplinary and the ability to deploy field teams depended in part on the number of escorts and vehicles the inspected state party could provide to support the inspection. ITF was the policy, but the platform on which it was performed was the computer based Integrated Information Management System (IIMS). All of this enabled the IT to submit its daily inspection plans to the ISP. ITF was a pretty good way of preparing, organising, and reporting inspection activity, and could gradually narrow down the Inspection Area to a handful of key targets for more detailed investigation. It was a tad rigid and ponderous at times, but despite this it proved to be a very good tool in the hands of well-trained and capable inspectors. IIMS on the other hand, whilst initially indicating much promise, showed signs during BUE that it might not be fully up to the task. This would become much more evident in IFE14 itself.

Most of the surrogate inspectors in the exercise had by this stage gone through the training cycle together, and of course a few, though mostly PTS OSI Division personnel, had participated in the two previous BUEs. We were therefore starting to see a strong esprit de corps develop amongst the inspectors, and this would of course be critical in a real OSI given the likely long timelines and uncomfortable working environments that would be encountered. In BUE 3 the control staff had set the maximum working day as between 0800 and 2000, after which the BOO would be closed and sealed up ready for the following day. This still made for a long day – boxes of sandwiches and other snacks were prepared for collection after breakfast, which inevitably led people, me included, to work through what was supposed to be their lunch breaks. At the post exercise wash-up one of the vegetarians complained that their sandwiches contained but a single leaf of lettuce. One wag – Peter Labak, deputy ITL – then piped up and said, 'why did you want two?' In contrast, breakfasts and dinners were well provisioned buffets both of which helped morale. By the end of the two weeks of hard work and proximity nerves were starting to fray a little at the edges, nothing major but an indication that the psychological aspects of a prolonged OSI such as those required under the CTBT need to be factored into inspection planning. Inspectors will need time to relax and rest otherwise there could be a risk of burnout, leading to mistakes and accidents as judgments become impaired through mental tiredness and physical fatigue. Interpersonal skills are essential attributes for CTBT inspectors since they need to be able to cooperate and get along in testing circumstances.[4] We had seen this before in the early days of UNSCOM inspections in Iraq when inspection teams were thrown together and deployed with virtually no prior training or knowledge of who else was in the team.

Overall BUE 3 was a great success. We at last saw clear signs of the integration of the information generated by application of the various inspection techniques set forth in the Protocol Part II. The managed access negotiations worked well too with satisfactory negotiated outcomes for both sides. Inspection team daily de-briefings as required by the ITF were also well-run and at the right level of detail so that everyone knew what had happened, what was planned next and the emerging findings from the inspection activity to date. These also included notice of any health and safety issues or near misses encountered during the day, so that everyone else could avoid any repetition. There were of course still issues that would need to be addressed before IFE14, and this was the reason for the high priority recommendations in the external evaluation report that we produced after the exercise. I also had to think of a new way of making some of our points in the hot wash up that we held at the end of the exercise. I wanted the message to be clear and not lost in a traditional PowerPoint presentation. As I had recently been browsing through the US Library of Congress on-line collection of American Civil War (ACW) photographs, it occurred to me that some of the images from there could be counterpoised with images taken during BUE 3 to either show progress or that things had not much changed since IFE08 or BUEs 1 and 2. A black and white image would illustrate a capability in IFE08, and if progress had indeed been made we could then show a colour photo of the current capabilities as demonstrated in BUE 3. If there had been no progress, then I would show the same B&W photo in the next slide. So, for example, for the state of play on sub-soil sampling we started with an ACW photo of a rickety set of a surveyor party's measuring poles and Union soldiers to be followed with a picture of the PTS' Geoprobe – a machine for drilling small diameter holes for sub-soil gas sampling accompanied by the head (Ranier Arndt) of the OSI Division's Equipment Section striking a noble and proud bearing standing alongside. For the RN lab status in BUE 2 I found an American Civil War photo of three Union officers sheltering under a makeshift structure made from trees and foliage, but as there had been insufficient progress I showed the same picture again in my following slide to show how things stood at BUE 3. However, I then dropped in a picture of the Confederate Cavalry commander in the Army of Northern Virginia – JEB Stuart noting that this time round we did have Harry Miley. Harry was a RN expert from the US Pacific Northwest National Laboratory and head of the RN inspection sub team. Harry also sported a large beard, which gave him a passing likeness for JEB Stuart. Harry took this in good part. As with the early CWC PCIs, humour was never far away and an essential ingredient in both the success and enjoyment of CTBT exercises.

IFE14 – The Dead Sea, Jordan, November- December 2014

IFE14 would, by some way, be the largest, longest, most complex, and ambitious arms control and disarmament on-site inspection exercise that I took part in during my career. That we were holding this exercise in the Middle East of all places with the brutal Syrian civil war raging only a few hundred miles to our north from our location at the north end of the Dead Sea made its significance even more acute. We had Israeli and Arab experts taking part as well as an Iranian. Overall, there was a very broad geographic representation throughout all the teams involved in the exercise; and there was a good gender balance too. In the External Evaluation team, we had me (UK) and one each from Algeria (Lotfy Simohamed), Canada (Gordon Vachon), Croatia (Ivo Valic), Brazil (Paulo Malizia), France (Thierry Fournier), Jordan (Samer Al Kharouf), Spain (Sara Figueras), Sweden (Anders Axelsson), and the United States (Julia Craven Jones). We also had two PTS experts to assist: Ian Oliver and Szabolcs Osvat. Gordon (an old colleague from CWC and BTWC Protocol days) remained in Vienna to monitor the work of the Operations Support Centre (OSC). Unlike IFE08, this time round we would not be running a survival exercise. All participants were accommodated in a high quality resort hotel on the Dead Sea, which was a short distance from the Base of Operations and a regular shuttle bus service ran from the hotel to the BOO to ferry participants to and from each location. We all had our own rooms and there was no shortage of food to keep body and soul together.[5] Moreover, we all had en suite rooms, so regular access to a hot shower was a huge advance on IFE08 as I could attest. All of which meant that the participants could concentrate on the task in hand and the process and technical aspects of the exercise.

The scenario created for IFE08 had been a bit of a disappointment as discussed in Chapter 5, however, there were mitigating circumstances. This time round a much greater scientific and technical effort was invested in making sure that the scenario for IFE14 was scientifically sound and would present a solid platform on which to test the PTS' OSI policies, procedures, and technologies. Ward Hawkins from the Los Alamos National Laboratory and a veteran of the US nuclear testing programme was appointed chair of the Scenario Task Force (STF). The STF would draw on expertise from other US National Laboratories (Brian Milbrath and Ted Bowyer from Pacific Northwest), AWE Aldermaston (Peter Sankey), AWE Blacknest (Neil Selby), FOI Sweden and Israel. It would operate in secrecy as it was vital that the details of the scenario were kept from the inspection team and anyone else not authorized to receive details. US engagement was one major difference from 2008 and this would have a major bearing on the quality of the synthetic data created for the exercise. The same goes for AWE Blacknest who were also resourced by the MOD to provide substantial technical input, and this took the form of synthetic seismic data to mimic the triggering event; Sweden provided RN data and the US would manufacture radioxenon and Argon-37 that would be used to spike samples during the inspection. A series of artifacts and injects were created for the inspection team to find and to be used to either delay or speed up the inspection if it looked as if it might not meet the STF's planning expectation as to where the IT should or needed to be by a particular point in the exercise timeline. A detailed master event list was drawn up to this end. Ward Hawkins was in a state of near permanent anxiety during the exercise in case the STF had missed something important. One of the key lessons from IFE08 was that the scenario should be peer reviewed by an expert group to check that the scenario was scientifically and technically sound before being finalised. A small group of experts, including UK and US weapons experts with experience of nuclear testing, were convened at a meeting held in Baden in 2013 to review the scenario. I was also present as the head of the external evaluation team and with Target 18 on my list I sat in on the experts' deliberations. Apart from a few very minor comments on the scenario design, including on what was described as the diversion site, the scenario was given the thumbs up much to the great relief of Gordon MacLeod and Ward Hawkins. Both the peer review process and the scenario itself, from my perspective, worked well and appeared to provide a solid platform on which to test IFE14's objectives. So, we were clear to go.

Given the nature of this exercise the PTS were not going to be able to ship the IT equipment plus all the other paraphernalia needed to support the exercise in real time. Much of it was sent in advance by sea and air, so this was one unavoidable artificiality in the exercise. No one however was under any doubt that for real this would be a major logistical undertaking, but not an impossible one since there is a good deal of expertise and experience within the UN system of moving large quantities of equipment and humanitarian aid in response to natural disasters. Drawing on this and establishing a set of standing arrangements with service and transport providers would be the way to go in future, but for now our focus would be on how various OSI techniques and equipment would function over a protracted period in the field. All the exercise participants required for the initial phase of the inspection assembled in Vienna so that we could start with some of the preliminary preparations before flying to Amman, which we did on two separate flights. When we arrived one of the first activities was to begin the Point of Entry procedures, which were held at a hotel adjacent to Amman international airport as would be likely in a real OSI. The ISP team, led by Malcolm Coxhead – my Australian colleague and co-OSI Manul Task Leader, immediately started to tax the patience of the IT led by Gregor Malich (Chief of the Equipment Section in the OSI Division) in a row over the admissibility of the Inspection Mandate, alleging that it contained mistakes with the names of the inspectors and until these were addressed the ISP Representative was not prepared to accept it. Meanwhile equipment checks continued elsewhere and these proceeded largely without any problem. The Mandate row was eventually resolved, but it was all part of an ISP strategy to delay proceedings; moreover, the arguments once again demonstrated the critical importance of the ITL and key team members having effective negotiating and diplomatic skills. (Much the same lesson identified at Coevorden.) It is never just enough to be an accomplished scientific expert in one of the CTBT OSI techniques.

As already noted, this time round we would not have to worry about the quality of accommodation and sustenance as we were all accommodated in a resort hotel on the Dead Sea.[5] The Inspection Area was set in a region of Jordan known as Madaba, this was a mountainous region and the western boundary of the IA ran close to the Dead Sea. The BOO was established opposite on a piece of hard standing, the down side there was that flies were a major problem and on one occasion in the first days when I went up to our working tents, I was greeted by a huge cloud of insecticide that was billowing the length and breadth of the BOO to deal with what Bela Balczo from the PTS had referred to as the 'Fly Storage Facility.'[6] It was not entirely successful as we were plagued by the things for much of the exercise, though they became much less of a nuisance towards the end as I recall. The evaluators were no doubt not the only ones to run a competition to see who could dispose of the most flies in their working tent.[6] The BOO was well designed, following the same layout as had been used in BUE 3, and was going to play an important part in enabling effective integration of all the inspection techniques and review of the accumulated data as had been the case during BUE 3. The ISP team had their own working tents set up outside the BOO working area, and one of the advantages for the evaluators was that we had a go anywhere pass that allowed us to see both sides at work and could thus review the issues from different ends of the same telescope. Meeting and work rooms were also established in the hotel for the respective teams. The Inspection Team Functionality policy and the IIMS were used to generate inspection plans for consideration and hopefully acceptance by the ISP. This daily cycle basically ran throughout the inspection and as time went by the IT having deployed field teams with visual observation, seismic aftershock measurements, radionuclide surveying and sampling, geophysical techniques, multispectral and infrared and overflights, gradually narrowed down the areas of interest to the point where they had in fact identified the two key locations created by the Scenario

Task Force. One of these was the diversion site, which looked as if it might well have the features of a test site and was intended to see if the IT could tell the difference between this location and the real site of the clandestine test and apply their efforts accordingly. These locations were known as sites N and K to the control team and as Polygons 18 and 29 to the inspection team. These sites were the main features engineered to simulate observables relevant to the preparation and conduct of an underground nuclear test and offered a solid platform to test the integration of the inspection techniques in play. IFE14 thus had posited a non-compliance scenario. The issue would be whether the IT would invest all its resources in the right place; the ISP was already insisting on strict managed access measures in a vain attempt to delay the IT and prevent inspectors from gathering the necessary information. The ISP hoped that its delaying activities and cover story for the presence of elevated radiation readings detected by the IT would convince the inspectors that there was nothing related to nuclear testing in the location – a disused quarry. Unfortunately for the ISP, though, the IT had not only found the site, but they also ultimately detected xenon and argon isotopes that were diagnostic of a nuclear test having taken place. The control team had swapped samples when the originals were brought back to the receiving area at the BOO for information collected in the IA. This showed the importance of the US material contribution to the exercise since they had manufactured the isotopes, a capability that was not open to us in 2008, and something that added immeasurably to the quality and utility of IFE14. The inspection team had been successful, and the ISP players had of course helped facilitate the process; it could not have replicated the sort of role that its counterpart had played at Coevorden as such levels of obstruction would have prevented key parts of the exercise as well as some of its objectives from being played out. One suspects that for real a guilty ISP would not have allowed an IT to get close to the scene of its cheating, but that can be an indication of non-cooperation and obstruction, which could convince states parties that the inspected state party had failed to demonstrate its compliance. Then again it is always a possibility that an ISP might miscalculate, thinking it might be able to get away with it and successfully prevent the IT from gathering incriminating facts. In fact, we saw this in the real world in Syria in 2013 when a UNSGM team already in the country collected clear and convincing evidence that chemical weapons were used against civilians, including children, on a relatively large scale in the Ghouta area of Damascus on 21 August 2013.[7]

The Evaluation Team gathered an immense amount of data about the exercise; EIMS made it easy to collate our key findings and recommendations. However, we had to produce two reports: one high level one containing the major points and a lower order technical report with all the detail for each of the evaluation targets. The overall process of identifying and learning all the lessons from IFE14 was a lengthy one; the OSI Division held two workshops to look in detail at the results – one of these took place in Tel Aviv with the other in Vienna at the VIC. It was going to take us about eight months to finalise the Evaluation reports in time for the planned target date of being ready for the summer Working Group B meeting in August 2015. An exercise of the magnitude of IFE14 deserved a thorough review, and to make sure that we had no re-run between evaluators and the PTS that had marred the follow-up to IFE08, Ian Oliver and I made sure that there would be extensive dialogue on the draft reports. As with the BUEs, we wanted to ensure that there were no factual errors in the reports and that our findings' recommendations were clear. We would share our drafts with the OSI Division and held a detailed seminar with PTS and subject matter experts from the IT from 29 June to 1 July 2015 before finalising the Technical Report. However, there remained a vital caveat; final editorial and substantive judgments rested with the Evaluation Team and me as team leader and principal drafter of the high level report. Fortunately, this process proved straightforward and relatively stress free. EIMS had provided all the evidence we needed for our judgments. I think this was also testimony to the hard work and professionalism of all the experts engaged in this process from the Evaluation Team, Inspection Team, and the PTS OSI Division. All this meant that the wider credibility of the final report, especially in the policy making organs of the Preparatory Commission, was all the stronger, and it was always one of my main aims throughout the process to achieve such an outcome. The Technical Report in the end ran to some 272 pages containing 425 key findings that led to 253 recommendations. These were included in a ranking system of high, medium, or low priority. Our intent here had been that those recommendations carrying a high priority ranking should ideally be addressed in a new OSI Action Plan that would be prepared by the PTS given their importance to the development of an effective and efficient OSI operational capability.

One of the main achievements in IFE14 concerned the extensive use of atmospheric and sub-surface sampling and analysis for radioactive noble gases as this represented a major step forward in the effectiveness of the inspection, compared to what had been deployed in any previous OSI activities and especially since IFE08. This shows that developing effective capabilities for OSI can take years, translating art into article is rarely a straightforward process. A similar story applies in the case of MSIR. MSIR techniques and technologies were not available during IFE08. While MSIR technologies were used in BUE 3 play was notional and focused on data analysis exclusively via a data inject provided by the control team. IFE14 was therefore the first OSI exercise where MSIR techniques and technologies were played through in their entirety and marked a significant improvement in operational capability for MSIR techniques for OSI. They did however generate vast amounts of data and there was only one already fully loaded expert in the IT who could process and analyse it. As we had pointed out in BUE 3, this represented a weakness in the inspection team as it was overly dependent on one individual; there would definitely need to be additional MSIR experts in future.

Not everything was perfect of course, and that should not be surprising as one of the aims of such exercises is to find out what works and what does not – a point explicit in one of IFE14's objectives and in one of the four high level evaluation questions: what are the capability gaps and areas that require further development and training? A CTBT OSI generates vast amounts of digital data. Finding sufficient time to assess, report and discuss the findings from field teams and translate them into technical mission reports continued to be a challenge in IFE14, much as was the case during BUE 3. The compression of time during the IFE may have been a factor here, but it was not the sole explanation. The evaluation team's recommendation following BUE 3 was that consideration should be given to ensuring that time was regularly scheduled for discussions at the sub-team level to review reports, strategies and survey designs. This problem was a potential Achilles' Heel in the ITF as it would mean that an IT could run out of time and/or simply be overwhelmed by the sheer volume of data as they chased the clock. We proposed that this shortcoming could be addressed in future OSI training programmes by putting more emphasis on effective time management. Overall, the ITF process needed to become less ponderous and much more fluent. We suggested too that further consideration needed to be given to steps that could be taken to shift the balance of effort within the inspection team to provide more time for analysis of data from the field. One way to do this would be to create specific slots at the BOO to be staffed expressly to conduct an analytical review of the data collected in the inspection area as part of the overall inspection planning and review process. Other options would be to reduce the number of field teams deployed on particular days or to assign the responsibility for data analysis to one sub-team member (who would be available for field teams if needed). This issue and a possible redesign of the way information is assembled, labelled and accessed in computer systems (the Integrated Information Management System (IIMS), field information management system (FIMS) and temporary hard drives) needed to be further investigated, as the then current arrangements, partly as a result of time pressure, hindered the effective dissemination and integration of inspection information. In fact the IIMS was a weak link in the overall process. It was not a stable enough platform, and its response rate was often slow. The servers in the receiving area and in the working area at the BOO did not work reliably, with adverse consequences for the sustained effectiveness and efficiency of the inspection planning and review process. The IIMS software that controlled the chain of custody process for environmental and gas samples was not mature enough for field use and appeared not to have been fully prepared for samples collected in the field and returned to the BOO. Software had to be fixed and updated on numerous occasions. Users also lacked sufficient training and practice with the system and were not provided with checklists to guide them through. For these and other reasons the evaluation team recommended that the PTS would either have to invest substantial resources to fix the problems, or develop a new more effective platform. As it happened the OSI Division opted for the latter, and a new much improved system has now been developed (GIMO – Geospatial Information Management for On-Site Inspection) and tested in a Build-Up Exercise on the launch phase of an OSI held in November 2019. This particular case study showed yet again the necessity of testing equipment and procedures in realistic field conditions as that is the only way of really being sure that they can stand up to the rigours of a real OSI, especially one held in a non-cooperative and environmentally challenging conditions in a remote location.

We also noted a serious deficiency in environmental sampling, namely the often haphazard recording of sampling locations, leading at best to significant unnecessary work at the BOO and at worst to doubts and in at least one observed case to grave errors in the sampling locations finally assigned to the analytical results. Obviously, even a small uncertainty as to what location a sampling result applies to will undermine its integrity, and a grave error (i.e. sample collected at a completely different site) will lead to a misdirection of inspection effort and a lack of credibility in the findings. We noted that there were sufficient issues with the radionuclide sample collation and chain of custody processes to lay them open to legitimate challenge whereby the integrity of an inspection's radionuclide analytical results could be called into question by an ISP and its allies; this is a major vulnerability in the OSI process that needed to be addressed as a matter of urgency. Much more work was needed here to improve on effectiveness, efficiency and sustainability. However, these problems were readily amenable to practicable and achievable solutions, and work was put in hand post IFE14 to address them. Any non-compliant state party would always be likely to challenge the findings of an inspection team, question its methodology, the reliability of its equipment, and the competence and allegiances of inspectors regardless of how good and solid they are. We saw this in spades with the Syrian and Russian responses to OPCW and UN investigations of Syrian chemical weapons use and Syria's wider compliance with CWC obligations between 2013 and 2020.[8] This means that inspectors, whatever the treaty regime, need to ensure that their reporting is solid, sound, contains no contradictions, is scientifically and technically credible and evidence based. Practice OSIs provide one key way of ensuring that come the day when they need to be deployed for real, an international inspection team will be able to report confidently with no exposed flank for a non-compliant, sullen and aggressive ISP to shoot at.

As for our assessment of then current level of preparedness to conduct an OSI using the technologies and techniques exercised during IFE14 – the last of the four high level questions, this was not an easy one to call. In general terms, significant progress had been made in developing and demonstrating operational capabilities across a broad range of the techniques and processes required for an effective OSI. It was difficult, if not impossible, to quantify these advances for several reasons. First, there were no agreed key performance indicators for what constitutes operational readiness, although some earlier WGB considerations (some of which I had proposed) in this area could help provide some general, albeit provisional, guidance.[9] Second, there were no agreed data quality objectives for radionuclide measurements and equipment sensitivity requirements. Third, the allocation of numerical values for states of OSI readiness was fraught with technical difficulties. Fourth, much of OSI operational capability would be based on qualitative factors, which are not always readily amenable to simplistic quantitative measurement. Despite these caveats and on the evidence of IFE14, and considering the exclusions from exercise play and other artificialities such as time compression and the advance deployment of equipment, much of it provided as contributions in kind, some solid operational capabilities existed for most of the techniques, procedures and infrastructure. Overall the evaluation team felt that with further development work those capabilities that were played could contribute effectively to the expeditious, sustainable and reliable conduct of an OSI.

Conclusion

I have been immensely lucky to be involved closely with many activities central to the history of arms control and disarmament since I joined the FCO on 19 March 1985. However, the undoubted highlight was the IFE14. As already noted, the exercise itself marked a major improvement on IFE08 and generated many important new lessons for the development and operationalisation of the CTBT's on-site inspection provisions. All participants pulled together for a common purpose, and the PTS' On-Site Inspection Division was instrumental in making it happen. IFE14 serves in a modest way as a reminder of what humanity can achieve when it puts its mind to it. It strikes me that it is a very great shame that the common spirit and purpose created during IFE14 did not translate into the day-to-day affairs of arms control and disarmament efforts whether they are in Geneva, The Hague, Vienna or New York.[10] The war in Ukraine has seen to that, but even prior to Putin's brutal war, things were difficult in multilateral fora and securing agreement on matters of substance an increasingly elusive aspiration. Exercises such as IFE14 as well as the smaller BUEs provide a meaningful tool to ensure that that development of capabilities and understandings can proceed in the meantime against the day when times are more conducive to progress. As with the UK original CWC PCI programme, it is through a continued process of realistic role play exercises that capabilities can be developed, validated and maintained, and it does not matter whether it is a nuclear, chemical or biological weapons context.

Chapter 8

Conclusion
The United Kingdom and on-site inspections

From 1988 until 2020 the UK was a key player in the development of how on-site inspections could and should work in multinational arms control and disarmament treaties. The work done on CWC and BTWC challenge inspection verification in particular was pioneering and set the trend for others to follow, and in the case of the CWC went a considerable way in shaping the final content of its Verification Annex Parts II and X. On nuclear matters the UK once again was in the vanguard with its role in the UK-Norway Initiative and in the CTBT UK experts contributed substantially along with many other state signatory experts to the development of OSI operational capabilities, culminating as we saw in the last chapter with IFE14. It was my privilege to be involved closely with all of this work and perhaps the only expert, certainly in the UK, to have worked on the practical aspects of nuclear, biological and chemical weapons arms control and disarmament. Over the years and after almost seventy inspections exercises there are a wide range of reflections, observations, lessons and insights that occur to me. Perhaps surprisingly there is a good deal common to all types of treaty challenge type inspections. The longer I worked on these issues, the clearer this conclusion became. One of my military colleagues (Wing Commander Pete Strachan) in the MOD's Military Operations 4 branch once commented that what we usually had in exercises was lessons identified, they had not yet been learned. Ideally next time round they would be applied, though this was not always the case in the CWC PCIs over the years. However, there seemed to me to be several major lessons that are worth highlighting by way of concluding remarks.

The first of these concerns the importance of setting clear objectives for exercises without overloading them with too many diverse aims since sometimes these can be incompatible and create conflicts over the best use of time within the exercise. Related to this is the pressing need to design a compelling and credible scenario that allows the exercise objectives to be met. This is, as we have seen, a major challenge for CTBT exercises, but less so for CWC/BTWC scenarios where it is comparatively easy to devise a scenario that fits the facility and its activities that have been selected to host the exercise. There are inevitable artificialities and time compressions in these exercises, but that does not degrade their utility. However, the context and nature of artifacts created for the exercise must have some underlying credibility otherwise the players, especially the home team/ inspected state party, will struggle to defend or negotiate effective managed access approaches. Empty ammunition boxes covered with a shroud and small derelict orange caravans do not cut the mustard.

Managed access was devised in the UK CWC PCI programme to ensure that adequate access could be given to inspectors whilst protecting highly classified information unrelated to the CWC (or any other arms control treaty for that matter as we saw in the BTWC, CTBT and nuclear disarmament verification exercises). I never saw any national security or commercially confidential information concern that could not be addressed by the judicious application of a range of managed access measures or techniques. Access within nuclear weapons facilities, pharmaceutical R&D laboratories and intelligence related facilities proved possible even though there were serious initial doubts harboured by the custodians and operators of such places. Problems were, and often are, generic and thus amenable to the same solutions regardless of location or state in which the facility resides, though many states were reluctant to accept that such a conclusion would apply to them citing unique conditions that excused them from such an outcome. Obsessive security and security cultures in authoritarian states were part of the problem, but such perceptions could be seen in western states too. The bottom line is that the concept is valid no matter where it originated. Sometimes bespoke solutions might well be required for specific situations as we saw in the case of some of the UK's nuclear weapon related facilities. There is a balance to be struck with managed access in that an overzealous approach, such as applying it when it is not needed, will only create suspicions and aggravate inspection teams unnecessarily as well as leading to delays. It was for this reason that the CWC makes clear that state parties are not to use managed access to avoid their obligation to demonstrate compliance. The CTBT has exactly the same principle. A well thought through strategy of managed access could well be applied and an inspection team might be oblivious of the fact. It does not do to be too obvious such as the occasion when we were at RAF Honington for the second time and the map used in the opening site briefing showed the SSA completely blanked out in grey. In the Q&A session immediately afterwards I asked about what was being concealed by this 'grey area' to which the JACIG Senior Escort Officer (an RAF Wing Commander Bill Snell) quickly said that he would prefer to characterise the colour as RAF blue. Understated humour again.

In the work on OSI a lot of what was done was designed to look at both how inspections would work for inspectors and how the hosts could manage such an intrusive investigation where security and logistical concerns needed to be addressed. One area where both sides needed to get things right was in the opening site briefing, which became an express requirement in the CWC's Verification Annex for example. For the hosts it is essential to start on the right foot and be as open as possible about what goes on at the site; it is important to avoid any subsequent surprises if the IT finds some activities or facilities not mentioned in the briefing. Maps and diagrams must be up to date and accurate as well as clear. The existence of any lodger units within the site needs to be highlighted as well as general health and safety requirements and hazards present on site. A description of where the site sits in organizational terms is also crucial – who owns and pays for it? In the UK there is a requirement for all MOD sites to have a CWC challenge inspection plan, which means that much of the opening brief should already be scripted and will follow a standard outline that is in the MOD Standing Instruction for Arms Control. The brief should also include a site windshield tour when the inspectors are driven around the site so that they can orient themselves and see the site layout and topography.[1] Ideally in very large sites this should also include the option of a helicopter overflight as even in this day and age of Google Earth, images of the ground may not be current. When the CWC was being drafted there were no such things as drones, but now these should become an essential tool for any inspection team. Inspectors can use the brief to raise questions on site activities and its internal organizational structure and use the details to help further flesh out its initial inspection plan. Windshield tours are excellent ways of identifying buildings and structures for priority inspection. This is the first instance where the Mark One Eyeball comes into play as an essential piece of inspection equipment.

Inspection equipment should never drive an inspection; just because there is a magic machine that goes ping does not mean that inspectors should determine their activities by a need to deploy such kit regardless of the context or information needed. This was one of the reasons why the CTBT's Inspection Team Functionality concept was developed. In a search logic, activities should be shaped by the need to answer specific questions in order to improve understanding of what is actually present at a particular location and how that relates to the non-compliance concern that triggered the inspection in the first place. Since the CWC negotiations concluded in 1992, technology has advanced apace and this has implications for the types of equipment that inspectors could usefully deploy in the field. Remote sensing is one key area applicable for multiple verification tasks in investigations of alleged use; drones equipped with high resolution digital cameras and other sensors such as LIDAR increases the capabilities of inspection teams especially in non-permissive environments such as a war zone, or where there is inaccessible terrain such as steep mountain sides or dense forestation. The CTBT faces similar advances compared to the technologies that were available when it was negotiated in the mid-1990s and reflected in the Protocol's paragraph 65. Such technologies could help make much more efficient and effective use of time during an inspection, thereby enhancing the team's prospects of acquiring all the information it needs. They can of course also add to information overload.

Time management is critical in any inspection, especially where the duration is limited as it is in the CWC challenge inspection (eighty-four hours). Even in the CTBT where in theory an OSI could last up to 130 days, time is important since the initial period is only twenty-five days and the continuation period is dependent on progress being made in the first phase in order to provide the justification for continuing the inspection. An inspection team has to cope with an inspection area of up to $1,000km^2$, so setting up and making operational its base of operations, deploying field teams and collecting and processing data quickly is of the essence. Processing and reviewing the collected data quickly but accurately is a critical task, even though this might be in a hostile environment and I do not just mean the climate, weather or terrain. Fluency and a thorough familiarity with procedures, equipment and techniques are essential attributes to making the most use of the time available. Ponderous, pedantic and rigidly mechanistic approaches will not succeed. Effective time management is thus one of the key requirements for an effective inspection, but it is also one of the hardest to achieve, which is why regular realistic field exercises are essential to practice and hone capabilities.

CONCLUSION

Interviews proved to be one of the most critical tools in a CBW challenge inspection/investigation. Drawing out detailed information about facilities and their activities added considerably to the inspector's ability to determine what was going on or had happened at a site. The cross-referencing of information found on the site, through document reviews, analytical results and briefings helps the inspectors determine whether the picture that they are assembling is a true and plausible one. If it is not, then suspicions might arise or new lines of enquiry emerge that need to be pursued. A persistent pattern of evasion or lies tells its own story. Effective interviewing is such an essential skill for inspectors, that it has become a core topic in training programmes for the OPCW, IAEA and UNSGM. Identifying the right people at a location to interview can be done through listing key functions that would very likely be performed on site such as a senior ammunition technical officer responsible for explosive storage or head of health and safety or emergency response. Others because they have been identified in documentation found on site or during the opening site briefings. Reliable sequential technical interpretation is of course essential as it is more than likely that the interviewee will not have a sufficient command of English – English is the working language of the OPCW and UNSGM for instance. Sequential interpretation takes time – doubling the time of the interview, which needs to be factored into inspection planning. Linguists well versed in the technical subject matter are also important to have available as time can be lost in misunderstandings and confusions caused by poor interpretation. Worse still, key pieces of information might well be missed. For example, in one of the UK/US/Russian Federation BTWC trilateral working groups the inelegant phrase 'sewage cookers' was used by a US expert to describe waste incinerators at a non-military biological facility in Russia seen by the UK/US visiting team, but the inexperienced US interpreter actually translated this as 'cookers of shit' much to the amusement and confusion of the Russian experts. However, the lessons work both ways, it is essential to avoid slang and colloquialisms when interviewing, which is not always easy – clarity and brevity are thus critical attributes for the interviewer. Whilst prepared questions are an important part of the process, the interviewer should not stick religiously to these as the dynamic nature of the conversation may take a new tack, which would require some follow-up questions not in the script. And if interviewing through an interpreter, it is important to look at the interviewee, not the interpreter, as body language offers important insights. The note taker should look at the interpreter.

Auditing or document review proved to be of great value in the CBW PCIs; there was and is such a diverse range of documents that could be requested and reviewed during an inspection. All of these, somewhat paradoxically, can be used by a site to help it to demonstrate its compliance, and this was a point that we laboured to our chemical and pharmaceutical industry colleagues that given the regulatory framework under which they operated a vast number of records had to be kept and these could be used by inspectors to help confirm the statements made about peaceful purposes at the site. Following a process through also helps build confidence; for example, noting the serial numbers on ammunition storages boxes in particular storage bunkers, picking one or two at random and then requesting sight of the relevant paper or computer based record. Language can of course be an issue; in the CBW PCIs we were operating in English, so a key learning point was an inspection team really ought to possess sufficient linguistic skills to be able to make use of records. However, it would be very easy to end up swamped in a deluge of paperwork, so careful and targeted selection will be important. It some cases it may not be necessary to review some of the documents as the mere fact that the inspected site produces them in the first place is the important point.

Negotiating skills are one of the key attributes that an effective inspection team would need to possess in abundance from the ITL downwards since interacting with escorts and facility personnel will be a continuing feature in all inspections. Negotiating access will largely devolve to the ITL and other senior members of the inspection team, but that does not mean that other team members can ignore some of the basics. It can be easy to be drawn into an endless and pointless set of arguments over Treaty rights and obligations as well as the correct legal interpretation of a treaty or protocol text. As we saw at Coevorden and IFE08, the ITL needs to keep options open, ensure that some inspection activity takes place whilst taking careful note of the ISPs arguments and behaviour. Listening carefully to the ISP and trying to take account of what might be genuine concerns and uncertainties or indeed a complete lack of authority to decide, should enable the ITL to make helpful suggestions for how access might be achieved in a manner to satisfy both sides. In one of our latter PCIs at RAF Honington we posited a scenario in which the ISP representative (played admirably by John Foggo from the UK National Authority) was uncertain, inexperienced and unsure on how to manage the inspection: naivety and incompetence rather than non-compliance, but this still presented a different set of challenges for the

IT. For these reasons possession of effective negotiating skills has become, rightly, a central feature in inspector training programmes. Of course the most able negotiator might not be able to shift the pig headed one inch off their ground, but the point is that such a negotiator will have been able to expose each and every evasion, lie and half-truth and reflect this in the final inspection report.

Keeping track of information in an inspection was also one of the recurring lessons regardless of the verification regime. If there are no procedures and means to record information collected during an inspection, then the team will easily become swamped and lose track of chains of custody and provenance of specific bits of information acquired during the inspection. All this will inevitably weaken the final report and make it ripe for criticism from the ISP and its allies. In the CTBT OSIs a dedicated inspector was tasked with managing the database, and although a CTBT OSI generates gigabytes of data in sharp contrast with a CWC challenge inspection, the need for an effective inspection archive is essential for both inspectors and inspected state party regardless of the treaty. It needs to be accessible, clear, chronological, and above all useable.

In the original UK PCIs we did not need to think about training either for the inspectors or escorts; we learned by doing and were working out how best to mount an effective CWC challenge inspection in order to influence the design of the CWC's provisions. The same applied in the BTWC PCI programme. However, once the CWC entered into force and the CTBTO Preparatory Commission started its work on building OSI operational capabilities, the need for an effective training programme for inspectors became clear. Field exercises became an essential part of this; classrooms and PowerPoint presentations are never enough. I certainly saw this through my participation in over seventy OSI exercises. Short of the real thing, there is no substitute for realistic field exercises as that is where you can see whether all the component parts of an inspection will actually hang together. You might have a laptop running off powerful servers in the base of operations, but if you do not have stabilised and reliable power supplies you are hobbled. It was good to see the OPCW, UNSGM and CTBTO put significant resources into training their personnel ahead of major exercises. This was certainly true for IFE14, for example, and had been instrumental in helping to build up a strong esprit de corps as noted in the previous chapter. In many ways large scale exercises are the culmination of a training programme, and help validate whether the training materials and curricula are fit for purpose. Well trained personnel are therefore a key ingredient in a successful practice inspection, especially where there is no permanent inspectorate as is the case for both the CTBTO and UNSGM. Even for the CWC training and practice in challenge inspection are essential as the skills required go beyond those acquired for routine inspections and need to be periodically exercised.

Continuity and institutional memory are essential in the development of OSI operational capabilities built up through training programmes, table-top and field exercises. Sadly this is much harder to achieve given the seven year tenure policies that constrain both the OPCW TS and CTBTO PTS, rotation in the posting of national experts means that there are fewer and fewer individuals who have extensive experience in these matters and that presupposes that they have on-going inspection exercise programmes in the first place, which is a doubtful proposition. In the UK I was the only expert who remained in post for over thirty years working on NBC arms control verification, something which certainly helped in a modest way the UK to maintain a leading and influential role in the CWC and CTBT in particular. More effective knowledge management, recruitment patterns, personnel training, continued coherent exercise programmes can all help mitigate the adverse effects on personnel capabilities from tenure and high turnover of staff in foreign and defence ministries.

In early UK thinking on CWC challenge inspection in the 1980s challenge was largely seen as a deterrent. At the time we had not really thought much more about this, but as the PCI programmes ran their course and we moved into training OPCW, UNSGM and CTBTO inspectors we increasingly thought about what would constitute an effective operational capability. For a deterrent to be credible, then an effective OSI operational capability needs to exist and be visible. A state party considering a clandestine NBC programme in breach of its treaty obligations would hardly likely be deterred by an international disarmament organization with few poorly trained inspectors, hardly any equipment, reliable analytical capabilities, and no validated procedures and policies; and which had never been exercised. Conversely, one with a large pool of well-trained and experienced inspectors, one that was well equipped with the latest measurement and detection technologies, regularly rehearsed and tested and continually improving operational capabilities presents a much more credible deterrent. It would be a brave or indeed foolish advisor who told his government that they could guarantee to get away with cheating even if such an inspection team turned up on their territory at short notice. A capable inspection team could well collect incriminating facts or ample evidence of obstruction, evasion, lies, deceit and a pervading lack of cooperation that would convince a doubting Executive Council that the state party had failed to demonstrate its compliance. Even if a smoking gun is not found, then the whiff of cordite tells its own story.

British policy for the handling of an in-bound inspection was predicated on the need to cooperate with the inspection team and address its requests as promptly and as comprehensively as possible. We debated whether a more proactive approach would be better; for example, having carefully analysed the inspection mandate we thought at one stage that it might be useful to identify likely areas of interest within the site given the non-compliance concerns for the inspection team and suggest that they might like to make these priority areas. This approach rarely went down well with inspectors; for instance, during an CWC PCI at RNAS Culdrose in 2000, which included three OPCW TS inspectors, the home team produced a comprehensive suggested plan, which was promptly rejected by the IT. The inspectors felt that they were being steered and possibly misdirected away from areas of real interest; too much cooperation can thus be counter-productive. Many years before, one of the UK IAEA safeguards experts (Frank Walford) at the UKAEA told me when we discussed the best approach to take in inspections that if the hosts were being too cooperative he would be thinking what were they trying to hide. There is thus a balance to be struck here between cooperation and appearing too willing to help, and it may not always be easy to find. However, on balance it is better not to offer up suggested plans, though there are occasions where offers of advice on the practicalities and timelines involved in inspection activities at complex sites can be helpful. A careful review of the non-compliance concern, however, can be useful for the home team in identifying areas where the inspectors are likely to prioritise. This can help with any managed access preparations that might be required.

Inspections are not just about a mechanical or procedural process of checking for the presence or absence of treaty limited items. There is an important psychological dimension too, especially in challenge inspection scenarios. To put it crudely, pissing the inspectors off is never a good strategy as it will make them more suspicious and less forgiving of the inevitable delays and missteps that can arise in a short notice inspection as the hosts try to find their feet. We saw this at PCI 3 at RAF Honington in 1989, the third BTWC PCI at Pfizer in 1994, Fort Halstead in 1996 and the challenge inspection exercise with the OPCW at Coevorden in 2002 for example. It is therefore essential to avoid creating situations where the inspectors face an endless succession of delays, denials, disputations, discord and disappointments. A failure to do so will not lead to an effective inspection where the demonstration of compliance by the inspected state party is achieved in a timely and efficient manner. That objective was and is at the heart of UK policy on handling in-bound inspections, and was the best approach to challenge inspections that we constantly emphasised in training courses for National Authority personnel over the years. You ignore the psychological dimension of an inspection at your peril.

Looking back at thirty years of inspection exercises at home and abroad, there were so many high points and memories as well as countless colleagues with whom it was both a privilege and pleasure to work. We tried to make the world a better place and reduce the risk of war through our efforts to negotiate and implement arms control and disarmament treaties. Sadly much of that work looks to have been in vain now given Russia's unjustified and brutal war against Ukraine and the consequent worsening of relations between Russia and NATO. That said, the OPCW's exposure of Syrian CW use and unresolved questions on its CW programme shows that at least one part of the verification architecture that we strove so hard to create has broadly functioned as intended. In the meantime the CTBTO now has plans in hand to conduct a new IFE, so the hard work of sustaining and developing OSI continues at the coal face, and it is now up to the next generation to build on past achievements and avoid the mistakes and failures made in earlier times. However, Russia has now withdrawn its ratification of the CTBT, which takes us even further away from that treaty entering into force, but that does not invalidate the need to keep working on OSI issues. As the nineteenth-century Scottish reformer and author Samual Smiles noted, 'The very greatest things – great thoughts, discoveries, inventions – have usually been nurtured in hardship, often pondered over in sorrow, and at length established with difficulty.'[2] This strikes me as an apt summary of our extensive efforts to design, develop and implement on-site inspections for arms control and disarmament treaties between 1988 and 2020.

Endnotes

Chapter 1

1. A much smaller exercise had also taken place at Semipalatinsk in 2002 known as FE02 – Field Experiment 2002. Semipalatinsk was the largest town nearest to the test site. Semipalatinsk was renamed Semey following Kazakhstan becoming independent in 1990.
2. John R. Walker, *Britain and Disarmament The UK and Nuclear, Biological and Chemical Weapons Arms Control and Programmes 1956-1975*, Farnham, Ashgate, 2012, pp 124-26.
3. John R. Walker, *British Nuclear Weapons and the Test Ban 1954-1973 Britain, the United States, Weapons Policies and Nuclear Testing: Tensions and Contradictions*, Farnham, Ashgate, 2010. See chapter 6.
4. The Convention on the Prohibition of the Use, Stockpiling, Production and Transfer of Anti-Personnel Mines and on their Destruction to give it its Sunday name.

Chapter 2

1. Albert Palazzo, *Seeking Victory on the Western Front: The British Army and Chemical Warfare in World War 1*, Lincoln, The University of Nebraska Press, 2000. On the first day of the German Operation Michael on 21 March 1918 German artillery fired 3.2 million rounds of ammunition against the British, one third of which had a chemical fill – mustard as well as other types. Robin Prior, *Conquer We Must A Military History of Britain 1914-1945*, Padstow, Yale University Press, 2022, pp 214-5.

2. Harvard Sussex Program Occasional Paper, Issue 05, *The 1925 Geneva Protocol: Export Controls, Britain, Poland and why the Protocol came to include 'Bacteriological' Warfare*, John R. Walker, June 2016.

3. John R. Walker, *British Nuclear Weapons and the Test Ban 1954-1973, Britain, the United States, Weapons Policies and Nuclear Testing: Tensions and Contradictions*, Farnham, Ashgate, 2010.

4. CD/500, United States of America, Draft Convention on the Prohibition of Chemical Weapons, 18 April 1984.

5. TNA PREM 19/1693, FCO telno 60 to Washington, Chemical Weapons, 13 January 1986.

6. TNA PREM 19/1184, R. B. Bone, Private Secretary, Foreign and Commonwealth Office to A.J. Coles Esq, 10 Downing Street, Chemical Weapons: US Draft Treaty, 18 April 1984.

7. Memorandum for the Assistant to the President for National Security Affairs, Subject: US Draft Chemical Weapons (CWC) Treaty and Mrs Thatcher's Visit, December 21 1984, Kenneth L. Adelman, US Arms Control and Disarmament Agency, Reagan Library/ Margaret Thatcher Foundation.

8. TNA PREM 19/1693, FCO telno 60 to Washington, Chemical Weapons, 13 January 1986.

9. TNA PREM 19/1184, Chemical Weapons Negotiations, Arms Control and Disarmament Department, Foreign and Commonwealth Office, 18 April 1984.

10. CD/715, Chemical Weapons Convention: verification and compliance: the challenge element, United Kingdom of Great Britain and Northern Ireland, 15 July 1986.

11. CD/921, CD/CW/WP.245, Verification of the Chemical Weapons Convention: practice challenge inspections of military facilities, United Kingdom of Great Britain and Northern Ireland, 14 June 1989.

12. Over the period covered by this book Porton Down went under different names: the Chemical Defence Establishment; the Chemical and Biological Defence Establishment, Defence Evaluation Research Agency, and then Defence Science and Technology Laboratory.

13. Division 1.1 (mass explosion hazard); Division 1.2 (severe projection hazard); Division 1.3 (fire, blast or projection hazard); Division 1.4 (fire or projection hazard).

14. The aim of this Agreement is to standardize within NATO Forces the minimum markings to be applied to ammunition and its packaging manufactured by or for the NATO member states.

15. O-Pinacolyl methylphosphonofluoridate.
16. The Royal Ordnance Factories were part of a government department until they were privatised in 1987. Today Glascoed is operated by BAE Systems Global Combat Systems Munitions. After the closure of other ROFs, Glascoed remains the only ammunition filling facility in the UK and exports its products, as well as supplying the Ministry of Defence. Glascoed now employs about 400 people and has invested heavily in R&D and improved production facilities. ROF Glascoed – Wikipedia Accessed 29 March 2023.
17. See 18th Century Research History, The Man-Midwife in the 18th Century, The Man-Midwife in the 18th Century – HistorianRuby: An Historian's Miscellany Accessed 31 March 2023.
18. The CAM was the standard British Armed forces battlefield chemical warfare agent detector. It used ion mobility spectrometry to detect the presence of chemical vapour. It was thus not really a verification instrument and we did not actually have one with us at the time, but its notional use was one of the managed access options discussed and agreed.
19. In the early stages of the CWC negotiations the term of art was 'Challenging State Observer' (CSO).
20. AMSO was a position on the Air Force Board.
21. One of the issues making agreement to the exercise difficult and made RAF personnel nervous about such an exercise was an unstated fear that we were similar to a NATO TACEVAL (Tactical Evaluation), which was a short notice inspection to test a flying station's readiness for wartime duties. Apparently these could be quite brutal and it could be career limiting for officers who failed to come up to the mark. We assured everyone this was not the case; we were only borrowing their facility and staff. The escort officer's careless use of words certainly did not blight his career as he later when on to be an Air Vice Marshall.
22. John R. Walker, *A History of the United Kingdom's WE177 Nuclear Weapons Programme From Conception to into Service 1959-1980*, BASIC, London, March 2019. See also Royal Air Force Historical Journal 26, *The Proceedings of the RAFHS Seminar on the RAF and Nuclear Weapons, 1960-1998*, Abingdon, 2001.
23. John R. Walker, *British Nuclear Weapons Stockpiles by Year: 1953–77*, RUSI Journal, August 2021.
24. Agreement between the UK and the USA for Cooperation in the Uses of Atomic Energy for Mutual Defence Purposes 1958.

25. John R. Walker, *British Nuclear Weapons and the Test Ban, Squaring the Circle of Defence and Arms Control, 1974-1982*, Abingdon, Routledge, 2023, p 116.

26. Atomic Weapons Research Establishment and successors: Foulness outstation, reports, The National Archives Accessed 14 April 2023.

27. John R. Walker, *British Nuclear Weapons and the Test Ban 1954-1973, Britain, the United States, Weapons Policies and Nuclear Testing: Tensions and Contradictions*, Farnham, Ashgate, 2010, pp 169, 180 and 189. The site would eventually close in late 1997.

28. CD/1012, CD/CW/WP.304, United Kingdom of Great Britain and Northern Ireland, Verification of the Chemical Weapons Convention: Practice Challenge Inspections of Government Facilities: Analysis of Results, 11 July 1990, p 18.

29. As it happens many years later Dr John Bartlett from Porton Down and I visited GCHQ for a *'walk through, talk-through'* visit to assess the implications of a CWC challenge inspection at its facilities. It turned out to be very easy from a CWC perspective as it was mostly offices and computers, which could be switched off if any inspectors were escorted round the offices.

30. CD/921, CD/CW/WP.245, United Kingdom of Great Britain and Northern Ireland, Verification of the Chemical Weapons Convention: Practice Challenge Inspections of military facilities, 14 June 1989.

31. *Chemical Weapons Convention Bulletin, News, Background & Commentary Relevant to Chemical Weapons & Chemical Arms Control*, Issue No.8, June 1990 p 16.

32. CD/PV.564, Conference on Disarmament, Final Record of the Five Hundred and Sixty-Fourth Plenary Meeting held at the Palais des Nations, Geneva, on Thursday, 12 July 1990, at 10 a.m., 12 July 1990.

33. CD/1012, CD/CW/WP.304, United Kingdom of Great Britain and Northern Ireland, Verification of the Chemical Weapons Convention: Practice Challenge Inspections of Government Facilities: Analysis of Results, 11 July 1990.

34. CD/1012, CD/CW/WP.304, pp 3-4.

35. Unfortunately, geophysical techniques never made it into either the CWC Verification Annex or the future approved OPCW Equipment list agreed at the First Conference of States Parties in 1997. They were, however, explicitly listed in the 1996 CTBT Verification Annex Part II paragraph 69. It would not be until 2014 that a gravity meter was

actually used in an arms control inspection exercise, this time in the CTBTO's Integrated Field Exercise 2014.

36. CD/CW/WP.269, United Kingdom of Great Britain and Northern Ireland, Instrumental Approaches to Non-Intrusive Analytical Techniques for Inspection and Verification, 12 January 1990.

37. Dr Graham Cooper, 'Inspections on Request: Coming to terms with their scope,' *Chemical Weapons Convention Bulletin, News, Background & Commentary Relevant to Chemical Weapons & Chemical Arms Control, Quarterly Journal of the Harvard-Sussex Program on CBW Armament and Arms Limitation*, Issue No.10, December 1990.

38. Ralf Trapp, *Verification under the Chemical Weapons Convention: On-site Inspection in Chemical Industry Facilities,* SIPRI Chemical & Biological Warfare Studies, Volume 14, Oxford, Oxford University Press, 1993.

39. CD/CW/WP.249, Report on a national trial inspection of an industrial chemical facility, United Kingdom of Great Britain and Northern Ireland, 21 June 1989.

40. TNA CAB 131/17, Cabinet Defence Committee, D.C. (56) 13 (Revise), 4 July 1956. By which time the GB pilot plant had produced about twenty tons of agent. See CD/ 856, Past production of chemical warfare agents in the United Kingdom, Working Paper, United Kingdom of Great Britain and Northern Ireland, 17 August 1988.

41. CD/15, Visit to Britain by chemical weapons experts (14-16 March 1979), United Kingdom of Great Britain & Northern Ireland, 24 April 1979.

42. See for example CD Working Papers CD/1101, CD/CW/WP.360, Working Paper submitted by Germany, Report on a trial challenge inspection at a large chemical plant site, 15 August 1991; CD/1100, CD/CW/WP.359, Working Paper Submitted by the United States of America, Report on the 3rd United States trial inspection exercise, 14 August 1991; CD/1021, CD/CW/WP.311, Working Paper Submitted by the Czech and Slovak Republic, Report on a trial challenge inspection at a chemical facility, 26 July 1990; CD/996, CD/CW/WP.292, Working Paper Submitted by the German Democratic Republic, Report on the trial challenge inspection in a chemical industry plant, 12 June 1990.

43. CD/1056, CD/CW/WP.330, Report on Two joint Chemical Weapons Practice Challenge Inspections, Germany and the United Kingdom of Great Britain and Northern Ireland, 8 February 1991.

44. CD/1102, CD/CW/WP.361, Report on an international trial challenge inspection, Germany, 15 August 1991.

45. TNA DEFE 13/2731/1, I.S. Manson, DACU (CW), Chemical Weapons Convention Challenge Inspection; Further Work on Managed Access at Nuclear Facilities, January 1991. This included reports from the practice challenge inspection site selection visits to BNFL Capenhurst and UKAEA Harwell.

46. John R. Walker, *Britain and Disarmament The UK and Nuclear, Biological and Chemical Weapons Arms Control and Programmes 1956-1975*, Farnham, Ashgate, 2012. See Chapter 6, 'The UK and the Biological and Toxin Weapons Convention Negotiating History: March-September 1971: The Key Months', pp 73-114.

Chapter 3

1. John R. Walker, *Britain and Disarmament The UK and Nuclear, Biological and Chemical Weapons Arms Control and Programmes 1956-1975*, Farnham, Ashgate, 2012. See Chapter 6, 'The UK and the Biological and Toxin Weapons Convention Negotiating History: March-September 1971: The Key Months', pp 73-114.

2. BWC/CONF.III/23 Part I, Geneva, September 1991, Third Review Conference of the Parties to the Convention on the Prohibition of the Development, Production and Stockpiling of Bacteriological (Biological) and Toxin Weapons and on their Destruction Final Document, p. 16.

3. John R. Walker, Harvard-Sussex Program Occasional Paper Issue 02, *The Leitenberg-Zilinskas History of the Soviet Biological Weapons Programme*, December 2012; for an account of UK and US efforts to get to the bottom of the Soviet BW programme see Milton Leitenberg and Raymond A. Zilinskas, with Jens Kuhn, *The Soviet Biological Weapons Program*, Cambridge, Harvard University Press, 2012; and David Kelly, *The Trilateral Agreement: lessons for biological weapons verification in* VERTIC *Verification Yearbook 2002*, Nottingham, Russell Press, 2002.

4. BWC/CONF.III/VEREX/WP.5, Working paper submitted by the United Kingdom, UN Special Commission BW Inspections in Iraq: Lessons for the Ad Hoc Experts Group on Verification, April 1992.

5. BWC/CONF.III/VEREX 9/Corr.1, Ad Hoc Group of Governmental Experts to identify and Examine Potential Verification Measures from a Scientific and Technical Standpoint, Report, 15 October 1993.

6. The formal title was practice compliance inspections rather than practice challenge inspections as had been the case in the CWC, but the terms were often used interchangeably. The main reason for this was to avoid any suggestion that it was a direct copy of the CWC provisions.

7. Dr Pearson had also decided in 1991 to change the name of Porton from the Chemical Defence Establishment to Chemical and Biological Defence Establishment to reflect the growing importance of the work on biodefence.

8. Changing the name of Departments and secretariats in the FCO and MOD was a recurring and sadly annoying feature over the years as fads came and went, usually associated with changes in Heads of Department and Under-Secretaries. In the case of ACDRU, its parent department changed several times over thirty-five years from the Arms Control and Disarmament Department to Non-Proliferation and Defence Department to Non-Proliferation Department to Counter-Proliferation Department and then to the Counter-Proliferation and Arms Control Centre, which was a joint unit staffed with FCO and MOD officials located in the MOD Main Building. ACDRU was briefly a separate department in its own right in 1987.

9. John R. Walker, 'Chapter 14, Verification of the Biological and Toxin Weapons Convention: the UK's Practice Compliance Inspection Programme' in *Verification 1994, Arms Control, Peacekeeping and the Environment,* Verification Technology Information Centre edited by J.B. Poole and R. Guthrie, London, Brassey's (UK), 1994, p 136.

10. John R. Walker, 'Chapter 14, Verification of the Biological and Toxin Weapons Convention: the UK's Practice Compliance Inspection Programme' in *Verification 1994, Arms Control, Peacekeeping and the Environment,* Verification Technology Information Centre edited by J.B. Poole and R. Guthrie, London, Brassey's (UK), 1994, p 135.

11. John R. Walker, 'Chapter 14, Verification of the Biological and Toxin Weapons Convention: the UK's Practice Compliance Inspection Programme' in *Verification 1994, Arms Control, Peacekeeping and the Environment,* Verification Technology Information Centre edited by J.B. Poole and R. Guthrie, London, Brassey's (UK), 1994, p 142.

12. Now the Medicines & Healthcare products Regulatory Agency.

13. Clinical trials testing new drugs are divided into different phases. The earliest phase trials may look at whether a drug is safe or the side effects it causes. Later phase trials aim to test whether a new treatment is better than existing treatments. A Phase 1 trial typically involves a small number of volunteers, perhaps twenty to fifty; Phase 2 may have about a few tens to over a 100 whilst Phase 3 would be in the region of the large 100s to 1000s.

14. John R. Walker, 'Chapter 14, Verification of the Biological and Toxin Weapons Convention: the UK's Practice Compliance Inspection Programme' in *Verification 1994, Arms Control, Peacekeeping and the Environment,* Verification Technology Information Centre edited by J.B. Poole and R. Guthrie, London, Brassey's (UK), 1994, p 143.

15. Samuel Smiles, *Self-Help: With Illustrations of Conduct and Perseverance,* John Murray, Albemarle Street, London, 1897, p 278.

16. BWC/AD HOC GROUP/WP.223, Working Paper submitted by the United Kingdom of Great Britain and Northern Ireland, The Role and Importance of Auditing in On-Site Activities, 19 September 1997.

17. Dr Graham Cooper, 'Inspections on Request: Coming to terms with their scope,' *Chemical Weapons Convention Bulletin, News, Background & Commentary Relevant to Chemical Weapons & Chemical Arms Control, Quarterly Journal of the Harvard-Sussex Program on CBW Armament and Arms Limitation,* Issue No,10 December 1990.

18. John R. Walker, Chapter 16, Update: Verification of the Biological and Toxin Weapons Convention: the UK's Practice Compliance Inspection Programme' in *Verification 1995, Arms Control, Peacekeeping and the Environment,* Verification Technology Information Centre, edited by J.B. Poole and R. Guthrie, Westview Press, Oxford, 1995, p 194.

19. Report by the Netherlands and Canada entitled "Bilateral Trial Inspection in Large Vaccine Facility," BWC/CONF.III/VEREX/6/WP.112, 1993.

20. John R. Walker, Chapter 16, Update: Verification of the Biological and Toxin Weapons Convention: the UK's Practice Compliance Inspection Programme' in *Verification 1995, Arms Control, Peacekeeping and the Environment,* Verification Technology Information Centre, edited by J.B. Poole and R. Guthrie, Westview Press, Oxford, 1995, p 196. See also BWC/CONF.III/VEREX/WP. 147, UK Practice Inspection: Pharmaceutical Pilot Plant, 27 May 1993. A full and detailed account of all the issues and lessons learned from the PCI programme can be

found in John. R. Walker, A.P. Phillips and Lorna Miller, 'Chapter 13, Verification of the Biological and Toxin Weapons Convention: the UK's Practice Compliance Inspection Programme: Final Report', in *Verification 1996, Arms Control, Peacekeeping and the Environment,* Verification Technology Information Centre, edited by J.B. Poole and R. Guthrie, Westview Press, Oxford, 1996, pp 171-191. See also United Kingdom BTWC Practice Compliance Inspection (PCI) Programme. Summary Report, BWC/SPCONF/WP.2, 20 September 1994.

21. BWC/AD HOC GROUP/21, The Role and Objectives of Information Visits, Working Paper submitted by the United Kingdom of Great Britain and Northern Ireland, 13 July 1995.

22. Dr Tony Phillips from Porton Down was invited to observe a Nordic practice visit organised by Norway, Sweden, Denmark, Iceland, and Finland. BWC/AD HOC GROUP/WP.298, Report of a trial random visit to a biopharmaceutical production facility: Working Paper submitted by Denmark, Finland, Iceland, Norway and Sweden, 21 August 1998.

23. The term non-challenge visits had been coined by Stephen Pattison who was the UK Friend of the Chair on Compliance Measures in the Ad Hoc Group. Stephen was Assistant Head of the FCO's Non-Proliferation and Defence Department at the time and used this term to group together all the diverse concepts and ideas for on-site activities other than challenge inspections and investigations of alleged use.

24. BWC/AD HOC GROUP/WP76, Report of a Joint UK/Brazil Practice Non-Challenge Visit, Working Paper submitted by Brazil and the United Kingdom of Great Britain and Northern Ireland, 18 July 1996.

25. BWC/AD HOC GROUP/WP76, Report of a Joint UK/Brazil Practice Non-Challenge Visit, Working Paper submitted by Brazil and the United Kingdom of Great Britain and Northern Ireland, 18 July 1996, page 8. We also submitted a list of equipment that could be used in a declaration format – BWC/AD HOC GROUP/WP.82, List of equipment for facility declarations, Working Paper submitted by Brazil and the United Kingdom of Great Britain and Northern Ireland, 23 July 1996.

26. BWC/AD HOC GROUP/WP.251, Working paper submitted by the United Kingdom of Great Britain and Northern Ireland, Use of a Simulated Declaration Format in a Practice Visit, 17 December 1997.

27. BWC/AD HOC GROUP/WP.258, Working paper submitted by the United Kingdom of Great Britain and Northern Ireland, Report of a Visit to a Pharmaceutical Research Facility, 9 January 1998.

28. BWC/AD HOC GROUP/CRP.8 (Technically corrected version), Protocol to The Convention on the Prohibition of the Development, Production and Stockpiling of Bacteriological (Biological) and Toxin Weapons and on their Destruction, 30 May 2001.
29. John R. Walker, 'Reflections on the 2001 BWC Protocol and the verification challenge' in *The Nonproliferation Review,* Vol.27, Numbers 4-6, July-December 2020.

Chapter 4

1. CD/769, Working Paper submitted by the United Kingdom of Great Britain and Northern Ireland, Making the Chemical Weapons Ban Effective, 10 July 1987.
2. See CWC Verification Annex Part II, General Rules of Verification, A. Designation of Inspectors and Inspection Assistants paragraph 2, 4 and 5; Part X Challenge Inspections Pursuant to Article IX A. Designation and Selection of Inspectors and Inspection Assistants, paragraph 1.
3. The radiation case surrounded the fission trigger in the weapon's 'primary' and the thermonuclear fuel in the 'secondary.' A key sensitivity was the geometry, shape and dimensions of this component.
4. William Penney was the leader of the nuclear work under the title Chief Superintendent High Explosive Research.
5. The site eventually ended up being part of the Defence Science and Technology Laboratory (Dstl), which was formed in 2001, but was finally closed in 2022 as Dstl left with Fort Halstead's functions transferred to Dstl Porton Down. Many years later long after Penney had retired there was a commemoration at Fort Halstead with a blue plaque unveiled on his former office in the early days of the programme. Walking back to the reception Penney whispered that this was all very well, but the plaque had been placed on the wrong building, his office had been in the building oppositive.
6. CWC Verification Annex Part II General Rules of Verification, paragraph 56.
7. Who Killed the Dugway Sheep? Why It Matters Fifty Years Later – Modern War Institute (westpoint.edu) Accessed 14 July 2023.
8. The US also hosted an exercise in July 2001 for the OPCW TS at Indian Head, US Naval Facility, Maryland, and my colleague Clive Rowland from the MOD represented the UK on that occasion.

9. U.S. Senate's Conditions to Ratification of the CWC – Full Text Accessed 15 July 2023.

10. The US finally completed destruction of its CW stockpile in July 2023 – 16 years late.

11. Christopher Hibbert, *Wellington, A Personal History*, Harper Collins Publishers, 1997, p 14.

12. There is of course a long tradition of the UK and US not seeing eye-to-eye on all issues; there were, for example, extremely heated and divisive debates between the Chiefs of Staff and Joint Chiefs during WWII on the best strategy to adopt in North Africa, the Mediterranean and on the timing of the landings in France. See Chapter 17 in Robin Prior, *Conquest We Must A Military History of Britain 1914-1945*, London, Yale University Press, 2022. Field Marshall Lord Allanbrooke, *War Diaries 1939-1945*, ed. Alex Danchev and Daniel Todman, London, Phoenix, 2002, gives a clear insight to the exasperations of working with the Americans.

13. *Dr Strangelove or: How I Learned to Stop Worrying and Love the Bomb*, Stanley Kubrick, Colombia Pictures, 1964.

14. A cromach is a Scottish walking stick and it is customary in Scottish Highland regiments for the officers to carry them as part of their dress. Colin used to say that he used his to keep wayward inspectors under control during inbound inspections.

15. Over the years we invited experts from Australia, China, France, Germany, India, Iran, Pakistan, South Africa, US and Russia.

16. C-21/4, Report of the OPCW on the Implementation of the Convention on the Prohibition of the Development, Production, Stockpiling and Use of Chemical Weapons and on their Destruction in 2015, 30 November 2016, p 14.

17. Colonel Mustard of course is a character in the Waddington's board game 'Cluedo', whilst Major Bloodnok, played memorably by Perter Sellers, was a character created by Spike Milligan in the British 1950s BBC radio comedy 'The Goon Show'. Bloodnok's army career was noted for cowardice and financial irregularities. My German colleagues told me afterwards that when we had sent the inspection notification by fax machine on the Friday afternoon for the inspection on the Monday, they saw the name Colonel Mustard and burst out laughing just as their commanding officer was walking past the comms room. He came in to see what all the hilarity was about: 'British joke sir' came the reply.

Chapter 5

1. Cmnd. 551, *Report of a Conference of Experts to Study Methods of Detecting Violations of a possible Agreement on the Suspension of Nuclear Tests*, Geneva, 1 July to 21 August 1947, London, HMSO, 1958.
2. See John R. Walker, *British Nuclear Weapons and the Test Ban 1954-1973 Britain, The United States, Weapons Policies and Nuclear Testing: Tensions and Contradictions*, Farnham, Ashgate, 2010.
3. See John R. Walker, 2010 Chapter 8.
4. Dr Charles C. Bates, Chief Vela Uniform Branch, On-Site Inspection for Underground Nuclear Tests, *in 'Developments in Technical Capabilities for Detecting and Identifying Nuclear Weapons Tests,'* Hearings before the Joint Committee on Atomic Energy Congress of the United States Eighty-Eighth Session, USGPO, Washington (March 1963), pp 201-202.
5. Charles C. Bates and Theodore F. George, On-Site Inspection for Underground Nuclear Tests, IEEE Transactions on Nuclear Science, Volume 10 Issue, January 1963.
6. TNA, AB 16/4681, The history of the Test Ban Treaty 1955-1965, W.G. Penney, S. Zuckerman to Prime Minister, *Nuclear Test Ban*, 15 May 1963.
7. John R. Walker, *British Nuclear Weapons and the Test Ban 1954-1973, Britain, the United States, Weapons Policies and Nuclear Testing: Tensions and Contradictions*, Farnham, Ashgate, 2010, pp124 and 132-34.
8. These paragraphs are drawn from the author's article, 'The Comprehensive Nuclear Test Ban Treaty (CTBT) and On-Site Inspection (OSI): A Historical Perspective' that appeared in VERTIC *Trust & Verify*, Issue Number 164, Summer 2019, pp 7-9.
9. John R. Walker, *British Nuclear Weapons and the Test Ban Squaring the Circle of Defence and Arms Control, 1974-1982*, Abington, Routledge, 2023, Chapter 2.
10. John R. Walker, *British Nuclear Weapons and the Test Ban. Squaring the Circle of Defence and Arms Control, 1974-1982*, Routledge, Farringdon, 2023.
11. Richard Starr had been the Australian Ambassador to the CD during the Treaty negotiations and had been invited by the PTS Executive Secretary to conduct an external review of the operation of the PTS.
12. Argon-37 is a synthetic radionuclide that is created from neutron capture by calcium 40 followed by an alpha particle emission as a result

of subsurface nuclear explosions. It has a half-life of 35 days. Argon-37 was eventually added to the CTBTO's *'OSI List of Radionuclides of Interest'*, which is an Annex to the draft OSI Operational Manual.

13. This did not apply to ISP-IT meetings since I always tipped them off when and where they would be happening.

14. The time and motion study expert played by John Le Mesurier in the Boulting Brothers' 1959 film *'I'm Alright Jack'* offers the perfect illustration.

15. John R. Walker, *Main lessons from the Integrated Field Exercise 2008* in CTBTO Spectrum CTBTO Magazine Issue 14 April 2010, p 27. The CTBTO produced a short promotional film on IFE08 - see https://www.ctbto.org/our-work/on-site-inspection-exercises/ife08

Chapter 6

1. John R. Walker, *Britain and Disarmament The UK and Nuclear, Biological and Chemical Weapons Arms Control and Programmes 1956-1975*, Farnham, Ashgate, 2012, see Chapter 10.

2. Hansard, House of Commons Debates, volume 79 column 334W, 20 May 1985.

3. Hansard, House of Commons Debates, volume 80 columns 613-20, 7 June 1985.

4. History – NORSAR Accessed 10 August 2023.

5. UK/Norway Initiative on nuclear warhead dismantlement verification – GOV.UK (www.gov.uk) Accessed 10 August 2023.

6. The UK – Norway Initiative: Report on the UKNI Non-Nuclear Weapon States Workshop. (7-9 December 2011).

7. The United Kingdom – Norway Initiative: Research into The Verification of Nuclear Warhead Dismantlement, Working Paper submitted by the Kingdom of Norway and the United Kingdom of Great Britain and Northern Ireland, NPT/CONF.2010/WP.41, May 2010.

8. Based on a joint design, the United Kingdom and Norway built two prototypes of the Information Barrier system, one in the United Kingdom by AWE and one in Norway by IFE and FFI. The system consists of a germanium detector and an electronic unit. The electronic unit records the detected gamma-radiation energies and runs a specially designed software code to determine if these recorded energies correspond to

the declared type of radioactive material. The outcome of the process is either a green light indicating the presence of the declared type of radioactive material in the sealed container or a red light indicating the absence or insufficient quantities of this material. No other information is available from the electronic unit, and all collected information is deleted immediately after the result has been presented. See The United Kingdom – Norway Initiative: Research into The Verification of Nuclear Warhead Dismantlement, Working Paper submitted by the Kingdom of Norway and the United Kingdom of Great Britain and Northern Ireland, NPT/CONF.2010/WP.41, May 2010.

9. The United Kingdom – Norway Initiative: Research into The Verification of Nuclear Warhead Dismantlement, Working Paper submitted by the Kingdom of Norway and the United Kingdom of Great Britain and Northern Ireland, NPT/CONF.2010/WP.41, May 2010.

10. The United Kingdom – Norway Initiative: Research into The Verification of Nuclear Warhead Dismantlement, Working Paper submitted by the Kingdom of Norway and the United Kingdom of Great Britain and Northern Ireland, NPT/CONF.2010/WP.41, May 2010, pp 19-20.

11. The United Kingdom – Norway Initiative: Further Research into Managed Access of Inspectors During Warhead Dismantlement Verification, 2010.

12. The United Kingdom – Norway Initiative: Research into The Verification of Nuclear Warhead Dismantlement, Working Paper submitted by the Kingdom of Norway and the United Kingdom of Great Britain and Northern Ireland, NPT/CONF.2010/WP.41, May 2010, p 24.

13. Jacob Benz, Jens Wirstam, Alicia Swift, Lars van Dassen, Robert Hughes, Tore Ramsøy, Jennifer Schofield, Steinar Høibråten, Facilitating a Nuclear Disarmament Verification Exercise Lessons Learned from the Quad Nuclear Verification Partnership and the LETTERPRESS Simulation March 2019, p 10.

14. NPT/CONF.2020/PC.III/7, National Report Pursuant to Actions 5, 20, and 21 of the Nuclear Non-Proliferation Treaty (NPT) 2010 Review Conference Final Document Report submitted by the United Kingdom of Great Britain and Northern Ireland, 25 April 2019, p 5; Letterpress: Post-simulation Report, 2020.

15. Letterpress: Post-simulation Report, 2020, paragraph 5.1.1.

16. For a detailed review of equipment and technology issues see Keir Allen, Anders Axelsson, Neil Grant, Robert Hughes, Styrkaar Hustveit,

Peter Marleau, Lisa Ovenden, Tore Ramsøy, Glen Warren. *Selection and Deployment of Verification Technologies Lessons learned from the Quad Nuclear Verification Partnership and the LETTERPRESS Simulation*, March 2019. See also Annex to *Report on the Quad Verification Partnership at the Third NPT Preparatory Committee in New York*, 2 May 2019, Summaries based on the reports on lessons learned from the LETTERPRESS Simulation, presented to the IPNDV Joint Working Group in Helsinki, 5 March 2019.

17. Jacob Benz, Jens Wirstam, Alicia Swift, Lars van Dassen, Robert Hughes, Tore Ramsøy, Jennifer Schofield, Steinar Høibråten, Facilitating a Nuclear Disarmament Verification Exercise Lessons Learned from the Quad Nuclear Verification Partnership and the LETTERPRESS Simulation March 2019, p 26.

18. *NuDiVe Nuclear Disarmament Verification Documentation of Nu Di Ve Exercise, September 2019*, Ministère de L'Europe et des Affairs Étrangères, Ministère des Armées, Auswärtiges Amt, Universität Hamburg and Forschungszentrum Jülich; https://www.fz-juelich.de/en/news/archive/press-release/2022/2022-04-08-nudive-en; Christoph Wirz, *UNIDIR Exercise: Menzingen Verification Experiment* in Annual Report Spiez Laboratory 2023, Spiez Laboratory May 2024.3

Chapter 7

1. CTBT/PTS/INF.1331, Principal Findings of the External Evaluation Team on the 2014 Integrated Field Exercise, 10 August 2015, p 4.

2. The following inspection activities may be conducted and techniques used, in accordance with the provisions on managed access, on collection, handling and analysis of samples, and on overflights: (a) Position finding from the air and at the surface to confirm the boundaries of the inspection area and establish coordinates of locations therein, in support of the inspection activities; (b) Visual observation, video and still photography and multi-spectral imaging, including infrared measurements, at and below the surface, and from the air, to search for anomalies or artifacts; (c) Measurement of levels of radioactivity above, at and below the surface, using gamma radiation monitoring and energy resolution analysis from the air, and at or under the surface, to search for and identify radiation anomalies; (d) Environmental

sampling and analysis of solids, liquids and gases from above, at and below the surface to detect anomalies; (e) Passive seismological monitoring for aftershocks to localize the search area and facilitate determination of the nature of an event; (f) Resonance seismometry and active seismic surveys to search for and locate underground anomalies, including cavities and rubble zones; (g) Magnetic and gravitational field mapping, ground penetrating radar and electrical conductivity measurements at the surface and from the air, as appropriate, to detect anomalies or artifacts; and (h) Drilling to obtain radioactive samples

3. Thomas Carlyle in his 1841 book *On Heroes and Hero Worship* noted that Edmund, 'Burke said there were Three Estates in Parliament; but, in the Reporters' Gallery yonder, there sat a Fourth Estate more important far than they all.' The three estates in the UK parliament were: the Lords Spiritual, the Lords Temporal and the Commons.

4. In this context one of the more bizarre sights in this, and indeed any OSI exercise that I had taken part, was a Karaoke evening in which members of the inspection team were singing along to a video of Eduard Khil – a Russian singer from the 1960s and 1970s – with his Trololo Song.

5. In the early stages of IFE14 we had quite a few cases of what Samuel Pepys called in his diary 'a looseness of the bowels', possibly caused by ice in the fruit juices served at breakfast. I steered clear of these so was unaffected, but a couple of my colleagues in the Evaluation Team were afflicted, and one of them was brave enough to go on the helicopter initial overflight – fortunately without incident for both him and the crew.

6. As already noted humour was never far away in these exercises and other PCIs. George Tuckwell, the Geophysics Team leader in the IT and one of the designers of the Inspection Team Functionality concept (the other was Luis Gaya Pique) and a veteran of IFE08 suggested that we ought to have a song list with titles relevant to what we were doing. I suggested inter alia The Eagles, 'Lyin' Eyes' Pink Floyd, 'Us and Them' and Bernard Cribbins 'Hole in the Ground.'

7. A/68/663–S/2013/735, United Nations Mission to Investigate Allegations of the Use of Chemical Weapons in the Syrian Arab Republic Final Report, 13 December 2013, p 21.

8. See for example Arms Control Association, Timeline of Syrian CW Activity, 2012-2022, Arms Control Association accessed 6 September

2023; OPCW, EC-104/DG.4, Report by the Director-General Progress in the Elimination of the Syrian Chemical Weapons Programme, 24 August 2023.

9. My proposal had been to see development in three phases: initial operational capability, interim operational capability and comprehensive capability. I got the idea from studying the early days of the UK nuclear weapons programme. In this scheme we would look to which of the OSI techniques would be available, the numbers of trained inspectors, the types and quantity of equipment available, the numbers of Policy documents, Standing Operating Procedures and Work Instructions that were available and had been tested in an exercise. We would also look at abilities to work in extreme environmental conditions such as sub-zero temperatures or on the high seas.

10. John R. Walker, 'A Farewell to Arms Control,' VERTIC, *Trust and Verify*, Issue Number 167, December 2020.

Chapter 8

1. I recall that there was some debate as to whether we should use the term 'windshield' as opposed to 'windscreen' – the former being the US term, whereas the latter is the British version. Since the CWC talks about 'windshield' that was the word used in the MOD's Standing Instruction.

2. Samuel Smiles, *Self-Help: With Illustrations of Conduct and Perseverance*, John Murray, Albemarle Street, London, 1897, p 278.

Glossary

ACDA	Arms Control and Disarmament Agency
ACDD	Arms Control and Disarmament Department, FCO
ACDRU	Arms Control and Disarmament Research Unit, FCO
ABM	Anti-Ballistic Missile
ABPI	Association of the British Pharmaceutical Industry
ACSA (N)	Assistant Chief Scientific Adviser (Nuclear)
AHG	Ad Hoc Group
APB	Ammunition Processing Building
AWE	Atomic Weapons Establishment
BFI	Bulk Fuel Installation
BNFL	British Nuclear Fuels Limited
BTWC	Biological and Toxin Weapons Convention
BOO	Base of Operations
BUE	Build-up Exercise
BW	Biological Weapons
CAM	Chemical Agent Monitor
CAMR	Centre for Applied Microbiology and Research
CBDE	Chemical and Biological Defence Establishment
CBW	Chemical and Biological Weapons
CD	Conference on Disarmament
CDE	Chemical Defence Establishment
CIA	Chemical Industries Association
CFE	Conventional Forces in Europe

CSO	Challenging State Observer
CTBT	Comprehensive Nuclear Test Ban Treaty
CTBTO	Comprehensive Nuclear Test Ban Treaty Organisation
CWC	Chemical Weapons Convention
CWCSG	Chemical Weapons Convention Steering Group
CW	Chemical Weapons
DACU	Defence Arms Control Unit, MOD
DERA	Defence Evaluation Research Agency
DML	Devonport Management Limited
DMO	Director of Military Operations
DOD	Department of Defense
DTI	Department of Trade and Industry
EIMS	Evaluation Information Management System
ENDC	Eighteen Nation Disarmament Committee
EOD	Explosive Ordnance Disposal
ESMF	Equipment Storage and Maintenance Facility
FCO	Foreign and Commonwealth Office
FFM	Fact Finding Mission (Ottawa Convention)
FIMS	Field Information Management System
GCHQ	Government Communications Headquarters
GIMO	Geospatial Information Management for On-Site Inspection
GLCM	Ground Launched Cruise Missiles
GMP	Good Manufacturing Practice
HAS	Hardened Aircraft Shelter
HEU	Highly Enriched Uranium
HMNB	Her Majesty's Naval Base
HSE	Health and Safety Executive
HT	Home Team
IA	Inspection Area
IAEA	International Atomic Energy Agency

IB	Information Barrier
ICI	Imperial Chemicals Industries
IFE	Integrated Field Exercise
IIMS	Integrated Information Management System
IMS	International Monitoring System
INF	Intermediate Nuclear Forces
ISP	Inspected State Party
IT	Inspection Team
ITL	Inspection Team Leader
JACIG	Joint Arms Control Implementation Group
LOSP	Logistics and Operations Support Plan
MDA	Mutual Defence Agreement
MO 4	Military Operations 4, DMO MOD
MOD	Ministry of Defence
MOU	Memorandum of Understanding
MSIR	Multi Spectral Infra-Red
NAA	Neutron Activation Analysis
NBC	Nuclear Biological Chemical
NCND	Neither Confirm Nor Deny
NNWS	Non Nuclear Weapons State
NPT	Non Proliferation Treaty
NRTE	Naval Reactor Test Establishment
NWS	Nuclear Weapons State
OPCW	Organisation for the Prohibition of Chemical Weapons
OSC	Operations Support Centre
OSI	On-Site Inspection
OSIA	On-Site Inspection Agency
PACS	Proliferation Arms Control Secretariat, MOD
PCI	Practice Challenge Inspection
PEE	Proofing and Experimental Establishment
PIRA	Provisional Irish Republican Army

GLOSSARY

POE	Point of Entry
PTBT	Partial Test Ban Treaty
PTS	Provisional Technical Secretariat
QA	Quality Assurance
RAF	Royal Air Force
RANSAC	Random Selective Access
RNAD	Royal Naval Armaments Depot
RNAS	Royal Naval Air Station
RN	Radionuclide
RSO	Requesting State Observer
S&A	Sampling and Analysis
SALT	Strategic Arms Limitation Talks
SAMS	Seismic Aftershocks Monitoring System
SOPs	Standing Operating Procedures
SSA	Supplementary Storage Area
START	Strategic Arms Reduction Treaty
STF	Scenario Task Force
STIC	Secure Transport Container
TNA	The National Archives
TRIS	Trusted Radiation Identification System
TS	Technical Secretariat
UCNI	Unclassified Nuclear Information
UKAEA	United Kingdom Atomic Energy Authority
UKNI	UK-Norway Initiative
UNSCOM	UN Special Commission
UNSGM	United Nations Secretary-General's Mechanism
VA	Verification Annex (CWC)
VEREX	Verification Experts Meeting
VIC	Vienna International Centre
WGB	Working Group B
WI	Work Instruction

Bibliography

The National Archives

DEFE 68/1263, International Arms Control: Chemical Weapons General; Technical Reports; Intersessional Treaty Discussions; Project Martello, 1989 Aug 7 – 1990 Jan 5.

DEFE 68/1264, International Arms Control: Chemical Weapons General; Negotiations, Talks and Discussions, 1990 Feb 28 – 1990 Mar 30.

DEFE 68/1265, International Arms Control: Chemical Weapons General; Negotiations, Talks and Discussions; Challenge Inspections; Johnston Atoll, 1990 Apr 26 – 1990 June 4.

DEFE 68/1266, International Arms Control: Chemical Weapons General; Negotiations, Talks and Discussions; Challenge Inspections, 1990 June 4 – 1990 July 6.

DEFE 13/2731, International Conferences and Arms Control: chemical weapons treaty negotiations and inspections, 1988 Feb 29 – 1991 July 15.

UK Parliamentary papers

Cmnd. 551, *Report of a Conference of Experts to Study Methods of Detecting Violations of a possible Agreement on the Suspension of Nuclear Tests*, Geneva, 1 July to 21 August 1957, London, HMSO, 1958.

Conference on Disarmament Working Papers

CD/15, Visit to Britain by chemical weapons experts (14-16 March 1979), United Kingdom of Great Britain & Northern Ireland, 24 April 1979.

CD/769, Working Paper submitted by the United Kingdom of Great Britain and Northern Ireland, Making the Chemical Weapons Ban Effective, 10 July 1987.

CD/ 856, Past production of chemical warfare agents in the United Kingdom, Working Paper, United Kingdom of Great Britain and Northern Ireland, 17 August 1988.

CD/921 CD/CW/WP.245, Verification of the Chemical Weapons Convention: practice challenge inspections of military facilities, United Kingdom of Great Britain and Northern Ireland, 14 June 1989.

CD/CW/WP.249, Report on a national trial inspection of an industrial chemical facility, United Kingdom of Great Britain and Northern Ireland, 21 June 1989.

CD/CW/WP.269, Instrumental approaches to non-intrusive analytical techniques for inspection and verification, United Kingdom of Great Britain and Northern Ireland, 12 January 1990.

CD/1012 CD/CW/WP.304, Verification of the Chemical Weapons Convention: practice challenge inspections of Government facilities: analysis of results, United Kingdom of Great Britain and Northern Ireland, 11 July 1990.

CD/1056 CD/CW/WP.330, Report on two joint chemical weapons practice challenge inspections, Germany and the United Kingdom of Great Britain and Northern Ireland, 8 February 1991.

CD/1080 CD/CW/WP.341, Verification of the Chemical Weapons Convention: practice challenge inspections at civil chemical plants, United Kingdom of Great Britain and Northern Ireland, 5 June 1991.

CD/1102, CD/CW/WP.361, Report on an international trial challenge inspection, Germany, 15 August 1991.

VEREX and Ad Hoc Group Papers

BWC/CONF.III/VEREX/WP.5, Working paper submitted by the United Kingdom, UN Special Commission BW Inspections in Iraq: Lessons for the Ad Hoc Experts Group on Verification, April 1992.

BWC/CONF.III/VEREX 9/Corr.1, Ad Hoc Group of Governmental Experts to identify and Examine Potential Verification Measures from a Scientific and Technical Standpoint, Report, 15 October 1993.

BWC/CONF.III/VEREX/6/WP.112, Report by the Netherlands and Canada entitled "Bilateral Trial Inspection in Large Vaccine Facility," 1993.

BWC/CONF.III/VEREX/WP. 147, UK Practice Inspection: Pharmaceutical Pilot Plant, 27 May 1993.

BWC/SPCONF/WP.2, United Kingdom BTWC Practice Compliance Inspection (PCI) Programme. Summary Report, 20 September 1994.

BWC/AD HOC GROUP/21, The Role and Objectives of Information Visits, Working Paper submitted by the United Kingdom of Great Britain and Northern Ireland, 13 July 1995.

BWC/AD HOC GROUP/WP76, Report of a Joint UK/Brazil Practice Non-Challenge Visit, Working Paper submitted by Brazil and the United Kingdom of Great Britain and Northern Ireland, 18 July 1996.

BWC/AD HOC GROUP/WP.223, Working Paper submitted by the United Kingdom of Great Britain and Northern Ireland, The Role and Importance of Auditing in On-Site Activities, 19 September 1997.

BWC/AD HOC GROUP/WP.251, Working Paper submitted by the United Kingdom of Great Britain and Northern Ireland, Use of a Simulated Declaration Format in a Practice Visit, 17 December 1997.

BWC/AD HOC GROUP/WP.258, Working Paper submitted by the United Kingdom of Great Britain and Northern Ireland, Report of a Visit to a Pharmaceutical Research Facility, 9 January 1998.

NPT

NPT/CONF.2010/WP.41, The United Kingdom – Norway Initiative: Research into The Verification of Nuclear Warhead Dismantlement, Working Paper submitted by the Kingdom of Norway and the United Kingdom of Great Britain and Northern Ireland, May 2010.

The UK – Norway Initiative: Report on the UKNI Non Nuclear Weapon States Workshop (7-9 December 2011).

NPT/CONF.2020/PC.III/7, National Report Pursuant to Actions 5, 20, and 21 of the Nuclear Non-Proliferation Treaty (NPT) 2010 Review Conference Final Document, Report submitted by the United Kingdom of Great Britain and Northern Ireland, 25 April 2019.

OPCW

S/659/2007, Note by the Director-General, Report on Challenge Inspection Exercise Delft, The Netherlands 10 – 14 September 2007, 26 October 2007.

CTBTO

John R. Walker, *Main lessons from the Integrated Field Exercise 2008* in CTBTO Spectrum CTBTO Magazine Issue 14 April 2010.

Secondary sources

Nathan E. Busch, Joseph F. Pilat, *The Politics of Weapons Inspections: Assessing WMD Monitoring and Verification Regimes*, (Stanford Security Studies, Stanford, 2017)

Dr Graham Cooper, 'Inspections on Request: Coming to terms with their scope,' *Chemical Weapons Convention Bulletin, News, Background & Commentary Relevant to Chemical Weapons & Chemical Arms Control, Quarterly Journal of the Harvard-Sussex Program on CBW Armament and Arms Limitation*, Issue No.10, December 1990.

David Kelly, *The Trilateral Agreement: lessons for biological weapons verification in VERTIC Verification Yearbook 2002*, (Russell Press, Nottingham, 2002)

Ralf Trapp, *Verification under the Chemical Weapons Convention: On-site Inspection in Chemical Industry Facilities, SIPRI Chemical & Biological Warfare Studies, Volume 14*, (Oxford University Press, Oxford 1993)

John R. Walker, 'Chapter 14, Verification of the Biological and Toxin Weapons Convention: the UK's Practice Compliance Inspection Programme' in *Verification 1994, Arms Control, Peacekeeping and the Environment*, Verification Technology Information Centre edited by J.B. Poole and R. Guthrie, (London, Brassey's (UK), 1994)

John R. Walker, Chapter 16, Update: Verification of the Biological and Toxin Weapons Convention: the UK's Practice Compliance Inspection Programme' in *Verification 1995, Arms Control, Peacekeeping and the Environment*, Verification Technology Information Centre, edited by J.B. Poole and R. Guthrie, (Westview Press, Oxford, 1995)

John. R. Walker, A.P. Phillips and Lorna Miller, 'Chapter 13, Verification of the Biological and Toxin Weapons Convention: the UK's Practice Compliance Inspection Programme: Final Report', in *Verification 1996, Arms Control, Peacekeeping and the Environment*, Verification Technology Information Centre, edited by J.B. Poole and R. Guthrie, (Westview Press, Oxford, 1996)

John R. Walker, *British Nuclear Weapons and the Test Ban 1954-1973 Britain, the United States, Weapons Policies and Nuclear Testing: Tensions and Contradictions*, (Ashgate, Farnham, 2010)

John R. Walker, *Britain and Disarmament The UK and Nuclear, Biological and Chemical Weapons Arms Control and Programmes 1956-1975*, (Ashgate, Farnham 2012)

John R. Walker, Harvard-Sussex Program Occasional Paper Issue 02, *The Leitenberg-Zilinskas History of the Soviet Biological Weapons Programme*, December 2012.

John R. Walker, Harvard Sussex Program Occasional Paper, Issue 05, *The 1925 Geneva Protocol: Export Controls, Britain, Poland and why the Protocol came to include 'Bacteriological' Warfare*, June 2016.

John R. Walker, *A History of the United Kingdom's WE177 Nuclear Weapons Programme From Conception to into Service 1959-1980*, BASIC, London, March 2019.

John R. Walker, The Comprehensive Nuclear Test Ban Treaty (CTBT) and On-Site Inspection (OSI): A Historical Perspective' ,VERTIC *Trust & Verify*, Issue Number 164, Summer 2019.

John R. Walker, 'Reflections on the 2001 BWC Protocol and the verification challenge' in *The Nonproliferation Review*, Vol.27, Numbers 4-6, July-December 2020.

John R. Walker, *British Nuclear Weapons Stockpiles by Year: 1953–77*, RUSI Journal, August 2021.

John R. Walker, *British Nuclear Weapons and the Test Ban, Squaring the Circle of Defence and Arms Control, 1974-1982*, (Routledge, Abingdon, 2023)

Index

A45, 28-9, 41, 79, 80, 154

A90, 154

Aberporth, 112

active seismic, 122, 161, 206

Ad Hoc Group (AHG), 4, 7, 52, 61, 69, 71, 73, 75

Advisory Committee on Dangerous Pathogens, 56

Air Force Board, 193

Al Hakam, 53

Algeria, 172

Altdorf, 112

Amman, 173

AMSO, 21, 193

Anglesey, 91

Animal (Scientific Procedures) Act 1986, 60, 67

Anti-Personal Landmines, 3, 59, 112-13, 167 *See also* Ottawa Convention

Antler underground nuclear test, 123

Arcania, 130, 134, 137, 141

Argon-37, 131, 139, 172, 175, 202-203

arms control, 1-3, 6, 8-9, 11, 15, 30-1, 48, 50-1, 53, 69, 73, 75, 95, 108-9, 113, 121-2, 144-8, 152, 157, 159, 171, 180-2, 188, 190, 195

Arms Control and Disarmament Agency (ACDA), 66, 100, 102

Arms Control and Disarmament Department (ACDD), 12, 197

Arms Control and Disarmament Research Unit (ACDRU), 7, 12-3, 15, 116, 138

Arndt, Ranier, 139, 171

Arvidsson, Henry, 109

Association of the British Pharmaceutical Industry, 53-5, 65

auditing, 51, 64, 70, 186

Avonmouth, 42-3, 45-6

Axelsson, Anders, 172

AWE Aldermaston, 1, 5, 11-3, 27-8, 30, 33, 39-41, 55, 78, 88, 116, 118, 120, 124, 131, 149, 155, 172

AWE Blacknest, 2, 172

AWE Burghfield, 26, 40-1, 85, 112, 116, 147, 149, 153

AWE Foulness, 30-1, 33-4, 149

Baden, 143, 173

Bad Kreuznach, 47, 49

Balczo, Bela, 174

Barlow, Andrew, 116

Bartlett, John, 13, 95